Going This Way

Stories from the Life of Charlie Yates

DIANE YATES

WESTBOW®
PRESS
A DIVISION OF THOMAS NELSON
& ZONDERVAN

WestBow Press books may be ordered through booksellers or by contacting:

WestBow Press
A Division of Thomas Nelson & Zondervan
1663 Liberty Drive
Bloomington, IN 47403
www.westbowpress.com
1 (866) 928-1240

ISBN: 978-1-4908-2726-1 (sc)
ISBN: 978-1-4908-2727-8 (e)

Library of Congress Control Number: 2014903504

Printed in the United States of America.

WestBow Press rev. date: 02/24/2014

CONTENTS

INTRODUCTION

About the Book "Going This Way"

In his 63 years, Charlie Yates lived in six different states, two foreign countries, attended at least thirteen different schools, was a member of seven churches, and had three different careers. If you knew him in one of these windows of time, you had only a glimpse through partly closed blinds. He was the son of Air Force aviator and spent much of his childhood on or near Air Force bases. He graduated from Texas Tech University where he was a member of the Alpha Tau Omega fraternity. Upon graduation he was commissioned into the United Stated Air Force. His first assignment after pilot training was flying OV-10s in Southeast Asia. During his 20 year career he also flew the T-38 and F-15. Upon retirement from the Air Force he flew B-737s, MD-88s, MD-90s and B-767s for Delta Airlines. After retirement from Delta he became the Chief Flight Instructor for Marcair, a flight school at Northwest Regional Airport in Roanoke, Texas. Throughout those years as an airman, a husband, father, and grandfather, he was a student of the Bible. As he grew in his faith, proclaiming the gospel became a greater passion than flight. In the last fifteen years of his life, he preached and taught in many different venues. When he introduced himself to a new audience, he would use the words of the apostle Paul, *"It is a trustworthy statement; deserving full acceptance, that Christ Jesus came into the world to save sinners, among whom I am foremost of all."* (1 Timothy 1:15)

The stories about Charlie are legend in his circles of influence. The young sinner and the older, wiser, forgiven sinner lived, created, told, and retold stories. He verbally recounted his stories with great energy and animation, and he also shared them through movies, pictures, and books. The stories were of his adventures, mishaps, jokes, near death experiences, joys, sorrows, struggles, and battles. Sometimes the stories were told merely to entertain, but more often than not, they were used to instruct. There was always a lesson in the learning and an application upon reflection.

He used to tell the joke about the prisoner in the jail cell. The prisoner would yell out a number, and the other prisoners would all laugh. A new inmate asked why the laughter. One of veterans explained that they had heard the jokes so many times that the jokes were numbered. If someone merely said the number, the prisoners laughed because they knew the joke. The new guy walked up to the bars and yelled, "number fourteen!" There was dead silence in the cell block. He asked the older prisoner, "What's wrong? Why didn't I get any laughs?" "Well," said the older man, "sometimes it's not the joke, but how you tell it."

So goes the joke with Charlie's closest friends; they numbered his stories, but only he could tell them the right way. Upon his tragic death, those who knew Charlie realized that exponential numbering was needed. There were more stories to be unearthed. The book is a compilation of some of the stories that reveal the character and transformation of a gifted, yet ordinary, person that God used for His purposes and His glory.

The Title

When the Yates family moved to Texas in 1991, we began teaching the rules and the art of waterskiing to many kids, young and old. We taught the friends of our children, and then we began having ski days for junior high, high school, and college age kids from our church. In 1996 we found it necessary to buy a newer, larger boat to better serve our "ministry." It was during the steamy Texas summers when we taught so many to ski that Charlie coined the phrase, **"I'm going this way; I suggest you do the same."** It was inevitable that a new skier would get tangled in the rope, struggle with putting on the skis, and would wind up facing the opposite direction that the boat was headed. Soon everyone in the boat knew what to say to the confused novice in the water. "I'm going this way; I suggest you do the same."

Charlie would always give an instructional briefing before the skiing began. The lessons on skiing inevitably led to a presentation of the gospel. Charlie compared the skier to the child of God. The skier could not ski under his own power. It was the power of the boat that brought him up out of the water. So it is with man; he is unable to save himself; it is only by the power of God through faith in Jesus Christ that man is saved. It was up to the skier to stand firm (on the skis) and to keep his eyes on the pole in the center of the boat. The child of God is to stand firm in his faith, keeping his eyes on the cross. Many beginning skiers did not pay heed to the admonitions. They tried to pull themselves up on the skis, and then they looked down, resulting in a fall. Of course, the falls provided a reason to reiterate the key components not only of getting up and staying up on water skis, but also the basic tenets of the faith. The analogy proved a great way to teach, as Charlie would say, "young skulls full of mush."

The Final Page

When Charlie died, two young women in his church, Alyssa Kern and Christe Chandler, set up a forum to collect stories about Charlie to put in a memory book. Friends of all ages and walks of life sent stories and pictures about the man who had influenced them or befriended them in some way. His precious daughter, Angela Guthrie, created the last page in the book. It was a picture of the sun setting, with a body of water in the foreground. There were only a few words on the page, "I'm going this way; I suggest you do the same – Charlie Yates." The ultimate meaning of this is fully understood by those who knew him. He had his heart and mind set on heaven. His son, Smedly, eulogized, "He got what he wanted."

Special Acknowledgements

The book was edited by Fern Gregory. Due to declining health, *my* book was her last editing assignment. Fern worked as an editor for the Master's College Biblical Counseling Department for thirteen years. She also edited many of Lou Priolo's books. I considered it a great privilege to have her red pencil marks all over my pages.

The book would not have been complete without contributions from Bob Fleer, Charlie's high school cohort and friend for life. Bob led a life as colorful and interesting as Charlie's. He needs to finish writing his book, but for now, his grandson can read this one.

A Note from the Author

I'm not sure "author" is the correct term. I woke up in the early hours of the morning one day about six months after my husband died. My mind was full of the stories of the 42 years we shared. I wanted to preserve those memories for our grandchildren. They would only know "Poppy" through those stories. That sleepless morning I made a list of stories and then I was able to go back to sleep. The next day I began to write. But the book is not just my record of memories. It includes some of Charlie's letters and testimonials, and some of the stories, eye witness accounts, and reflections of people whose lives intersected his. I am grateful to all who contributed. My prayer is that the story of God's work in Charlie's life will be an inspiration to others.

– Diane Elizabeth Yates

Each strand of sorrow has a place
Within this tapestry of grace;
So through the trials I choose to say:
"Your perfect will in your perfect way."

From "The Perfect Wisdom of Our God"
Hymn by Keith Getty and Stuart Townsend

CHAPTER 1

Be Careful

2012

"You have taken account of my wanderings; Put my tears in Your bottle. Are they not in Your book?" – Psalm 56:8

I looked in my rear view mirror and saw the flashing lights. It took a moment for me to realize that I was being pulled over. I turned the corner, passed the gas station, and stopped near the curb on the service road. As the officer approached, I rolled down my window, leaned out and asked, "What did I do wrong?" He responded, "Well Ma'am, you were going 40 on Kimball." I said, "I'm sorry, I wasn't thinking. I'm on my way to my husband's funeral." As soon as I said funeral, I knew that wasn't the right word. It wasn't the funeral. This was Tuesday and the funeral was yet to be on Friday. I was on my way to a memorial service at the airport in the hangar where Charlie worked. It didn't matter. The officer looked in my car and asked, "Why isn't anyone with you?" I told him, "There are so many grandchildren that I couldn't fit in the car, so I had to drive myself." I could tell he was skeptical. I asked, "Did you hear about the plane crash on Saturday?" "Yes Ma'am." "That was my husband." The officer paused, looked at me and said, "You can go on. Be careful."

How many times had I said that to Charlie? "Be careful." I said it in those early days of flight training in Lubbock, Texas. I said it when I left him at the airport on his way to Jungle Survival School and then on to Southeast Asia to fly in combat. I said it when he went to Las Vegas to fly F-15s in simulated war games in the Red Flag exercises. I said it every time he told me about a near miss, an accident, or the death of a fellow aviator. Usually, the "be careful" was followed by "I love you." The last time I said it to him was with regard to his flight check with a pilot who had a problem with his plane the prior week. This pilot took off from Northwest Regional Airport in Roanoke, Texas, in a Piper Cherokee with his wife and two children. Observers on the ground said the plane had difficulty gaining altitude and the engine was misfiring. Despite the malfunction of his craft, the pilot radioed that he was continuing to his destination. The dispatchers who received his communication and were aware of the plane's disturbing performance instructed him to turn around and put the plane on the ground immediately. Upon landing, the pilot was met by the owner of the airport. Concerned for the safety of flight operations at the airport, the owner confronted the pilot and told him that he wanted him to hangar his airplane someplace other than this airport. But before he flew that aircraft again, the owner directed him to get a flight proficiency check from Charlie Yates, the chief flight instructor at Marcair, a flight school on the airport grounds, and he told him to get his plane checked out by a mechanic.

Fears

As Charlie told me about the request concerning flight instruction, I had the same uneasiness that I felt when his friend, Tommy Meyer, asked him to take a commercial flight to Florida and ferry a small, open cockpit biplane called a "Little Toot" back to Texas. I voiced my concerns about the trip. He would be alone, exposed to the elements with limited instruments, flying from central Florida to Roanoke, Texas in one day. That would be fourteen hours of flying, map in lap (no GPS), with six stops for fuel. I was his dispatcher. He called me at sunrise when he took off. "Be careful," I said. He gave me his plan with the designated fuel stops, phone numbers and estimated times of arrival at each one. He had diligently planned his route to follow main highways and to avoid the swamps and forests in the southern coastal states. A little over an hour into the flight, he called to tell me that the plans had changed. The plane had two fuel tanks. There was a problem when it was time to switch from the empty tank to the full one so he landed short of his first planned stop to see if he could figure out what was going on. After a few phone calls to Tommy, he realized that the fuel switch was installed in a different orientation than on a similar plane he had flown before. What he thought was "on" was really "off." With that problem solved, he proceeded, but by now the carefully laid plans he had given me were null and void. The next stop would be about two hours from this one. He told me approximately where that would be and that he would call me.

The Little Toot

Meanwhile, as his dispatcher, I was tracking the weather on my computer. It was April, which meant it was tornado season. He had timed his trip between two weather fronts, one exiting the east coast of Florida and one approaching Texas from the northwest. I did not doubt Charlie's abilities, but I was anxious. I had to remind myself of something that I believed and had come to accept when Charlie was flying combat missions in South Vietnam 40 years ago – God numbers our days. We knew all the clichés and sayings at our house, such as "A watched pot never boils." This day, I had a new one: "As the crow flies, time does not." Throughout the day, I took the calls and prayed for his safety. The front was moving faster than expected. The weather service predicted that the line of severe thunderstorms would produce large hail and tornadoes. The line was expected to pass through the Dallas/Ft. Worth area between 8-10 p.m. I gave him the weather forecast about 3:30 when he called at his fuel stop. He said that his next fueling would be in Corsicana, Texas, and then he would fly directly to Northwest Regional Airport from there. By 6 p.m., I still had not heard from him. The blobs of green, yellow, red and purple on the weather radar steadily approached the Red River at the border of Texas and Oklahoma. It was close to 7 p.m. and I was ready to put out an alert for him when he called. Before I could say anything, he blurted, "I would have called sooner, but I had to take care of another problem. When I landed, a tire blew on the plane. The blowout damaged a strut and ripped the wheel pant. Almost everything at the airport was shut down for the day, but a mechanic who was on his way home stopped to help. He was able to locate a new tire, remove the damaged wheel pant, and rig a "Band-Aid" for the strut. I'm departing now and should arrive just after sunset." I asked him how the weather was there. "It's hazy with scattered clouds. I'll be able to make out familiar landmarks on my route. It will be a straight shot." "The storms are close," I said. "Be careful. I love you."

I was watching the radar when the final call came. "I'm putting the plane in the hangar here in Roanoke. Come pick me up." It was dark except for the flashes of lightning which lit up the ominous towers of storms that were rolling in our direction. As I drove toward the airport, with the squall line before me, I was thankful Charlie was safely on the ground. I was awed by the magnificent but terrifying sight and sounds bearing down upon us. I prayed for those who would be in harm's way throughout the night. *"God is our refuge and strength, a very present help in trouble. Therefore we will not fear, though the earth should change and though the mountains slip into the heart of the sea;"*

That night I could not know that a year and five months later, those words from Psalm 46 would comfort my soul in my darkest hour.

Preflight

The week of September 16, 2012 was a busy one. Charlie had a full flight schedule. He had done a ground check with the Piper Cherokee pilot and would fly with him again after he flew some initial flights with other instructors. Charlie had an elder meeting on Thursday night at the church. He was also preparing to teach an adult Sunday school class and to preach at the assisted living center on Sunday afternoon. I babysat our grandsons, Reese and Ryder, on Monday. The rest of my days that week were filled with meetings, Bible study, choir practice, a haircut, a social event for women at the church on Thursday night, and a trip to a Biblical counseling workshop in Granbury on Friday and Saturday. Looking back, it is obvious that God afforded the opportunities for Charlie to do his favorite things with some of his favorite people during the last days of his life on this earth. Those of us who shared them have the precious memories. Monday afternoon while I stayed with baby Ryder as he napped, Charlie took the boat out with his protégé, college student Andrew Hale, and our three-year-old grandson, Reese. Charlie and Andrew ripped up the water on the slalom ski. Reese learned how to be a "helper" with the ropes and the skis and gloves. He wants to ski but not until he's eleven. Andrew took movies of Reese and his "Poppy" swimming, talking, singing, and yelling "fish jump" whenever they saw one.

Our dates during boating season, usually May through September, were on weekdays at sunrise. Charlie would set the alarm and get up before the sun was up. If the winds were calm, he would hook the boat to the trailer and then come wake me up. In September, the water at Grapevine Lake is still warm but the air temperature at dawn is in the low 70's. Add the chill factor of a boat zipping across the water at 32 mph and I said, "No, thank you; no skiing for me. You ski and I'll drive the boat." Charlie felt guilty that he was having all the fun skiing and I was in my long pants and sweatshirt with driving duty. I really didn't mind. This was my private, personal time with him. So many people had a part of him the other hours of the day. Besides, I loved being there on the lake as God ushered in the day with multiple hues of red, orange, and yellow splashed across the sky and spilling over the water. It was spiritual refreshment. On Tuesday, September 18, as I sat in the captain's seat, he took my picture, the sun behind me just splitting the horizon. He skied well that morning, his timing perfect as he cut back and forth across the wake like a knife through butter, walls of sunlit spray framing every turn. Not bad for an "old guy." This was the one sport he could do that didn't bother the arthritis in his hip.

Back at the house, I fixed breakfast while he dressed for work. I didn't hear him come down the stairs. As I stood at the sink, he put his arms around me and said, "You're a wonderful wife." I turned around and hugged him and said, "That's all I want to be – your wonderful wife." I could have said so much more.

On Friday morning, September 21, Charlie left for the flight school and I headed for the workshop in Granbury. I picked up my friends, Sandy and Cindy, and we arrived early enough in the day to visit some shops in the historic town square. We met up with our other friend, Carol, for a quick supper before proceeding to Grace

Bible Church for the first session. I was in my hotel room by 9:30 and I called Charlie, eager to tell him about it. He was just as eager to tell me what an incredible day he had. He had flown aerobatics in the morning with several of his buddies. Not many things gave him as much pleasure as saying "check six guns" to another aircraft in his imaginary gun site. That day he also delivered a "practice run" of his Bible lesson for Sunday to group of guys at the Blue Hangar Café during lunch. After work, he and Andrew Hale skied until the sun dropped into the water at the west end of Grapevine Lake. Andrew later told me that Charlie promised I would fix them some good food and then he remembered I wasn't home. Charlie worked on his lesson the rest of the evening. On Sunday he would be teaching from Revelation. The lesson was on heaven.

The Accident

On Saturday morning, September 22, I woke early enough to go to the self-serve breakfast at the hotel in Granbury. I cooked a waffle and picked up a newspaper. The news was on and I halfway listened to it as I read the paper and eavesdropped on the conversation at the next table. There were five guys at the table, varied in age and stages of beard. They were dressed in jeans and T-shirts. From their conversation, I gathered they were on a work crew. There was a little rough language. They talked about the job, how much beer they had consumed the night before, and the status of their relationships with the women in their lives. I thought that if Charlie were here, he would find a way to engage them in some banter and then steer them into deeper conversations, all with the intention of sharing the gospel. But Charlie was not here. He was on his way to the airport for a busy day of flight instruction. I turned off my phone and headed to the church for a full day of classes.

At the airport Chuck Grice inspected his RV6 mid-morning and taxied to the run-up area. His plane was a bright red, low wing, tail dragger, and it was fast. Charlie gave Chuck his annual flight checks

7

and they became friends. Chuck gave Charlie a set of keys to his airplane and told him to fly it often. Charlie and I took it on several excursions – a lunch date at the Hard Eight barbecue restaurant in Stephenville, a fly-by of the Chandler Ranch on Rattlesnake Mountain, a weekend at the Hangar Hotel in Fredericksburg. Charlie also introduced many young people from our church to the joy of flying in this plane.

The Marcair Decathlon was sitting in the run-up area in front of the RV6. Chuck suspected it was Charlie. The Decathlon taxied onto the runway, and he heard the words that had become all too familiar, "Check six, Chuck" – meaning that Charlie would be at Chuck's six o'clock – on his tail in Charlie's "gun site." In Charlie's world there were only two kinds of planes, fighters and targets. Charlie and the student took off and Chuck soon followed. It took a few minutes, but Chuck caught up with them about 3-4 miles northwest of the airport and they proceeded to fly in formation to the practice area. Once in the practice area, Charlie put some distance between them, rolled inverted for a few seconds, and then disappeared. A few minutes later, Chuck heard the three words again, "Check six, Chuck," and this time Charlie was on Chuck's six. They played some aerobatic games for a few seconds and then Charlie left to begin instructing the student. The last time Chuck saw his friend, Charlie was doing what he loved...flying.

Just past noon Charlie was in the office talking to Glenn Herrington, Director of Operations for Marcair, about the flight characteristics of the Piper Cherokee. One of his students, precocious 10-year-old, Alex Vanover, chatted with him. They shared a "gotcha handshake" as Charlie left to go fly. Around 1:15, Charlie climbed into the passenger seat of the Piper Cherokee. He was scheduled to fly with another student at this time but for some reason did not. Perhaps the student canceled. The owner of the plane had fulfilled the requirements of the airport owner with regard to flight checks. These were all done in the flight school airplanes. Charlie said he knew his "stuff" and he flew well. The pilot told the airport owner and presumably Charlie also that his plane had been repaired. He probably asked Charlie to fly with him in his plane as a confidence builder. The pilot did the usual checks and engine run-up and then they took off from Northwest Regional Airport headed south.

The plane quickly lost altitude and crashed into a wooded area in Northlake.

Doug Dunbar, KTVT/Channel 11 news staff reporter, was in the office at Marcair with his two kids and his wife. They were there to support their friend Justin, a paraplegic, who was about to begin his FAA check ride. Brooks Higginbotham, a Marcair flight instructor, burst into the office, saying that a plane has gone down off the south end. Doug had his car keys in his pocket and without hesitation, he, Glenn Herrington, Brooks, and Marc Barth all jumped in his car and raced south along the taxi way. The car was quiet; there were anxious thoughts but not many spoken words. Someone called 911.

They reached the area, jumped out, hopped the fence and began to run through the woods. About 50 or 60 yards in, they could smell the AVGAS and could hear something. It was definitely a sound coming from the airplane, something electrical, but they didn't realize what it was until they arrived. Within seconds, Glenn shouted "I see metal." The fuselage was all that remained. The wings were gone. The fuselage was pointed nose down at a somewhat steep angle and tilted to the right. The smell of fuel was now very heavy despite the fact that the wings were gone. And by now, they realized that the sound was the fuel pump, still running. Glenn made his way around to the passenger side of the plane which was partially obscured because the fuselage was tilted toward the passenger side. On the pilot side, Doug and Brooks looked through the window. The pilot was slumped forward, not moving. In that initial moment, they could not tell whether or not there was a passenger. With his fist, Doug began to bash in the left side window. Once it was broken, he and Brooks grabbed the pilot's shirt and pulled him up and back. Brooks checked his wrist for a pulse, while Doug tried to find one on his neck. In the same effort, as they lifted the pilot,

Glenn looked into the cockpit from the nose of the plane and said, "Oh my God, it's Charlie." He was underneath the pilot of the plane. What followed was a rapid mash of questions and answers: "Is he breathing?" "Is he moving?" The answer from Glenn was, "Yes, he's breathing." They began talking to Charlie, letting him know that they were there. Marc, the owner of Marcair and Charlie's employer, knelt down beside him. Charlie asked about the pilot and then he asked Marc, "Are you okay?" Even in this circumstance, he was still "Charlie", thinking of others first. Marc put his arm around Charlie's shoulder.

At this point, Charlie said that he didn't feel any pain. Charlie touched his face. It was bleeding; teeth were broken, and his chin was split. With a lisp, he said, "I guess I might need a few stitches." He grabbed Marc's hand and their eyes met, communicating more than words ever could at that moment. Marc prayed and recited the 23rd Psalm; "*The LORD is my shepherd, I shall not want. He makes me lie down in green pastures; He leads me beside quiet waters. He restores my soul; He guides me in the paths of righteousness For His name's sake. Even though I walk through the valley of the shadow of death, I fear no evil, for You are with me; Your rod and Your staff, they comfort me. You prepare a table before me in the presence of my enemies; You have anointed my head with oil; My cup overflows. Surely goodness and lovingkindness will follow me all the days of my life, And I will dwell in the house of the LORD forever.*"

The pilot was limp and lifeless; Doug and Brooks had not found a pulse. Since they believed him to be dead, they held him up by his bloodied shirt from underneath his arms to keep his weight off Charlie. In the moments that followed, someone had the great idea to rip a branch from a nearby tree. They shoved the branch down the middle of the cockpit, resting it on the front windshield spar and the passenger seat. Then they laid the pilot on the branch.

The spinning sound of the fuel pump was of great concern. Doug and Brooks searched the mangled control panel and around the pilot's body trying to find the fuel pump switch. They could not find it.

With the pilot stabilized Doug made his way to the front of the plane while Glenn moved toward the tail. Charlie was moaning, but his eyes were open. Doug reassured him that they were there and would take care of him, not to worry. Charlie was badly hurt, the facial wound ugly and bleeding. Doug wanted to keep Charlie conscious and talking so he told him, "We'll have to have a visit with the person who gave you that nasty split lip." There was blood everywhere. Charlie's white Marcair shirt, always finely pressed, was mostly full of blood. Doug had been through a few traumatic events in life, and he knew that a facial wound can often bleed to a degree that looks far worse than it is. He was hopeful and from that moment, when he made eye contact, he didn't let Charlie close his eyes. Foremost in Doug's mind was, "Keep talking. Keep telling him that we're going to get him help, and that he was going to make it." Later, Doug remembered, "I'm not sure why, but I believe it was a special moment between me and my friend."

As Doug looked to assess Charlie's injuries, the split on his face the most obvious, a tree leaf slowly drifted down from nearby. The small, green leaf came to rest right in the middle of the skin that had been opened at Charlie's lip. Doug could tell that Charlie saw it falling, watching how it gently settled into his wound. Because of the severity of the split lip, Charlie's words weren't overly clear. Doug recounted that once the leaf landed, their eyes focused on each other again, Charlie simply said, "That sucks; can you get that for me?" Here they were, in the midst of a plane crash. Doug is doing all he can to save his terribly injured friend, and his dear friend is still the same Charlie that Doug had known for eight years, the master of the one liner, a guy who could get a smile out of you, no matter how bad your day. Doug reached in, grabbed the leaf, careful not to touch Charlie's face, and tossed it aside. Charlie smiled. Doug tried to smile too, but it was hard. He knew his friend was in trouble; he just didn't know how much at that moment."

Charlie wanted out of the plane. With difficulty, because of his facial injury, he managed to communicate that desire. He also heard the spinning of the fuel pump and could smell the fuel. It was a bad combination. The men knew that it was better not to move someone with a traumatic injury. But as they all talked and worked together to keep Charlie alert, they and Charlie agreed that they needed to get him out of the wreck because of the high risk of fire or explosion. With the decision made, they faced another problem. The fuselage had come to rest at an angle that put most of Charlie's door facing the ground. Glenn made his way to the rear of the fuselage in search of the battery. He now realized if he could unhook a cable, he could stop the fuel pump. They determined that they could roll the fuselage and get Charlie's door open if they removed one small tree. Doug told Charlie what they were going to do and he nodded. By this time Glenn Hyde, the airport owner, and his friend John Richardson arrived on the scene with an axe. Several of the men took turns chopping at the base of the tree and in short order; they chopped the tree down and then moved the fuselage to an upright position.

They set to work on the crumpled and jammed metal door. With few tools available, they pried it open mostly by hand. Doug kept talking to Charlie the entire time. He was moaning, but still responding to Doug's commands. When they got his door open, it was a team effort to get him out. They were now able to get a better look at the rest of their friend's body. Even through his blood stained pants they could tell that his legs were in bad shape. They proceeded to tell Charlie that they were about to move him and that they would try to not hurt him. In one move, as gently as they could, they lifted their friend out of the passenger seat, and sat him down with his back leaning against a tree a few feet away. Moments later, Glenn found the battery and disconnected it. The fuel pump stopped. The only sound that filled the air was heavy breathing, theirs and Charlie's. He was trying his best to stay awake. His friends were doing their best to care for him and comfort him. I believe those men had already demonstrated their love by risking their own lives to try and save his.

It wasn't long before they heard the sirens. Alex, the young student Charlie greeted 20 minutes earlier, had gone into the hangar to look for his sunglasses. He came out just in time to see ambulances racing toward the end of the runway. John Richardson knelt down beside Charlie. John was visiting from Washington and didn't know Charlie. He asked him if he knew the Lord as his Lord and Savior. Charlie gave a broken smile and shook his head up and down to indicate a most definite "yes." John told him, "That's great! God has spared your life from this aircraft accident and you are going to have quite a story to tell. Would you like for me to call your wife?" Charlie nodded yes. John took his phone out of his pocket to make the call, but he had no signal and realized he couldn't reach anyone. Charlie's phone was missing, lost in the wreckage. Turning back to Charlie, John noticed that his foot was broken at the ankle. He said, "Charlie, don't worry about these wounds. You will get the best medical care and in six months, you will be as good as new." Charlie was calm and relaxed. He was fully taking in his surroundings, and he kept looking upward. John thought to himself, "Charlie has no fears. He knows Who is in charge, and he belongs to Him."

Those on the scene could hear the Fire Department's rescue fighters calling through the thick mesquite foliage. John and Glenn Hyde repeatedly yelled, "Over here!" The paramedics ducked in and out of trees, thorns, and branches as they made their way to the wreckage. They asked everyone to back away. Charlie grabbed Marc's wrist. The paramedics talked to Charlie, trying to determine the extent of his injuries. They put an oxygen mask over his face, cut open his shirt and hooked him to several monitors. John continued to encourage Charlie as the paramedics made sure he was stable enough for helicopter transport. As the other men waited and watched, Doug stepped on something. He looked down and saw a watch. The impact had ripped it from Charlie's wrist and hurled it about 20 feet or so in front of the nose of the airplane. It had blood stains on it, but he recognized it right away. It was Charlie's. Doug knew it was his because they joked about watches, Doug's watches. He has a bunch of them. Charlie would often tell him when they flew together, "In the eight years we've flown as instructor/student and friends, you have never worn the same watch." Charlie never wore one other than the old Casio. He was proud of the fact that his well-worn thirty dollar watch would outlive any of those fancy watches Doug wore. They laughed about the little watch that just would not quit. Now, Doug was hoping that the same applied to his friend who was in a fight for his life.

Right after paramedics lifted Charlie onto a backboard and prepared to transport him to the arriving helicopter, Doug walked over to him and held up the watch so he could see it. He told him that he had found "his crappy watch, and it was still running!" He promised to bring it to him at the hospital, but said that he would hang on to it so that these fine folks could do their work. Charlie smiled and nodded. After Charlie was strapped into the helicopter, he caught John Richardson's eye and gave him two "thumbs up."

Fears Confirmed

I mentioned that Chuck Grice was one of Charlie's flying buddies. Chuck also taught Bible Classes with Ernie Black at McFadden Ranch, a juvenile detention center. After flying that morning, Chuck joined Ernie at the ranch and participated in baptizing some of the youth. The baptism lasted about an hour and then he went home to do some work. At 2:20 p.m. he got a call from Don Langhorne, the owner of the hangar where he stores his plane. Don told him that the 52F was closed due to a crash off the end of the runway and it was his understanding that Charlie was on the plane. Chuck told his wife, Bettye Ann, what happened and then called Marc. Marc told him that Charlie had been airlifted to John Hopkins Hospital and that he was banged up but should be okay. When he told Bettye that he was at John Hopkins, she told him, "No, it has to be John Peter Smith Hospital (JPS)." She called the ER and was patched to the trauma center immediately. A nurse answered the phone and confirmed that Charlie was there and that they needed to contact next of kin immediately. Bettye handed Chuck the phone, and he told the nurse that he would find Charlie's wife. He asked how Charlie was doing. The nurse told him that she didn't think he was going to make it. It was 2:30. Chuck and Bettye got in the car and headed for the hospital. He called Marc again and found that no one had been able to get in touch with me. He called Ernie and told him they needed to find me. Ernie told him that he saw me at a seminar in Granbury the night before and thought I might be there today. Bettye called her son-in-law, David Rush, an ordained minister who lives a few miles from JPS and asked him to get to the hospital and try to get into the ER and pray with Charlie. Chuck called Ernie again and asked him to contact Charlie's pastor, Tom Pennington, and see if he could meet them at the hospital.

Thumbs Up

As the air ambulance medics were wheeling the gurney to the trauma room, a young chaplain ran up beside them. Seeing that Charlie was still conscious, he asked if he could pray for him. Charlie nodded and the chaplain prayed, ending with "The Lord be with you." Charlie gave a "thumbs up" and said "I know." Then Jeff Hood, the chaplain, stayed with him as the trauma team took over. This was only his second week on the job. As he watched, he found himself thinking, "This man is an adventurer, a brother in Christ. I want to get to know him. Lord, let him live."

Find His Wife

It was now about four in the afternoon. I was listening to the final speaker in the counseling workshop in Granbury. William Tyler was sitting across the aisle and a couple of chairs back from Sandy and me. His phone had repeatedly vibrated in his pocket. He finally decided to take the call and left the auditorium. It was Ernie Black. Ernie sat next to William in the session on Friday night. I had met William before and I know that Charlie had several lunch meetings with him. Among other things, they discussed his son, Daniel, who was about to be deployed to Afghanistan. William came back into the conference room and tapped me on the shoulder, motioning for me to come with him. When we reached the hallway, he told me that Charlie had been in an accident and that I needed to call the hospital. Instantly, inwardly I prayed, "Help Charlie, God! Help me!" The first image that came to mind was not an airplane. I pictured him in his pickup truck. William led me to Pastor Terry Enns's office. Pastor Enns handed me a piece of paper with the name and phone number of the nurse in charge of Charlie's care. I called the number. Someone else answered and then went to locate her. We were disconnected. I waited a minute and called again. This time the nurse answered, and she told me that she had been taking care of Charlie. She asked, "How soon can you get here?" I told her it would take me 45 minutes to an hour. Keith Palmer, the organizer of the workshop, walked in as I put down the phone. Ten years ago, Keith had been a classmate of my son, Smedly, at Master's Seminary. Charlie and I met Keith in 2011 at a friend's wedding. I stood up and William offered to take me to the hospital. I knew I would need my car so I declined. He insisted on leading me. He would find the best route and all I had to do was follow his car. The four of us, Terry, Keith, William, and I prayed. Later on, I would see Keith at the ER.

Carol met us as we left the office. I asked her to let Sandy and Cindy know and give them a ride home. I was trembling as I got in my car. Then I realized that there must be messages on my phone. There were several from Marc. He just said, "Call me." There was one from Chuck Grice. He said that Charlie had been in a *plane* accident, that he was at JPS and that the hospital would not release any information on him. Plane accident! I thought he was in his truck. No information on his condition! They must be waiting for next of kin. That was me! I prayed, "O God, give me the strength to bear what lies before me. Use me as an instrument of Your grace and a testimony of Your goodness. If it be Your will, save his life." I thought of Charlie's mom, Dottie. Her husband, Charlie's dad, died last year (November 2011). Her son, Bill, Charlie's younger brother died seven years ago. I prayed again for her and for my precious children and grandchildren.

I had to call my daughter Angela, my son Smedly, Charlie's mom, and his sister, Vicki. I have Bluetooth in my car so as I followed William, I made the calls. I told them that Charlie was in a plane accident and is in critical condition at JPS Hospital in Ft. Worth. That's all I knew. Smedly had to book a flight from Phoenix. Angela lives an hour away in Roanoke and had to find a babysitter for Reese and Ryder. Her husband, Ryan Guthrie, an American Eagle pilot, was on a trip and just happened to be at DFW Airport getting ready to fly to Arkansas. As he was doing the preflight checks around the plane, he put his hand in his pocket and felt his phone vibrate. He would meet Angela at the hospital. Dottie lives in Ft. Worth and Vicki in Flower Mound. My heart is breaking, but I can't let myself cry yet. I must hope. I must be strong for them. Psalm 46 was on my heart. I began to sing Martin Luther's hymn based on that Psalm. Verse three was tough.

A Mighty Fortress is Our God

A mighty fortress is our God, A bulwark never failing;
Our helper He amid the flood Of mortal ills prevailing.
For still our ancient foe Doth see to work us woe –
His craft and pow'r are great, And, armed with cruel hate,
On earth is not his equal.

Did we in our own strength confide, Our striving would be losing,
Were not the right man on our side,
The man of God's own choosing.
Dost ask who that may be? Christ Jesus, it is He –

Lord Sabaoth His name, From age to age the same,
And He must win the battle.

That word above all earthly pow'rs, No thanks to them, abideth;
The Spirit and the gifts are ours Thru Him who with us sideth.
Let goods and kindred go, This mortal life also –
The body they may kill; God's truth abideth still:
His kingdom is forever

As I walked into the hospital it wasn't by my own power. I was being carried on the shoulders of my Savior and Shepherd, Jesus Christ. It was His peace and His strength that sustained me. The emergency room was filled with our friends, many from Countryside Bible Church. Our pastor, Tom, his wife, Sheila, and most of the elders and their wives were there. The ER staff was waiting for me. They led me to a small room furnished with two chairs, a small table and a box of tissues. Dottie was sitting in one of the chairs, tissue in hand. A nurse told us she would get the chaplain. It seemed like a long time before he came. He was a young man with a gentle voice. He told us that the trauma team would come down shortly and talk to us. My questions were yet to be answered: Is Charlie critically injured? Is he in a coma? Is he even alive? In my heart, I believed he was dead. A staff member knocked on the door and told us they had another room for us. It was a conference room with a large table and a number of chairs along the walls. Dottie and I took a seat facing the door. I held her hand. My church family began to fill the room. Vicki and her daughter were there but my dear daughter was still in transit and my son would not get in to the DFW airport until 11 p.m. All of these people loved Charlie, too, and their hearts were aching, not only for Charlie but for themselves and for me.

Three members of the trauma team walked in and sat down facing me. They all looked tired, distraught, and sad. They recounted what had happened when Charlie arrived in the ER. The team assessed his injuries and began a blood transfusion. Soon, Charlie's breathing became more difficult so they tried to intubate him to give him oxygen. They were not successful because of his injuries. They asked Charlie if they could sedate him and try again. He said, "Yes." Before long his heart stopped. The doctor took the extreme measure of opening his chest and massaging his heart to try to revive him. In the conference room, the team chief related, "He didn't make it. We are so sorry."

Ryan arrived at the ER at the same time as Angela and her friend Grace. They walked in just after the doctor gave us the news. The room was silent. No one knew what to say to the young woman who just lost her father. Each one was still absorbing the terrible truth. She knew something was horribly wrong; it was written on the faces of everyone staring at her. Dottie was shaking her head back and forth and Sheila was crying. I got up from my chair, trying to make my way around to Angela as quickly as I could. I put my arms around her, she buried her face in my shoulder, and I told her he was gone. He is in heaven with Jesus.

Angela, Vicki, and I went together to see his body. I thought, "He has entered into his eternal home with the words, 'Well done, good and faithful servant.' He can rest from his labors and sing praises to his God with the heavenly choirs." I wanted to go with him, knowing full well that his race was over and mine was not. When Angela saw him she said, "He's making the face, that silly, crooked smile, knocked out look that he made when he wrestled with his grandsons and nephews." He always wanted the last laugh. I took one final look and remembered, "He is not here; he is home with the Lord." The chaplain met me as I walked down the hall. He told me that my husband and the family and all the friends from our church had made a great impact on his life. This was his first death experience in his position as chaplain. Later, he would tell his wife, "When I die, I hope people can say that I lived my life like Mr. Yates – that I lived a life that was significant."

Death Is Not the End

Some books start at the beginning. This one opens in the middle. The middle is the day Charlie died. The beginning is the eternity before he died, and the end is the eternity after. I don't know that I could explain this in my own words, but I don't have to. God explained it in His book, the Bible. God breathed His words to men that He chose so that we might know and understand His character, His plans, and His purposes.

King David, the man after God's own heart wrote, *"If I say, "Surely the darkness will overwhelm me, And the light around me will be night, Even the darkness is not dark to You, And the night is as bright as the day. Darkness and light are alike to You. For You formed my inward parts; You wove me in my mother's womb. I will give thanks to You, for I am fearfully and wonderfully made; Wonderful are Your works, And my soul knows it very well. My frame was not hidden from You, When I was made in secret, And skillfully wrought in the depths of the earth; Your eyes have seen my unformed substance; And in Your book were all written The days that were ordained for me, When as yet there was not one of them." - Psalm 139:11-16*

- God made each one of us sometime in eternity past. Before we were born He saw us and He numbered our days on this earth.

Paul, God's apostle to the Gentiles, wrote, *"Blessed be the God and Father of our Lord Jesus Christ, who has blessed us with every spiritual blessing in the heavenly places in Christ, just as He chose us in Him before the foundation of the world, that we would be holy and blameless before Him." - Ephesians 1:3-4*

- God chose us, those who would believe in the saving work of His Son, Jesus Christ, to be His children. He chose us sometime in eternity past.

Paul also wrote, *"For we are His workmanship, created in Christ Jesus for good works which God prepared beforehand so that we would walk in them."* - Ephesians 2:10

- God has a plan and purpose for our lives that He prepared in eternity past.

In his letter to the Corinthian church, Paul wrote, *"For we know that if the earthly tent which is our house is torn down, we have a building from God, a house not made with hands, eternal in the heavens. For indeed in this house we groan, longing to be clothed with our dwelling from heaven, inasmuch as we, having put it on, will not be found naked. For indeed while we are in this tent, we groan, being burdened, because we do not want to be unclothed but to be clothed, so that what is mortal will be swallowed up by life. Now He who prepared us for this very purpose is God, who gave to us the Spirit as a pledge. Therefore, being always of good courage, and knowing that while we are at home in the body we are absent from the Lord-- for we walk by faith, not by sight-- we are of good courage, I say, and prefer rather to be absent from the body and to be at home with the Lord.* - 2 Corinthians 5:1-8

- God prepared us in eternity past for our eternity future in His Presence where there will be no more sin and no more sorrow, and we will experience His pleasures forevermore

CHAPTER 2

Lump of Clay

1949-1969

"But now, O LORD, You are our Father, we are the clay, and You, our potter; And all of us are the work of Your hand."
- Isaiah 64:8

There are many words that could be used to describe Charlie Yates. He was funny, talented, driven, generous, friendly, loving, dependable, trustworthy, courageous, and sometimes annoying and aggravating. However, the most significant word I would use to describe him is "transformed." When he came into this world, he was but a lump of clay in the Potter's hands. Through the years, God kneaded, rolled, turned, shaped, tested, and fired the vessel that became His faithful servant.

Beginnings

Charles E. Yates, Jr. and Dorothy (Dottie) Nell Minter met at Texas Tech University in the fall of 1947. Charles was a war veteran, recently returned from serving in Italy where he was a bombardier on a B-24 named "Boomerang." Boomerang flew 50 missions over

Nazi Germany during World War II, living up to the meaning of her name.

Dottie was from the town of White Deer in the Texas Panhandle. She was eighteen, seven years his junior and she was quickly won over by the suave war hero from Cisco. They married August 22, 1948. Less than a year later on July 14, Charles Dwight Yates was born. He earned his first nickname while still in the womb. His soon-to-be parents attended the newly released Disney movie, "Bambi." As Thumper the rabbit hopped through the forest, baby Yates kicked and bumped and thumped. Baby Charles D. was thus nicknamed Thumper. Anyone who knew him the first eleven years of his life called him Thumper. It took a change of schools in the seventh grade for him to get rid of that moniker. He liked to laugh, but he didn't want to be the butt of the joke. Until the day of his death, that name was not mentioned in his hearing by the family nor was it shared with others.

Charlie "Thumper" (1952)

I guess I should also set the record straight with regard to the color of my husband's eyes. Many people mistakenly thought they were blue. They were green – various shades of green, depending on what he wore and the color of the sky – but they were most definitely green like his father's. They were Christmas eyes, red and green, on many occasions. He was sensitive to cigarette smoke which caused the whites of his eyes to become very bloodshot. His eyes reddened when he laughed and that was often. With age and a heart tenderized by his own sorrows and love and compassion for others, his eyes would get red and tear up as he shared sentiments of joy, sorrow, hope, and encouragement. The eyes were green.....and red.

In May, 1951, the Korean conflict escalated and Charles was recalled to active duty. He became a bombardier instructor in B-25s and was stationed at Mather AFB in Sacramento. Son number two, Billy Wayne Yates, was born in the Mather hospital on January 19, 1953. In late 1954, Charles was transferred to Harlingen AFB where he was assigned to the wing supply organization and doubled as a navigator instructor in the T-29. Vicki Lubeth Yates was born at San Benito near Harlingen 'supposedly' on February 1, 1955. The birth date remains in question. Charlie (Thumper) insisted that she was born on February 2, Groundhog Day. He always celebrated her birthday on Groundhog Day. Once he made her a cake topped with a ceramic groundhog peeking out of a mound of crushed Oreos. In retrospect, his parents and sister were a little confused over the issue, and had Charlie lived a few more years, he probably would have had his mother and sister totally convinced.

The family moved to Laon, France, in 1956 where Charles served as the supply officer as well as a B-57 crew member for the 71st Bomb Squadron. The engines on the B-57 were started with a "cart start." There was a big black powder cartridge loaded on each engine. When the pilot hit the cart start switch, the cartridge went off like a giant blank shotgun shell. It made a big bang and clouds of angry black and gray smoke came from the exit ports below each engine, sometimes entirely shrouding the plane for a moment. That force would rotate the engine while fuel was fed to the compressor. Then, the engine would slowly wind up. Watching his dad launch was a magical moment. Another plane, the F-86 Sabre, was also based at this French town. It was loud, sleek, fast...and lethal. The plane was noted for its excellent all-around performance and ease of handling. It had a gyro gun sight, four 20 mm cannons, and flew at speeds exceeding 600 mph - a young boy's dream machine. It was in Laon that eight-year-old Charlie decided what he wanted to be when he grew up. As he watched F-86 fighters fly in and around the air base, he determined that he would be a fighter pilot.

While living in France, the family took the opportunity to travel to Brussels, Belgium, to visit the 1958 World Exhibition. Charlie had his first beer there (the only drink available) under the shadow of the Atomium. The Atomium was built for the World Exhibition. It is a massive structure shaped on the model of an elementary iron crystal enlarged 165 billion times. The visit made a great impression on the young lad. He would visit the site again almost fifty years later.

The Yates family moved to Bossier City, Louisiana, in 1958. Captain Charles Yates became a navigator on a B-52 in the SAC Bomb Wing at Barksdale AFB. It was during this time that the Cold War between the United States and the Soviet Union escalated. In 1956, Soviet Premier Nikita Khrushchev made this comment while addressing Western ambassadors at a reception: "Whether you like it or not, history is on our side. We will bury you." The United States' response was a greater reliance on nuclear weapons against enemies in wartime and the doctrine of "massive retaliation," threatening a severe response to any Soviet aggression. The B-52 was a vital part of the strategy. The bomber crews were on alert four times a month, twice on call at home and twice on airborne alert. They also flew training missions three times a month. In the event of an attack, the crews would be called into immediate action. Therefore, their families were trained in how to prepare for a nuclear attack. Charles taught son Charlie, by then a Cub Scout, how to pack up the family boat with camping gear, hunting and fishing gear and survival equipment. He was to be the man of the family and take care of his mom and younger brother and sister at a lakeside camping spot far from the military base. This was a lot of responsibility for a young kid, but he was still a kid.

Thanksgiving at the alert facilities on base
(left to right) Vicki, Charles, Dottie, Bill, Charlie (1962)

In 1965, his dad's squadron was sent to Guam to support the Vietnam War. This was a temporary duty (TDY) assignment usually lasting six months, with a short return to home base and then back again for six months. While he was deployed, the squadron was reassigned to Carswell AFB, Ft. Worth, Texas, and the TDYs continued until 1973. Dad was not home much. Charlie's most memorable birthday party was the time his mom made him a cake that looked like a covered wagon. He enjoyed his "Alamo

Fort" with the hundreds of soldiers, cowboys, Indians, and horses so much that he bought another set on eBay when he was in his fifties, much to the enjoyment of his grandsons. He made model airplanes, flew them on wires, and crashed and burned them at a time when he should not have been playing with matches. After school, he and his buddies shot rabbits and snakes in open fields near his house. He loved music, but he didn't particularly care for band when he got braces and had to temporarily play the clarinet instead of the trumpet.

Charlie and his brother Bill shared a similar sense of humor. Their dad and their maternal grandfather, Ed Minter, were known for their "funny bones," so it was no surprise that the juicy fruits didn't fall far from the tree. As they were growing up, Bill annoyed Charlie and Charlie bullied Bill, but it was the Yates' humor that bonded them in brotherhood. Charlie had a nickname for Bill. On most occasions he referred to him as "Newton" as in fig, or "Newt" for short.

Charlie didn't call his sister by her real name either. His parents named her Vicki, because that was the name Charlie wanted. There was a cute girl at school whom he liked; her name was Vicki. That girl was quickly forgotten. So, Charlie began calling Vicki "Lucy," as in "I Love Lucy," and together Charlie and "Lucy" watched all of the television episodes multiple times. Charlie would threaten her with maximum punishment (tackling or squeezing of the knee) if she would not hold up his foot or fetch something for him. She would have to report for duty and salute him. I believe this is called sibling slavery. Once when their mom was making a cake, they asked her to put food coloring in it to make it green. When Mom replied, "I could never eat green cake!" the light bulb came on and a tradition was born. The kids really wanted to have more raw batter than was left in the bowl or on the beaters. They realized that if they made the cake themselves and made it green, or blue, or gray or 'yuk,' they could then have as much as they wanted – raw or baked. Mom, and presumably other adults, wouldn't eat it.

Friend for Life

In school, Charlie was a good student and a leader. His problems in school generally had to do with citizenship. He was prone to fooling around and making wise-cracks. He enjoyed the role of class clown. Some teachers could handle him and some couldn't. The more memorable stories of his antics occurred in high school. In 1965, Charlie turned 16 years old. It was in late summer when he met Bob Fleer. They had been auditioning for trumpet chair positions with the Pascal High School Band. They were both new to the area and neither of them had made many friends yet. Charlie gave Bob a lift home. Within 35 minutes of meeting each other, Charlie and Bob realized that they had an enormous amount in common, so much so that they made plans to meet the next day. As Bob got out of the car, he turned, leaned into the window and said, "Thanks a lot Charlie! I'll see you later!" And Charlie said, "Gee, I hope not, but thanks for the warning!" Then he put the car in reverse and sped out of the driveway, leaving Bob in a fit of laughter and the knowledge that he had just met a friend for life.

Boys in the Band

The car Charlie drove was an English Ford, a 1959 Anglia he inherited from his Grandmother Yates. It was a nondescript little car, maybe six feet long. There were not many foreign cars on the road back then in the United States, save for a few Beetles maybe, but most of the road belonged to cars from Detroit. One day, Charlie and Bob were late for an early morning band practice. The band was playing when they walked in. Mr. Hewitt, the band director, was not happy that his first and second trumpet players were tardy. He stopped the music and asked if they had a good reason for interrupting practice. Charlie retorted, "I'll have you know we were in a wreck." He paused. There was silence. "I drive it to school every day." There was bedlam in the band. It's amazing that Charlie survived to play his trumpet another day, but he did. He and Bob marched and played their way through football season and competitions.

The next big band event was the Christmas party. They drew names and each band member was to buy a toy and bring it gift wrapped to the party. They would exchange the gifts and unwrap and play with them so they would be classified as "used." At the end of the party they would put all of the toys in a box for the annual citywide "Toys for Tots" gift donation program. Charlie and Bob weren't real keen about the party so they lollygagged and didn't go shopping until they were on the way to the event. They stopped by TG&Y (a five and dime store often referred to as "Turtles, Girdles, and Yo-yo's") and browsed the aisles. They didn't have to think about it or vote on it; they both knew what they were going to buy the moment they saw it. It was a great big red plastic fish with large glassy eyeballs. It wasn't a toy with moving parts. It had no batteries and didn't make noises. It was just a fish. Perfect! They decided they needed to get a second toy so they bought a three foot long matching red rubber shovel. Two red bows completed the purchase. As they headed out of the store to that odd, little cartoon car of Charlie's (from the side you could not tell if it was going to the right or the left), the two of them decided they could fix that with a hood ornament. Something like a ... fish. That should do the trick. They went back into the store, bought some masking tape and attached the fish over the metal doohickey on the hood and voila!

At the party, the kids who received the fish and shovel were visibly disappointed. Toward the end of the party, Charlie and Bob reluctantly crowned the box of "Toys for Tots" with their fish. The boys were the first to leave the shindig. They had to get back to the store to buy another fish. The next day the box of toys topped with party fish made the front page of the Fort Worth Star Telegram. The twin, the other bright red fish (now famous) turned the faded grey-blue dinky car into an enviable ride. Charlie could hardly wait to pick up the neighbor girl for school. Her name was Diana (not the

Diane he married). Diana's mother paid Charlie fifty cents a week to take her daughter to school. Charlie's mom thought it was a great idea. This was a recent development. The boys thought Diana was pretty but humorless. Bob wasn't too excited about the arrangement because being responsible for giving her a ride hampered their activities. Even though Bob lived several blocks away, Charlie picked him up first before he parked the car adorned with the fish in front of Diana's house. After a few moments, it was her mother who came to the front door. She was saying something but Charlie played hard of hearing. He nodded, smiled, cupped his hand to his ear and said, "What?" She pointed to the fish on the car and said, "The fish!" Charlie nodded and said, "The fish! Yes, yes, we have a fish. We like it too." She gestured and pointed again and then waved them on. The issue was settled with regard to paying passengers. Charlie and Bob began to see the potential of the sea creature.

Cruising

The big red plastic fish with the glassy eyeballs sat proudly on the hood of the little blue Anglia. And, of course, Charlie and Bob had filled the glove compartment with packs of cigarettes. There was quite a ridiculous debate between them the first time they bought the cigarettes. Charlie didn't smoke. Neither did Bob. The fish smoked like a chimney. Marlboros – filtered tips. They would light one up and stick it in a little hole between the fish's lips. The fish smoked two or three cigarettes on the way to school and two or three on the way back home. On the weekends when they were cruising around, it could go through two or three packs at the rate of two and a half miles per cigarette. It cost those boys more to keep that fish in cigarettes than it did to put gasoline in the car. Charlie was good. He would delay going up to the next light to ensure that they were the first car up to the crosswalk in downtown Ft. Worth. People would walk by and there would be that fish: big green eyes and tendrils of smoke curling up over those big grouper lips.

Model of Charlie's car with "the fish" hood ornament
(Unfortunately, no actual pictures exist.)

The car also had a phone. This was before cell phones, and there were probably only a handful of limousines in Ft. Worth with car phones. Few cars on the road even had air conditioning back then, so most people drove with the windows down on a pleasant evening. Charlie and Bob had no air conditioning, but they had a phone. It was a big black old fashioned receiver that fit perfectly - vertically – on the dashboard. It looked like it was made to go there. They tied the cord under the dash. They also had an old, loud alarm clock from which Bob's sister had twisted off the arms. Bob would pull the alarm button, "B' RING!" "B'RING!" Charlie would wait until he was certain he had the attention of the car next door. He would then pick up the receiver and answer the phone, "Hello!... just a minute." Then he would hand it out the window to the next car. "It's for you!"

Sometimes Charlie and Bob rode to school in Bob's '57 Mercury. It had a broken speedometer cable. One day upon leaving Paschal, Bob got a speeding ticket. Their friend Judd was in the back seat and Charlie was in the front passenger seat. The car was "orchid" (lavender) and white. As the cop was writing out the ticket, he asked what color it was. Charlie blurted out, "brown." The cop leaned down and stared, unsmiling, at Charlie for a good 45 seconds. Bob was sure he was going to get another ticket. Hanging out with Charlie could be risky.

The Band Trip

The Paschal High band director made preparations for a band competition near Houston. He asked for volunteers to make signs for the buses. Charlie and Bob immediately recognized this as an opportunity to make the trip especially memorable, so they signed on for the job. As they set about their task, they had another great idea. The band should have gifts for helpful people they met along the way. On one of their drives around downtown Ft. Worth, they circled several blocks where the buildings had been torn down to make way for the new convention center. They stopped to browse around the remains of a demolished hotel. In the rubble, they found some boxes, similar in size and shape to a box of chocolates. The words "Patrician Knob Bodies" were printed on the side of the box. Each box contained a dozen of the "knob bodies." They were round, two inches in diameter and one inch thick. On the top side was a one-inch circular indentation, maybe a 32nd of an inch deep. There was a rectangular cutout with rounded ends in the center, and the underside of the hard plastic object was hollowed out. The "bodies" came in three colors: peach, cream, and green. The boys didn't know what they were used for but they looked kind of neat so they stashed a bunch of boxes in the car. It didn't matter that they didn't know what they were nor would anyone else, but so what? The pretty "bodies" turned out to be parts of door knobs, but they gave them away nonetheless as if they were some valuable commodity. Whenever someone asked what they were, they went on some idiotic rabbit trail about when the knob bodies were first used, who invented them, where the plastic came from, etc. – all of it made up on the spot, of course. Bob's mom neatly gift wrapped the boxes. Charlie and Bob planned the speeches that would be given with the presentation of the gifts.

On the morning of departure, the kids met at the school with their instruments and suitcases. Charlie and Bob also had the bus signs and a large bag of "presents." Mr. Hewitt was not particularly enthused with the signs. He had expected "Paschal High School Band," "We're #1," "Ft. Worth, Texas-Home of the Proud Purple Panthers," etc., but he had not been specific in his directions. It was too late to do anything about it now. Firmly fastened to the sides and back of the buses were professionally made signs – "Just Married," "For Sale," "Drink More Milk." The boys found these signs in the same vicinity as the boxed "bodies."

The buses stopped throughout the day for fuel, lunch, and bathroom breaks. As everyone gathered near the bus to load up after the first stop, Charlie and Bob engaged the manager of the fuel station in conversation. They told him they had something for him and asked him to come over by the bus. Bob retrieved a package and Charlie began to speak. "Fred, as a token of our sincere appreciation for all your help and patience, we have this small gift for you." Band members gathered around. This was very curious and they all knew the first and second trumpet players well. Fred untied the ribbon, tore off the lovely paper, opened the box and stared at the peach-colored knob bodies. There was a tear in his eye as he said, "I don't know what to say. Thank you. Thank you very much." The band members clapped, whistled and yelled, "Way to go, Fred!" They clamorously boarded the bus, took their seats, and wondered what entertainment they could expect at the next stop.

One stop was a tour of the Astrodome in Houston. When the tour guide told the band how tall the arena dome was above second base, Charlie asked, "Is that with or without the bag?"

That's Right, Mel!

In 10th grade in Bossier City, Louisiana, Charlie selected French as his foreign language class because he had lived in France. His teacher was French and he earned a B in the class. When the family moved to Ft. Worth, Texas, in the summer of 1965 and Charlie began the 11th grade at Paschal High School, he needed another year of foreign language. He signed up for French 2. The first day of class he realized that he was in trouble. The teacher wasn't French, but that is all she spoke. The kids who had her for French 1 were responding to her questions and laughing at what she was saying. Charlie had no clue. She may as well have been speaking Greek.

All year long, he struggled through the class. He was failing, and there was only one more major assignment, a five-minute speech in French. He fretted and thought and fretted some more about what he could talk about for that long in a foreign language that was still foreign. He realized that he would be so bad he would have to be funny. It was out of that realization that he decided to translate a Bill Cosby comedy routine into French. The routine he chose was a parody of television commercials that were popular in the mid-1960s. In the commercials, a famous sports figure with no acting skills would promote a product. In the Cosby routine "Little Tiny Hairs," a baseball player is doing a razor commercial. The routine goes something like this: the jock looks into the mirror and says, "That's right, Mel! I always use a razor........on my face...........I use it every time.....to shave...it. I go into the bathroom and look at my face in the mirror and I see little tiny hairs growing outta my face. And I say, lookee there at those little tiny hairs growing outta my face. I call my wife. I say come here wife and see these little tiny hairs growing outta my face. So I get my razor, schib- schop, and I rip my face to shreds. Those little numbers on that razor don't mean nothing. I only wanted a clean shave, not self-sacrifice."

So Charlie translated the routine with his limited French vocabulary. Depending on how one viewed it, meaning was either lost or enhanced in the translation. The things he could do well were the costume (a bathrobe), the facial expressions, the body language, the voice inflection. He did the routine without *any* French accent, and his head would move as if he was reading from a giant teleprompter, and like a typewriter carriage, when he got to the end of a line his head would pop back to the left, pausing until he could "read" the next word. "That's right, Mel! I always use a razor on my face to shave.... it." By this time, the other kids were rolling in the aisles. Even his French teacher is in hysterics. As soon as she can control herself, she says to Charlie, "Don't move; don't go anywhere; just stay here; I'll be right back." She ran down to the office to get the cart with the reel-to-reel tape recorder. With some effort, she rolled the big heavy machine into the room. She set everything up, placed a microphone on a stand in front of Charlie and said, "Do it again." Charlie passed French with a "D."

Emery Ate My Note

The school year 1965-66 was not good for Mrs. Yost. She taught history at Paschal High School, and she had been teaching many, many years. She had been teaching so many years that she was tired of teaching and was very near retirement. During most classes, Mrs. Yost had the students take turns reading portions of the textbook aloud. She would then periodically call on students to answer a question. You can imagine that the boredom meter was pegged pretty high. The environment was ripe for mischief. Whenever she would call on Charlie Yates to read, he would do so in such a strong voice with such expression that it brought some life to the class. The problem with "Mr. Yates" reading, however, is that he never seemed to be on the same page as everyone else. In fact, he could be several hundred years ahead of the current day's lesson. After several pages of reading, Mrs. Yost would realize there was some confusion among the students and would call on someone else. Charlie was also helpful to a young man that often sat next to him. Their seats were in close proximity because the first letters of their last names were near the end of the alphabet. His first name was Nate and he was not a good student. When Mrs. Yost would ask him a question, he looked like the proverbial deer in the headlights. Charlie helped him on more than one occasion by whispering the

35

answer, a ridiculously wrong answer. All but the teacher and poor Nate got the joke. Mrs. Yost often removed her shoes and left them under her desk until they repeatedly ended up somewhere else in the room during third period. Throughout the rest of the year, she had to hide her shoes so she could find them.

Paschal High was built in 1955. By 1965, numerous portable classrooms had been added to the campus. Mrs. Yost's class was the farthest from the main building which housed the cafeteria. This was a problem for third period. When class was over, the kids from this class were the last ones in the lunch line. By the time they got their lunch, there was no time to eat it before the next class. One day Charlie decided to fix that. He briefed the class on what to do. He had someone in the class adjust the blinds so that Mrs. Yost couldn't see the comings and goings from the other classes. When he gave the signal about five minutes before the bell actually rang, everyone packed up their things and left. Mrs. Yost seemed a little confused when the class emptied each day near lunch period, but they were able to get away with it for about a week.

Then she insisted that she didn't hear the bell. Charlie fixed that. He brought an alarm clock with a bell ringer. Bob was in math analysis in the barracks building next door to Charlie's class. He remembered hearing that tinkling bell and watching the class leave like a windstorm. His teacher, Mr. Bodiford, would look at his watch and say, "What on earth is going on over there?" This ruse worked for a couple of weeks until she became suspicious again. When the kids began to abandon her class she went to the windows and opened the blinds. Her hunch was right. No one else was leaving the portable classrooms. She put a stop to the early migration by barricading the door with her body until she was sure she had heard the official bell and could peek out the door and see that other classes had been dismissed.

For a while Charlie managed to avoid repercussions from his antics. The teacher knew he was a cutup and had a quick wit, but he was also a good student. He got away with a lot until the day his friend Bob showed up at the portable. He knocked on the door and asked if he could speak to Charlie. Mrs. Yost said, "No." Charlie knew Bob needed to give him some information so he just got up from his seat and walked to the door to talk to Bob, who told him, "I don't need a ride home from school today because Mom's picking me up now for a dental appointment." Bob left. Charlie went back to his seat. And Mrs. Yost sat down at her desk and scribbled out a note. "Mr. Yates, take this note to the principal's office." Charlie dutifully took the note and walked across the campus toward the main building. Before he reached his destination, he ran into Emery who asked him what he was doing. Charlie told him and Emery asked to see the note. Charlie showed him and then Emery ate the note! Now what? Charlie hadn't even read the folded note. What was he going to do – go to the principal's office and say, "I had a note but Emery ate it." He went to the cafeteria hoping Mrs. Yost would forget. She did.

On another day he wasn't quite as fortunate. Normally, the spit wads were aimed at the ceiling - with great success. There were so many stuck to the acoustic tiles that to the uninformed or uninitiated they might appear as an architectural feature. On this occasion, there was a lapse in judgment (as if teenage boys had much judgment). While Mrs. Yost was writing on the chalkboard with her back to the class, a student took aim at the board and splatted a big one. The noise startled her a little, but not knowing what it was, she kept on writing on the board. The dummy decided to see if he could get away with it again. He chewed a big wad, loaded it on a rubber band, and let it go. This time it landed on the back of Mrs. Yost's head. She reached up, pulled it out of her hair, and turned around. Her face was red as a beet. She stood at the front of the class and pointed at each student one by one and asked, "Who did this?" Most did not know because it was done quickly and surreptitiously. The few who did know were not going to let on.

Since she couldn't get a confession, she selected five suspects and sent them with a note to the vice-principal. He was the one who took care of "vice." Charlie didn't do it. That wasn't his style, but he was still suspect and she thought he might know who did. Mr. Cherry was the one who gave the "licks" with the leather strap. He read the note, lined the boys up, stood in front of them, and asked, "Who hit Mithiss Yoth with the spit wadth?" No one answered. Mr. Cherry got angry when he read the note. With no response to his question, his anger ratcheted up, his face also became rather beet-like, and he put his red face inches in front of the first young man and said, "You boyth had bether listhen up!" He moved to the next one in line. "Thith will not happen again." He kept walking and talking. "Unleth I find out who did thith, none of you will path thith clath." He stared into Charlie's eyes and said, "Do you underthan what I'm thaying?" Charlie was as shaken as the other guys but was mesmerized by Mr. Cherry's speech. His brain was so keyed in to Mr. Cherry that he spontaneously answered, "Yeth Thir!" They all received lashes and the culprit confessed.

The last time Bob visited Charlie in Mrs. Yost's class was after he had actually finished classes as a senior. Charlie, a junior, was still attending classes. Bob was at school turning things in and preparing for the graduation when he discovered he needed five bucks for a deposit on his cap and gown. So, he dropped by Charlie's class and asked to talk with him. At this point in the year, Charlie had earned the honor of sitting in the front row with his desk tight up against Mrs. Yost's. Of course, she said, "No." Charlie just asked Bob what he needed and then reached into his wallet while Mrs. Yost found her paper and pen and asked Bob for his name. As Bob put the money in his wallet, he noticed she had a piece of legal paper taped to the desk pull out with Charlie's name at the top. Under it was a long laundry list of sins with dates. Bob told her his name but she got it all wrong. The conversation went something like this:

"What is your name, young man?"

"Bob Fleer."

"Rob Gler?"

"No, Bob Fleer."

"Bob Gler?"

"No, Bob Fleer."

"Bob Fuller?"

"No, Bob Fleer."

"Bob Flower?"

"Yes."

"How do you spell that?"

"Let's see...B-O-B F-L-O-W-E-R, I think."

She wrote that down. Charlie could hardly contain his giggles as he stood up to escort Bob to the door. He said, "Hang around, we are about to be dismissed early." While he was talking, another student put the trash can near the door, and Mrs. Yost told Charlie that he couldn't talk to Bob and he was to return to his seat immediately. A minute later, while Bob stood outside, the alarm clock bell went off, the door flew open, the four-foot-tall trash can sailed out, and the room quickly emptied of students. About ten minutes later, the real bell rang.

The Driving Range

Bob was hired to work at the Green Oaks Inn in Fort Worth in the summer of 1966, but the job didn't start for two weeks. Charlie could not get on at Green Oaks because he was still too young, but he got a job at the driving range located on the property where the Tandy Mart was later built. He worked evenings for Mr. Walter Burke when the place got busy. After Charlie's first evening at work, he called Bob to say there was another opening and that Bob should work there with him until his other job began. He said it would be a lot of laughs. So, Bob went to work with Charlie, who was then promoted to Chief Employee, and Bob was the new underling. Mr. Burke ("Walter") walked Bob through the process that he had taught Charlie the night before. Bob was to wash the golf balls and box them for the next customers. Each little box held five rows of five. If one was using irons, he was provided with a box of "culls." These were balls with dents and cracks. But for those using woods, the box packing got more complicated. There were good balls with stripes and balls where the stripes had been washed off to mere speckles. The striped balls were to be called "stripe," oddly enough. The speckled balls were to be called "specklety." They were to be put into the boxes in a very strict order, which Bob pretended to misunderstand to Walter's considerable frustration and Charlie's considerable enjoyment. Walter even asked Charlie if he didn't have some smarter friends, which made Charlie roar with his patented laugh. (Bob rapidly smartened up, to Walter's relief, when he found out that smarts was a criteria to drive the range tractor that collected the balls.)

The boxes were on a slanted rack. After the balls had been washed free of grass stains, they were loaded bottom row up by getting a striped ball with the little finger of each hand, right then left, followed by the ring finger of each hand picking up a specklety (R then L), then picking up the fifth striped ball with the right index finger. You inserted those balls on the bottom row and then started on the next. However, the next row would start with speckled balls and you would continue to rotate the order until the box was full and the balls evenly distributed. So, it was "stripe-stripe, specklety-specklety, stripe. Then it was specklety-specklety, stripe-stripe, specklety. Then back to stripe-stripe, specklety-specklety...well, you get the idea. You were supposed to say that out loud for each box so you wouldn't get it messed up. Good night!

Speaking of which, when it was time for Bob to get briefed on the big stadium lights that lit the range at night, Walter explained that you simply pulled the big breaker switch down to shut down the lights at quitting time. As soon as he said that, Charlie said, "Like this," and cranked the lever down, putting the range and all of the customers in the dark. Every time Walter would show Bob something, Charlie would put on his best "Barney Fife" imitation and reiterate some point as if world peace depended on it.

Soon, another employee came along which elevated Bob to a higher status of some sort. His name was Ernie. He was as sharp as Bob had pretended to be that first night, and he brought the senior employees some side-splitting moments. It took them a week, and Bob didn't have a lot more time to spare, to convince Walter that Ernie was bright enough to drive the range tractor. On Ernie's first outing, Charlie volunteered to hook up the trailers for him. One trailer was simply a wheeled funnel rig with a paddle wheel at the bottle neck to launch the balls into the second trailer, a large wheeled cage. Charlie put the ring of the first trailer just on the lip of the tractor's pintle hook and Ernie took off. It took a surprisingly long time before the trailer tongue finally fell to the ground while Ernie kept trucking. Finally as he came back, he saw the two trailers standing there. Instead of backing up to the tongue, he tried to wrench the two trailers around by hand while outside of the tractor's protective cage! Walter saw this act and went nuts, shouting at Charlie, "He's out of the cage! He is going to get hit!" So, Charlie yells to the crowd driving their balls, "Look! He's out of the cage!" whereupon almost everyone began aiming at Ernie. They thought Walter was going to bust a neck vein. Both Bob and Charlie were in a fit of uncontrollable laughter. Walter once again banned Ernie from driving the tractor. It took the boys a couple of days, Bob's last few there, to convince Walter to give him another chance. This time, Ernie carefully inspected the trailer hitch of the first trailer. However, Charlie put the ring of the last trailer on the lip of the first trailer's pintle hook. As soon as Ernie left, the second trailer came off and Walter ran out screaming at Ernie. But, Ernie couldn't hear Walter over the tractor motor and spent the next half hour lining up all of the golf balls on the driving range in very neat rows about twenty feet apart.

The Lake

All work and no play would make for a pretty dull existence. When they weren't working, Charlie and Bob waterskied. Charlie's dad (Charles) returned from one of his deployments and the Yates' family invited Bob to ski with them at Benbrook Lake. It was there that Charlie taught Bob to slalom. On his first attempt, Bob asked, "Charlie, shouldn't I learn to ski with two skis first?" "Nope," Charlie answered, "I need a partner. We don't have time for that."

They used that little red and white boat with the outboard motor a lot. Charlie's dad was very generous in giving the two teenagers free use of the boat. All he asked was that they put gas in it and leave it spotless. They did. Bob remembered that he never wanted to disappoint Major Yates because he never treated him like a kid but rather as a friend. Like Bob's own dad, he was demanding but gave the boys a long leash and liked a good laugh. Charlie and Bob gave Charles a set of boat rules they put together. The rules were typed on onion paper on an old portable Smith-Corona typewriter with gummed up keys. The importance of the document was further enhanced by an encasement of contact paper and a cheap metal picture frame. Charles proudly displayed the rules on the dashboard of the boat.

One day Charlie and Bob hit the dock with the boat and tore out the bow flag mast. They cleaned up the boat, parked it by the base dock and set their course to scour the boat shops, concerned that parts for that old boat would be tough to find. Fortunately, they found the exact same mast, installed it, and then told him what had happened. He just said, "Okay."

Actually, the boys enjoyed skiing the most when Charles was available to drive. He was not interested in skiing but he was an outstanding boat driver. That gave Charlie and Bob a chance to ski together and show off. His dad got a kick out of towing them around, especially in front of the dock where the TCU sorority girls sunned themselves. Charlie's mom made knee length, flannel pajama nightshirts for the show-offs. She sewed big puppy dog faces to the front of the shirts. The puppy dogs had rolling plastic eyes and eight inch long doggie ears that flapped in the breeze. Charlie picked the red and white striped PJs so Bob wore the paisley ones. The boys made the seven foot long nightcaps out of old bed sheets. They made patterns, cut them out, and painted red spots on the fabric with a stencil and red model airplane paint. Bob's mom sewed the two halves of the cap together. They *really* impressed the girls when they wore the nightshirts, skiing side-by-side with their caps flapping in the wind.

Boat Rules

Rule #1 Follow all rules.

Rule #2 Power boats must always give way to sail boats because the sailboat debris is difficult to get untangled from the prop.

Rule #3 When a man falls overboard, immediately throw him a life saver. In an emergency like that, any flavor will do.

Rule #4 When approaching a dock, always approach from the water side since the land side is extremely hard on the propeller.

Rule #5 If you spring a leak, pull up some floor boards to let the water out.

Terminology: To fully appreciate the nautical life, it is important to have a thorough understanding of the terminology. Such technical terms as *boat* and *water* will be unavoidable. There are four sides to a boat—front, back, left, and right. The front of the boat is called the *bow*. The back of the boat is called the *stern*. The two sides are called *port* and *starboard*. These are often confused. A reliable way to recall which is which is to remember that *port* has four letters and *left* has four letters. We have thus far discussed three sides of the boat, *bow, stern,* and *port.* It should be obvious to the casual observer that there is only one other side left and that is *starboard.* Therefore, *starboard* is left. Right? (The "rules" were adapted from one of Bob's old *Mad* magazines.)

Charlie and Bob in puppy dog nightshirts (1966)

The Patient

In the late sixties, wisdom tooth extraction was a more serious surgery than now. It often required recovery hospitalization for a day or two. Charlie was so swollen after his surgery that he barely looked like Charlie. Visitors were restricted so Bob told the nurse that he was Charlie's brother. The nurse asked Charlie if he would like to see his brother and he said "yes." Bob entered the room solemnly carrying a big bouquet of brown, dead roses (acquired at no cost). He asked the staring nurse if Charlie would make it. Charlie had been told not to laugh and he was shaking, trying to keep his mouth still. Then Bob very seriously asked the nurse if she could provide a large vase of water for the flowers. Tears started to roll out of Charlie's eyes, and he was trembling all over. His legs were jumping and he was howling with his mouth closed. When the nurse brought the vase, Bob spent a lot of time arranging the flowers, occasionally backing off to view them from various angles. Charlie nearly choked to death. It really wasn't very thoughtful but Bob sure had fun.

College Days

Charlie's goal with regard to college was to complete his degree as quickly as possible so that he would qualify to become an officer in the United States Air Force. He loved geology, but that was a five year program so he decided to major in personnel management. He joined ROTC and maintained good enough grades to earn a scholarship for his last two years of school. He wasn't much into uniforms and marching. He had grown up as a military dependent, so that was "old hat." Besides, he had worn a band uniform since junior high school. He was just "jumping through hoops" with regard to the undergrad military training and the college classwork. He needed to do well enough in both to earn the required recommendations to be accepted to pilot training. Several factors were in his favor. He had Air Force connections through his father; he had grown up on or near military installations and knew what military life was about. Most of his peers were doing everything possible to avoid the draft because they did not want to go to Vietnam; and some, who knew they would be drafted because of the new lottery system, applied for pilot training slots with the intention of failing out of the program and waiting out the war in a desk job. On one occasion, Bob reminded Charlie to toe the line in order to achieve the goal. Bob was the ROTC IG (Inspector General) during his senior year. He knew there was some talk among the officers about Charlie's fraternity haircut. So, when he gave the cadet officers an inspection, he looked for any flaw he could find on Charlie. Bob was particularly hard on him, partly to "pull his chain" and partly to get his attention. A lower classman recorded the demerits on a sheet of paper and then handed them back over to Bob to post at the end of the semester. If a cadet received enough demerits, his overall ROTC grade would be lowered. Bob gave Charlie dozens, more than all the others combined, while Charlie stood at attention, seething. Of course, when the demerits were posted, he only had a few, none of them from Bob. Friends are friends forever, or so they say.

There was a lot of turmoil on college campuses in the late sixties. The "hippie/free-love/drug culture" and the war protests were just beginning to creep into conservative West Texas when Charlie started school at Texas Tech. On one occasion, a guy in the dorm confided to Charlie that he had tried a little "pot." Charlie looked at him quizzically and asked, "What were you cooking, beans?" The young man responded, "No, man, I tried some grass, you know, hemp .... weed .....marijuana." The light came on in Charlie's mind as he remembered something about that from his high school health class. He responded, "You mean you smoke that stuff? Man, not me, I'm going to fly airplanes." So while some in the dorm were doing drugs, Charlie and his roommate were trying not to get caught dropping water balloons from their fourth floor room onto the pedestrians below. The pranks were memorable, but his best college memories were related to his fraternity, Alpha Tau Omega (ATO), and his new found freedom in flight.

Wings

Uncle Gene Minter lived in Waco where he was a flight instructor at a flight school located on a former military base. He was just ten years older than Charlie and was more like an older brother than an uncle. Charlie lived with Gene and his wife, Gracie, and young cousins Marc and Michelle for six weeks during the summer after his freshman year. While there, he learned to fly. His first flight lesson was August 2, 1968, and six days later he made his first solo flight. Gene often recounted that Charlie was the best student he ever had. He was also a natural at the controls. For those reasons, Gene expected perfection from Charlie with regard to the academics and execution of flight maneuvers. Teacher and student worked hard, drank a little beer, and entertained themselves. Gene's father, Ed, had a great sense of humor and loved to joke and tease. He worked in the petroleum industry in West Texas. On his desk, he kept a picture of himself, sitting on a jackass. He loved people and liked to engage them in conversation so he would often ask his visitors, "Which one in the picture is the jackass?"

Well, Gene learned a trick or two from his father and engaged his impressionable nephew in shenanigans. On one occasion, Gene ferried an airplane from Waco to Love Field in Dallas for a customer. He took Charlie with him. After they delivered the plane, they waited at Gate 11 to catch a commercial flight back to Waco. There was a large crowd waiting at the adjacent gate. It appeared that most in the crowd were parents waiting for a group of kids to return from a trip. (This was before the security restrictions were put into place after September 11, 2001.) The attendant at that gate announced that the plane was late and that there would be a gate change which she would announce shortly. Gene told Charlie to follow him, and he went and stood in the middle of the crowd. After a few minutes, he said in a voice loud enough for those around him to hear, "I heard that the plane is coming into Gate 21." He nudged Charlie's arm and they started walking to Gate 21. The crowd followed. They stood around and waited a few minutes and then Gene strolled up to the desk and made a pretense of talking to someone in a uniform. He returned to Charlie's side and said, "The gate has been changed to gate number two." He and Charlie started walking. There was a buzz of voices behind them and the lemmings started making their way to Gate 2. At Gate 11, Gene and Charlie took their seats in the waiting area because their plane was about to board. The crowd passed on by, much to their amusement. A bunch of kids entered the terminal at Gate 13 as Gene and Charlie headed down the boarding ramp, laughing all the way.

Brotherhood

Charlie loved being a part of the fraternity. He enjoyed people and he reveled in the activities –the harassment of being a pledge and of putting others through the process, the parties, the intramural sports, the annual musical competition, and best of all the friendships.

Every year there was a competition among the fraternities and sororities. Each one would perform several numbers from a famous musical production. One year, the ATOs did "South Pacific." Charlie had never sung with a group before, but he discovered that he was a first tenor and realized it was almost as much fun as playing the trumpet. The club needed someone to play the conch shell in one of the numbers and of course, he volunteered. He had never played one before, but he figured it out. The next year the fraternity picked a western-themed musical and needed someone to play the harmonica. You guessed it – he had never played one of those before either, but he figured it out.

His closest relationships in the fraternity were his big brother, his pledge brothers, and his little brother. Some of those relationships were to remain tight throughout his life-time. It was on the flag detail duty where he met the cadet who was to become his little brother. His name was Gary Flynt. Charlie was a junior and a Flight Commander in AFROTC. Gary was a freshman and a Cadet Airman. Several hurricanes hit the Gulf of Mexico that September, sending a lot of rain throughout West Texas. On the day of the flag detail, it was raining cats and dogs in Lubbock.

The ROTC was responsible for raising and lowering the American flag on campus each day. Charlie was in charge of the flag detail, and Gary was one of two younger cadets who had the detail with him. Gary had never done flag detail before, so the day prior he found out where they were supposed to meet, what the uniform of the day would be, and the nature of his responsibilities. He got up early the next morning, put on the uniform, and walked from the Wiggins Complex over to the ROTC building. It was wet, and even with the raincoat there was no way to stay dry. Charlie showed up a few minutes after Gary. Both of them were soaked with rain dripping off their hats and faces. Gary aspired to be a pilot also, and he was digging this military "stuff" so he was grinning from ear to ear. Charlie asked him, "What are you smiling about?" Gary retorted, "Does it always rain this hard when *you* command the flag detail?" Charlie laughed and told him that he looked like a drowned rat. He then asked him to drop by his room that afternoon. A friendship was born. Gary pledged the fraternity and Charlie was his "big brother" even though Gary towered over him by nine inches.

Gary's pledge class took a trip (a pledge cut) to the University of Oklahoma. The pledges kidnapped some of the ATO brothers they particularly liked and took them on the bus. Charlie was one of them. The boys had an overload of fun in Norman, so on the way home everyone just wanted to sleep – everyone except Charlie and Dave Lamb. They commandeered the PA system on the bus and began to tell jokes. The jokes were really, really bad jokes - groaners. Finally, one of the actives, Bill Snyder, told Charlie that if he told another bad joke, they were tossing both him and Lamb off of the bus. Charlie took that as a challenge and begged the brothers to let him tell just *one* more joke. Snyder told him he could but it had better be a good one. Charlie picked up the microphone and began, "There were these three tomatoes, a poppa tomato, a momma tomato and a baby tomato, walking down the road. Baby tomato kept falling behind and finally the poppa tomato turned to the baby tomato, hit it on the head squishing it, and said, 'Ketchup!!!!'" The bus was in the middle of nowhere, between Seymour and Guthrie. Snyder told the bus driver to pull over and had some of the guys hold Charlie and Dave while he handcuffed them. Then the jokesters were unceremoniously tossed off the bus. The door shut and off went the brothers, leaving the two of them looking pretty dejected.

About ten miles down the road there were a couple of state troopers in the median. Snyder had the bus driver stop and he asked the troopers if they wanted to have some fun. Of course, being cops (in the middle of nowhere), they did. After the "crimes" had been explained, the troopers dutifully went to find and "arrest" the criminals. As the troopers neared them, they screeched to a stop, hopped out of the vehicle, grabbed the handcuffed dynamic duo and searched them. One of the troopers said they looked just like the description of two guys who had escaped from the Seymour jail. Charlie and Dave told them it was just a fraternity prank and the trooper said, "What's a fraternity?" The troopers put them in the cruiser and drove back to the bus that was waiting for them. The bus driver got out and walked up to the patrol car. Charlie and Dave were going nuts. "Hey, we know this guy. He's our bus driver. He will tell you who we are." The trooper turned to Bud, the bus driver, and said, "Do you know these boys?" Bud replied: "Never saw them before in my life!" The trooper played along, "Well, guess we'll just have to take them back to the Seymour jail." Charlie blurted out, "But I've got a test on Monday!" The hooting, hollering, and laughter from the bus were raucous. They were crying – the laughing hurt so badly.

Finally, Snyder walked over to troopers and told them that he really hated to spoil their fun but the brothers had to claim them. Besides, he confessed, "If they start telling you guys some of their bad jokes you'll be after all of us!" Charlie and Dave were ushered out of the cruiser and back into the bus where they sat, quiet as church mice, for the rest of the trip.

CHAPTER 3

This, That, and the Other

1969-1972

"Then the LORD God said, 'It is not good for the man to be alone; I will make him a helper suitable for him.'" – Genesis 2:18

The Blind Date

In his middle-aged years, Charlie took on the roles of uncle, instructor, Sunday school teacher, and mentor to many boys and young men. He would ask "What do you want to be when you grow up?" If they answered, "A pilot!" he would respond, "I'm sorry son, but you can't do both." Most often the boys would think about that for a moment, and then ask, "What do you mean?" Charlie's pat answer was, "You can't be a pilot *and* grow up." As his wife of forty-two years, I can affirm the truthfulness of that statement, at least with regard to Charlie. However, in the beginning of our relationship I thought that the college man who wanted to be an Air Force pilot was quite mature. Others, including his mother, his best friend, and my siblings knew better and failed to give me a heads up. Dottie, his mother, first noticed me and my sister, Janet, on the first Sunday we attended the Carswell Air Force Base (AFB) chapel with our family. My father, Major Joseph Coggins, was introduced as the new chaplain. Dottie determined to find a way to have her two sons meet those two girls with the dark hair and eyes. My younger brother, David, described the fateful progression of events: "I loved Billy Yates. It did not take long when we moved from Elmendorf AFB to Carswell in 1968 for us to become best friends. It took me thirty seconds on my bike to get down to Billy's house, so I spent a lot of time there. His mother, Dottie, was one of the sweetest women I had ever met. His dad, Charles, was a lovable bear, once you got past his bark. His sister, Vicki, was the cutest girl on the base, hands down. His off-to-college brother, Charlie, loomed larger than life for two high school boys. We used to visit his room on occasion to play with his model airplanes hanging from the ceiling. We knocked one down once and hoped Charlie wouldn't notice the uneven glue joints. We got reamed out for that one. It wasn't long before Billy and my sister Janet cooked up a scheme to introduce Charlie to Diane – a double date bowling night on one of his home visits! And the rest, as they say, is history."

Charlie wasn't eager to go out on a blind date that spring break. He already had girl troubles. He had two girlfriends. One was a junior in high school and lived in Ft. Worth, and the other was a girl he met at Texas Tech. One, he befriended while he was in high school, and the other he began dating at college when he was required to have a date for certain fraternity functions. His life became complicated. The college girlfriend was from Ft. Worth also and was home for the holiday. Both girls were expecting to spend some time with him. He gets home and his siblings have arranged for him to meet some *other* girl who lived down the street. Charlie responded to their plot with, "I'm sure she's a real nice girl. Dogs don't bark at her; she sews her own clothes; and babies don't cry in her arms. But, I really have other things I need to do." At the urging of his mother and the cajoling of Vicki and Billy, he agreed to a double date – Billy and Janet and he and I. Billy and Janet were sophomores in high school, and they planned the evening. All

Charlie had to do was show up with his car, drive, and be nice. We went to the golden arches of McDonalds and to the bowling alley. I was a senior in high school, the new girl, bussed across town to Arlington Heights High School. It wasn't easy to make friends in the huge school, especially since I lived so far from the campus. I had all the credits I needed to graduate except Texas history, so I went to school half days, worked at Neiman-Marcus in the afternoons, and anticipated attending college at Baylor University in the fall. I thought the blind date might be an interesting break in my routine. It wasn't. Billy and Janet whispered and giggled in the back seat, enjoying their private jokes, and keeping close watch on any interactions between Charlie and me. There weren't many. I could tell he would rather be somewhere else. His bowling was atrocious.

Give a Man Enough Rope....

The Yates were a boating and skiing family. A lot of ropes are used in the boating game. Often heard phrases were: "I spend half my life untangling ropes." and "Give a man enough rope..." The meaning of the last one is that if you give someone too much rope (or freedom), he could get tangled in it and "hang himself." Well, Charlie had somewhat of a tangled mess with his girlfriend situation. At the end of the spring semester, Charlie went to Officer's Training School in Montgomery, Alabama, for six weeks. It was like he had joined the Foreign Legion. He did not let either one of his girlfriends know when he got back in town. His mother hadn't given up on the chaplain's daughter.

One hot July day, she suggested that Charlie invite some of the neighbors to go waterskiing. Lake Worth was only a couple of blocks away from base housing. Billy knocked on the door and invited Janet and me. He also invited his friend, Larry Moertel, and his older brother, Randy, a sophomore at Louisiana Tech, who was home for the summer. I had waterskied a couple of times before in my life and had recently met Randy, so I thought this could be a fun time. I had a great time! I got right up on the skis - no disastrous falls and no wardrobe malfunctions. Randy was very attentive. Charlie and Billy showed off their admirable slalom skills and made great sport of Randy and Larry, who were beginners. As the day wore on, I recognized there was a little competition going on between Randy and Charlie. After skiing for several hours, we motored to a restaurant on the lake. While I was in the ladies' room, the boys figured out the seating arrangement. When I joined them, I was seated next to Charlie. Randy was at the other end of the table.

Charlie and I dated the rest of the summer. We skied, went on picnics, went to airshows and movies, and took walks by the lake - but no bowling. He loved to take pictures. He took his 35mm camera almost everywhere we went. Before, his primary subject was airplanes, but by the end of the summer he was taking a lot of pictures of me. Then he went back to Texas Tech, and I left home to begin classes at Baylor in Waco.

Another Lump of Clay

I see my life in three parts - life before Charlie, life with Charlie, and life without Charlie. I'm just beginning the third part, as of this writing, but I recognize that God used the first part to shape me into the woman that He planned would be Charlie's helpmate. The shaping wasn't finished in those first seventeen years; it would take more than four additional decades for the two of us to be continually molded and put through the fire before God said, "It is finished."

Life before Charlie was under the loving nurture of Joseph (Joe) Harold and Jean Elizabeth Coggins. Joe had just returned from serving in the Navy in the Pacific in World War II. He and Jean had known each other since childhood because they attended the same church and Jean was a friend of Joe's sister, Dorothy. Both felt they had been called by God to spend their lives in Christian service. They began dating during their sophomore year in college. Upon graduation, they married and moved to New Orleans where Joe attended seminary. I was born May 24, 1951 and Janet was born December 5, 1952. Those seminary years were lean years. Joe preached in rural churches in Louisiana and Mississippi and was able to earn a little money. On one of these occasions, I had just learned to walk and was toddling across the dirt yard of a small farm house. The resident rooster took offense and hopped on my head. I was terrified and began to run. The rooster hung on, claws digging into my forehead, flapping his wings, and screeching. The terror ended when I stumbled and fell, causing the rooster to land a few feet in front of me. Someone intervened and chased the wicked creature away. I had recurring nightmares about that rooster well into my teens. Mom had a degree in sociology with a desire to be a social worker, but she was unable to find a job. So, on weekdays she cooked hamburgers to sell to the other seminary students. One day there was another close call. I crawled up on a chair to watch my mother cook. I leaned over and the open flame licked the edges of my dress and set it on fire. My mother screamed but my father was there. He smothered the fire with his "big bare hands." Joe Coggins had noticeably big, strong hands. The hands that gently held his baby girl saved her life. In later years, my remembrance of this event would have even greater significance. Big hands wrapped in bandages are even bigger. Big hands nailed to the cross are infinitely big.

When Joe graduated from seminary, God began to open the doors that fulfilled his desire to minister to the great spiritual needs of those in the military. He became an Air Force chaplain in 1954. By 1958, my brothers David and Michael and my sister Kathy had been born. Kathy was only six weeks old when Joe was sent to Japan without his family for a one year remote assignment. I was seven years old. Mother was recuperating from a very difficult pregnancy and surgery. There was a newborn and three other siblings, ages 2, 4 and 5, and my daddy was gone. During the year I learned to depend on my heavenly Father. I had been taught about God's plan of salvation from my earliest years of comprehension. I understood my sin. I believed that God sent His only begotten Son to die for my sin, and I knew that because of my faith, God forgave me for my sins. I was now his adopted child. I was baptized in First Baptist Church of Rocky Mount, North Carolina where my grandparents attended, and where my parents were raised in the faith. The next year, in 1959, the family joined Joe in Japan where he had the opportunity to minister to a people he had fought against fifteen years earlier in the war. He and another chaplain started a mission in the town next to the military base. The family spent many weekends with Japanese families at the mission. By the time we left Japan, I decided I wanted to be a medical missionary when I grew up.

Jean and Joe Coggins, (l to r) Diane, Kathy,
David, Mike, and Janet (1958)

The first time I saw my parents cry was several weeks after we left Japan. We were on our way to our new home in North Carolina and were visiting my grandparents when they received a special delivery letter. The cargo plane that was bringing all of our belongings to the United States had crashed in the Pacific Ocean. The tears were not only for our personal material loss, but also for the loss of the crew of the plane. There was not much compensation for our household goods. Our grandparents purchased some bed linens and a few clothes, but a family of seven has a lot of needs. It was now necessary for my mother to find a job. Four of the children were in school, so she went to work in a childcare center on the base that allowed her to take Kathy (the youngest) to work with her. The rest of us became very independent and self-sufficient. The "ironing lady" came to the house in the afternoons when we got home from school. She did "the ironing" (no permanent press or polyester in these days) while we did our homework. Dad planted a garden and we shucked corn and shelled peas.

The second time I saw my parents cry was when my twelve-year-old sister, Janet, became deathly ill. At the time we were living at Elmendorf AFB, Anchorage, Alaska. Janet was hospitalized on the base, and she was very weak and losing weight. After several weeks she was diagnosed with Type I diabetes. Once her blood sugar levels were stabilized, she came home. The same week that she was hospitalized, our cat was hit by a car and severely injured. Ordinarily, Dad would have had the animal put down, but he didn't think the family, especially Janet, could bear it. So, he paid the hefty vet bill to have the cat's broken leg set. Janet and the cat recuperated together.

Dad was assigned to Seymour Johnson AFB in Goldsboro, North Carolina, from 1961 until 1965. During the Cuban Missile Crisis, military members and their families were instructed to prepare for nuclear war. We stockpiled supplies, and practiced huddling in the hallway of our home. This was less frightening than the drills we practiced in Japan where we had to go into underground tunnels.

When President Kennedy was assassinated, there was another period of great tension on the base and then more reason for alarm. There was a conflict going on in Southeast Asia. Some of the pilots from Seymour Johnson had been shot down. By that time, I was babysitting the young children of our neighbors. Many of the fathers were pilots, and I knew that it was my father who would bring the news to the families. I could not imagine anything more horrible.

In 1965, we moved to Alaska. The conflict in Southeast Asia grew into a war. The brother of my dear friend was killed in Vietnam. And then, there were several who graduated from my high school the year before, who were killed in action also. We moved to Texas in the summer of 1968. In 1969, when I entered college, there was violent opposition to the war in many parts of the country. It was still peaceful at Baylor, but during the course of my freshman year, the wave of change that had already rolled over most of the rest of the country washed through Texas. The most noticeable sign of the change was the "dress code." I began the year wearing the dresses I bought at Neiman-Marcus with my employee discount. I ended the year wearing bell-bottom jeans, tee shirts, beads, sandals, and Charlie's fraternity pin.

The Bear and the Red Raider

In college, every freshman was a "new kid." The playing field was leveled, and it was much easier to make friends. I wanted to be involved in something so I ran for the office of President of the Freshmen Spirit Committee. There were several of us who stood before a crowd of freshmen and made a rah-rah speech. I don't remember what I said, but I was elected. That meant I was in charge of the freshman float for homecoming. There were four other officers. The five of us set out to make a lot of friends quickly because we needed volunteers to help put something together. Charlie and I had exchanged addresses, and we had each written a couple of letters. I told him how busy I was with different committees, and how I was trying to get the float finished on time. I was also tasked with planning activities that would get the freshmen excited about being Baylor Bears. One of the activities was a cookout at a city park the day before homecoming. I guess Charlie figured I wasn't sitting in my room at night waiting for the phone to ring, so he wrote and asked if he could be my date for the Baylor homecoming.

He drove seven hours on that Friday before the game and was there for the park event. We went to the parade on Saturday morning, the football game in the afternoon, and then on Saturday night he took me flying by the light of the full moon. Charlie was staying with his Uncle Gene, and Gene had given him the keys to an airplane and told him to show me a good time. During my year at Baylor, I had a number of dates, but he was the only one who took me flying in the moonlight. We began writing a couple of times a week, and then we planned more opportunities to see each other – Thanksgiving, Christmas, a sorority dance, spring break, a fraternity party. Most of the young men I met at Baylor had yet to figure out what they were going to do with their lives. Many spent a lot of time partying and looking for ways to avoid being drafted into military service. No one wanted to go to Vietnam. By the end of my freshman year, Charlie convinced me that I should become a Texas Tech Red Raider. I had a small scholarship to Baylor and a part-time job on campus, but attending Baylor was still more expensive than Tech. With two other kids at home preparing to begin college after my sophomore year, my parents agreed that a transfer to Tech would be a good idea.

The Engagement

That summer, Charlie worked as a lifeguard at the Carswell AFB pool, and I returned to my job at Neiman-Marcus. In July, we decided to get married in December. He knew that the day after he graduated from Tech in May, he would receive his commission into the Air Force and would begin pilot training the following week.

We had a plan but we needed to break it to the folks. Charlie thought that we could have a little party, invite both families, and then he would give a slide show presentation. The camera had been our companion on most of our times spent together. We bought some poster board and painted titles and credits. He took pictures of those and made slides of them. The name of our presentation was "This, That, and the Other." The words on the final slide were "The End of the Beginning," and there was a picture of two intertwined rings. We made punch, a multicolored cake, and some popcorn. Charlie set up the screen and the slide projector. Just before he said "lights out," he put a Henry Mancini album on the phonograph. He started the slide show and timed it to the music. When the show was done, Charlie got up, turned on the lights, and turned off the music. There were claps and hoorays; the siblings were especially noisy. There was only one problem that I could see. He stopped the show on a picture of us together, but he did not show the last slide. Now what? "That's all folks!" My family walked home and Charlie put up the equipment while I cleaned up the party mess. Within a half hour, Charlie got over his cold feet. We went to my house, and he asked my dad for my hand in marriage (as if they hadn't guessed what was up). Then, we traipsed back down to his house and talked to his parents. Over the next few weeks, we worked out the details. Our parents would help us with school expenses the semester after we were married, and then 2 Lt. Charlie Yates would pay for the rest of my schooling.

That next week, Charlie said, "I guess we ought to get a ring." I said, "That would be nice." Except for Bob, we were the first of our peers to embark on this adventure. Charlie made $125 a week as a lifeguard at the base pool. We drove to Service Merchandise, a discount store that carried appliances, clothing, cameras, and some jewelry. We looked at the sparkling diamond rings in the glass case, and he said, "Pick one." We were military brats; I made most of my own clothes and carefully counted every penny I ever made baby-sitting and working in the department store. "Pick one?" I picked the least expensive ring on display, a narrow gold band with a small diamond for $125. The ring needed to be sized. Two days later, we went back to the store; I tried it on to see if it fit. The salesman put it in a nice ring box, then put the box in a small white paper bag, stapled it, and gave it to Charlie. We got in Charlie's red bug, buckled up, and then he tossed the bag to me. I stared at him a minute and said, "That's it?" I was thinking we should go out to dinner, go sit on a bench by the lake under the stars....something.... special. I lamely asked, "Shouldn't we make this a special occasion?" My fiancé responded, "Well, we can't really do anything today. I already arranged with all the guys in the neighborhood (Randy, brothers David and Billy, and others) to play flag football this afternoon. How about french fries and a coke?" That afternoon he broke his leg playing "football with the guys." We spent late afternoon and most of the evening in the emergency room as his leg was put in a cast.

The Honeymoon

I've always been a little embarrassed to tell this story, but it is what it is. Our wedding was December 29, 1970. I made my dress out of white velvet and trimmed the v-neckline and hem with white rabbit fur. All of our brothers and sisters were in the wedding, the girls in cobalt blue velvet and the boys in black suits. Bob Fleer was Charlie's best man; Bill Yates, Randy Moertel, and Gary Flynt were his groomsmen. My dad guided us through our marriage counseling and officiated at the ceremony. The night before at the rehearsal dinner, Charlie gave me a pair of earrings as a wedding gift. I gave him a Bible with a black leather cover, his name embossed in gold on the front. I taped a note inside– "Dear Charlie, Our lives with God, that we share, will be the most important thing that we share. Wherever you go, I hope that you will take this Bible with you, for as God loves you and is with you always, I am also. I love you, Diane"

Charlie and Diane Yates
December 29, 1970

The wedding was at the Carswell AFB Chapel, and our reception was a few blocks away at the Officers' Club. Charlie's parents gave us a two-night stay at the Royal Coach Inn in Dallas as a wedding gift. On January 30th, we returned to Lubbock in Charlie's little red bug, stuffed with some of our wedding gifts - enough to set up housekeeping in our newly-rented apartment. We hung out at the apartment over New Year's Eve. Since we still had a few days before classes started, we decided to go to Juarez, Mexico, right across the border from El Paso. Charlie had been there with his fraternity and had a really good time. We stopped to climb El Capitan, an impressive escarpment in the Guadalupe Mountain National Park, about 100 miles east of our destination. We didn't arrive in El Paso until after dark. The neon sign and the cheap room rate caught our attention so we checked in at the State Motel. Think, "stapled white paper bag." There was one light in the room, a bare light bulb hanging from a cord over the center of the bed. The mattress was deeply bowed in the center. It was covered with a faded, yellow, popcorn-chenille bedspread. There were several large holes in the spread, and threads hung from the tattered edges. We were dirty and tired from the mountain climbing, so we decided to stay. At the very least we could take a shower and rest. The outside wall of the bathroom was constructed of glass tiles which contorted the light from the neon sign out front. It was creepy, and I wasn't convinced that someone outside couldn't see what was going on inside. Skip the shower. It's a good thing that we didn't mind sleeping close together; we may as well have been in a hammock. We woke early, and checked out of the place before we could look at it more closely in the daylight, then picked up some fast food breakfast. After crossing the Rio Grande and having declared ourselves as tourists at the checkpoint, we entered Ciudad Juarez. Charlie told me that if I married him we would see the world. It was January 4th and it was a weekday. The streets were nearly empty, and only a few shops were open for business. We purchased a couple of malachite wall hangings for our apartment and bought two carved pelicans for our parents.

What Charlie, the trumpet player and Herb Alpert/Tijuana Brass fan, really wanted to see in Juarez was a mariachi band. When he was there before with his fraternity brothers, they found a great bar and listened to mariachi music for hours. We wandered around the streets of the city looking for a band. We finally found a bar/restaurant that was open. A cardboard sign by the front door advertised "live music," so we walked in, and the hostess sat us at a table barely a foot from the stage. We ordered some cokes and munched on some chips and salsa. Soon a man, a Mexican man, dressed in an ornate green outfit (tight pants and bolero), stepped out on the stage and began to sing in an Irish brogue "When Irish Eyes Are Smiling." We nearly choked on our chips. We tried to smile politely. When he finished, Charlie clapped enthusiastically and exclaimed, "Bravo! Bravo!" There was another couple in the place sitting by the front window, but they weren't paying attention. The singer, egged on by Charlie's appreciation, sang a few more songs.

We were hoping that the next act was a mariachi band. No such luck. This time a middle-aged, overweight, heavily made up woman walked to the center of the stage. The music played through the sound system, and she began to dance. As she danced, she dropped pieces of her costume about the stage, first a head piece, then the shoes, etc., etc. Before you knew it, she was standing two feet from us wearing almost nothing but her greasy sweat. I put my hand over my eyes and said, "Can we leave NOW?" Charlie left money on our table, grabbed my hand, and pulled me out the door. I mused, "What would my sweet grandmother, who taught me to pray when I was still in my crib, think about this?"

Air Force Commissioning Ceremony, (l to r) Charles E. Yates, Jr., Charlie Yates, Diane Yates (1971)

Do You Hear a Train?

We lived in the Varsity Village complex which was across 4th street and the railroad tracks from Texas Tech University. I was a better roommate than the two fraternity brothers Charlie lived with the previous semester. I knew how to cook and keep the place clean. We had a great time as married college students before the stresses of "real life" began. Upon graduation in May, he was commissioned as a 2nd lieutenant in the US Air Force. He bought a bicycle for me to ride to school and he took the VW ten miles down 4th Street to Reese Air Force Base where he was assigned to a pilot training class. Some weeks he would report for duty at 5 AM. When he had the predawn report time, we would go to bed early because he wanted to be rested and alert for his flight. Charlie would become very irritated if his sleep was disturbed.

It was one of those nights when we retired early. A short while after lights were out, I heard a noise. It sounded like a train that was far away, which wouldn't be unusual since we lived close to the tracks. The sound stopped. I began to drift off to sleep. I heard a noise again. What is it – the train? Quiet. I could hear Charlie breathing. Relax, go to sleep. The minutes passed. Is that another train? "Charlie, I hear a train!" Charlie stirred, "Uhhh ...what? Why did you wake me up? Leave me alone and go to sleep. I don't hear anything." I rolled over, pouting at his sharp tone. My mind was busy. I tried to think about my German vocabulary words. That should put me to sleep. More time passed. That noise, I heard it again! The train should have moved on down the tracks by now. I put the pillow over my head. The noise got louder and louder. I clamped the pillow tighter. The sound got louder, and I could feel Charlie leaning over on me. That's not a train! It's a harmonica. I pushed Charlie off the bed.

That wasn't the last time he would get in trouble with a harmonica.

Flight Training

The routine of pilot training was study, brief, fly, debrief, study, brief, fly, debrief, study, brief, fly, debrief, etc. Bob had done the same routine the year before Charlie, and Bob became a flight instructor in the T-38 when Charlie became a student. They were in different squadrons, but Bob did fly one instructional sortie with Charlie. Charlie was in the front seat and Bob, the instructor, was in the rear. It was a night instrument ride, and Bob decided to have a little fun with him. The T-38 had a nose wheel steering safety cut out when the burners were lit. What few knew was that the nose wheel steering could be cut out by simply hitting the engine ignition button since it was the same system. It only cut out for thirty seconds. So, every time Charlie came to a turn, Bob punched the ignition button, and he would lose steering. Charlie would yell, "I can't steer it." Bob would take it, and as the 30 seconds ran out, he would negotiate the turn and tell him, "It worked fine for me." Then at the next turn, he did it again. In the debrief Bob asked Charlie how he expected to graduate if he couldn't even taxi the plane. That is when Charlie suspected a rat. What are friends for?

CHAPTER 4

Lt. Charlie Yates Goes to War

Part 1

1972

"Blessed is the Lord, my Rock who trains my hands for war, my fingers for battle...."- Psalm 144:1

Charlie graduated from flight school in May, 1972. He studied hard, striving to be at the top of the class. He knew that his next assignment hinged on his class ranking. His burning desire since boyhood was to fly fighters, but there were five fighters in the block of assignments for his class. Two would automatically go to former navigators who had flown in the back seat of fighters in combat. He ranked high in his class, but the other 3 fighters were taken just before him. The remaining choices were tankers, bombers, T-37 and T-38 instructor slots, and 2 OV-10s. At that time, he didn't know a lot about the OV-10 except that it flew in support of the fighter operation in Southeast Asia. The OV-10 was not a fighter, but he would get to fly in combat. He took the assignment, knowing he would be headed to Vietnam. How ironic; he was the guy with a lottery draft number that assured he wouldn't be called up. He volunteered to go when he could have stayed stateside and taught others to fly.

He did not consult his wife about the decision.

OV-10s

After three months of training in the OV-10 at Hurlburt AFB, Florida, Charlie left his bride and headed for Vietnam via Prisoner of War (POW) training in Washington State and Jungle Survival School in the Philippines. The date was August 19, 1972. He was 23 years old. His experiences in the training camps were the "graduate school" of his previous boyhood and young manhood experiences – scouting, camping, hunting, fishing, tactical war board games, and pledging a fraternity. He shared with me some of his experiences in Washington. He and his partner were in the forest evading capture from the "enemy." They stumbled across another group's supply of meat hidden in a cold mountain stream. They "borrowed" some of it to add to their own rations. When Charlie was eventually captured, his torturers endeavored to put him in a small wooden box to "break him." As they stuffed him in the box and then adjusted the box to make it smaller in order to make him extremely uncomfortable, Charlie started screaming in excruciating pain. His captors believed him to be tightly crammed and contorted and set the adjustment. When his tormentors left the area, Charlie settled himself in a comfortable seating position to wait it out. When the guards finally came to release him from the torture, they were not happy to find him relaxed and grinning at them. Charlie may have won the battle but he lost the war.

In spite of the unpleasantness of the training, its culmination was one of the most memorable experiences of his life. One morning, the weary, broken, depressed group of trainees was called to the usual dawn report by their harsh captors. After they lined up before a guard dressed in the enemy uniform they were told "Criminals – About face!" When they turned around, the sun was rising before them. The "enemy commander" was now dressed in Air Force blues, saluting the men he had just put through the wringer. The sound of the bugle echoed through the forest, the American flag was raised, the men placed their right hands over their hearts, the national anthem played, and there was a tear in every eye. God bless America. The men were ready to fly and to fight.

During this time, Charlie's parents lived on Ward Street at Carswell Air Force Base in Ft. Worth, Texas. My parents still lived three houses down the street. Both sets of parents and Charlie insisted that I live with my parents while Charlie was in Southeast Asia. I had just turned 21 and was accepted as a medical technology intern at All Saints Hospital in Ft. Worth. I would be engaged in a year of intense study while he was gone. Charlie traded in our "red bug" for a lime green Cutlass so that I would have reliable transportation. We spent our last night together in a hotel, and then we drove to the airport in that new green car. I waited with him at the gate, tightly holding his hand, trying not to cry. I didn't dare speak. When his flight was called, he put on his sunglasses and walked down the enclosed ramp.

I lived the war through his perspective. The only way we were able to communicate was through letters. We wrote to each other almost every day. I usually received the letters in clusters and sometimes not in sequence. Those letters were my lifeline. If I didn't get one, I lost my appetite and imagined the worst. The nightly news was filled with stories of war protests, war casualty numbers, scenes of destruction, and the progress of peace talks. The war was not popular, and I did not make it a topic of conversation at work. I buried myself in my studies and prayed during my forty-five-minute drive to and from the hospital.

Letters

What follows is Charlie's war story through excerpts from some of his letters. Parts of those letters were for my eyes only and remain so. Interspersed through the letters are explanations and elaborations that Charlie wrote 40 years later as he compiled a photo-journal on the war called <u>Nguyen's Shadow</u>.

September 7
Dearest Girlfriend ...We're getting ready to move out — don't know exactly what we're going to do but will find out....The view of Washington is just beautiful. This is almost as hard as our mountain climbing trip...Everybody's complaining about being here except me and my partner-we're the only ones that think it is fun....after this all escape and evasion.

September 18
Dear Diane, Started Snake School (Philippines) yesterday. They put a lot of emphasis on the POW (prisoner of war) and escape and evasion issues.

Snake School – Clark Air Base, Philippines

San Francisco is in plain view out the left side of the aircraft in route to the Philippines where the Jungle Survival Course, a.k.a. Snake School, waits. My tour has officially started, DEROS established. That's "Date Eligible for Return from Overseas." Thus the expression "365 and a wake up" becomes the measure of your remaining days. After your one year tour in Southeast Asia (SEA), you'll wake up (hopefully) and be home, back in the land of the" round eyes." The jungle-covered mountains of the Philippines are very much like the terrain of Vietnam, Laos, and Cambodia. The first order of business in Snake School is building a dry shelter and making a fire in a torrential rainstorm. Next, evade the "enemy." Negritos gave the Japanese fits during WWII. Hiding in the densest part of the jungle was of little use against these jungle experts. No one was able to hide successfully. While I was sitting in academics at Snake School, two realities hit me. First, the instructor, a super sergeant, one with a lot of stripes on his sleeves, pointed directly at me and said, *"The man that was sitting in your chair was shot down this week and is evading the enemy as we speak!"* My initial thought was, *"It's just a scare tactic to make you pay attention."* My eyes shifted to the SAR (Search and Rescue) board that chronicled every 'shoot down' since 1965. The last two names on the list were guys I knew personally, one from college and one from pilot training. I was paying attention. Second reality: my original orders assigned me to the 23rd TASS (Tactical Air Support Squadron) stationed at Nakhon Phanom (NKP), Thailand. A young airman called out, *"Lieutenant Yates? You've been reassigned to the 20th TASS. Here are your new orders sir."* I was not going to Thailand with my buddies; I was going to Vietnam! I was not going to the resort by the Mekong River; I was going to Rocket City!

September 21

Finished snake school yesterday- didn't even see one snake. That had to be one of the best survival schools yet. There was no B.S... .P.S. I decided to finish this letter later. I've arrived. Da Nang is really a hole but I'm impressed so far with the squadron. I rode with a Catholic chaplain on the C-130 in here. He said he was a jinx because every time he comes back to Da Nang they take a bunch of rockets. Then, somebody else told me that the VC (Viet Cong) always knew when a new guy came in and they would greet him with a rocket attack. Ha! Ha! – Well, both stories are true. At 5:00 AM, the first three hit and the alarm went off. My roommate grabbed his helmet and flak vest and hit the floor. I didn't have one yet so I got under the covers – nothing can hurt you under the covers. At 5:05, the next rounds slammed in – just a little bit scary! But you don't have to worry about me – just think about me, okay?

Covey 25

I was met at the terminal and escorted to the squadron by the commander and introduced to the other pilots who were singing the FAC theme song, *"Dear Mom, Your Son is Dead,"* in honor of three of our pilots shot down that day. One was KIA (Killed in Action) and the other two were rescued. Reality was quickly setting in. The next greeting was from the Viet Cong at 0500--27 Soviet made 122mm rockets hit the base. Welcome to Rocket City comrade! I'm the 'New Guy' in the squadron, technically the FNG, but that acronym will go undefined. My official call sign is Covey 25 (that's two-five in the lingo). The first order of business is being declared 'Combat Ready', CR for short. That process involves 10-15 combat sorties and a check ride. Most are dual with an instructor; several are in the backseat observing the procedures. All involved directing airstrikes with real bombs and Gomers shooting back. Once combat ready, the missions are solo.

A brief explanation is required here. Throughout the history of warfare, nicknames are applied to the enemy. Japs, nips, krauts, Boche, Gerry's, Reds, Ivans, gooks, rag heads, etc. Tommys and Yanks for the 'good guys' with Yankee Air Pirate being my favorite. This war was no exception. The allied Vietnamese were the ARVN (pronounced *arvin*--Army of the Republic of Vietnam).

The Vietnamese enemies, the North Vietnamese Army (NVA) and Viet Cong (VC--*vee cee*), were referred to as Gomers and Charlie (short for the phonetic alphabet *Victor Charlie*, and *not* my favorite term). Nguyen was the most common Vietnamese surname like Smith or Jones. Everybody was named Nguyen. As a FAC, you got to know your AO (Area of Operation) real well. Your job was to shadow Nguyen and keep him from disrupting the lives of folks on the ground.

September 29

Today I flew my first combat mission...It was hard to believe that there was a war going on down there but there was. We put in two sets of strikes. The total fly time today was 6.8 hours and I'm a little tired.

The OV-10 Bronco

The Bronco was specifically designed to carry a wide variety of ordnance on seven external stations. Included were four M-60 machine guns and a total of 2000 rounds of 7.62mm ammunition. Four stations located on the sponsons could carry up to 500 lbs. each with 1000 lbs. on the centerline station. Two wing stations could carry AIM-9 air-to-air heat seeking missiles. The typical FAC load was three to four pods of Willy Petes on the sponsons, a 230 gallon centerline fuel tank and 2000 rounds of 7.62 ammunition. Night missions included illumination and defensive flares. A base defense Bronco carried a mix of MK-82 500 lb. general purpose bombs and LAU-3 pods each loaded with 19 2.75 inch high-explosive or flechette rockets. Flechette rounds were like shotgun shells. Instead of pellets, each rocket had 3000 or 6000 finned nails. FACs were tasked for visual reconnaissance, close air support, interdiction on the Ho Chi Minh Trail, base defense, or Search and Rescue (SAR) missions.

October 4

Dear Girlfriend, I got your letter today and I must say it did me a lot of good...I put your Lord's prayer (pressed on a flattened penny) on my dog tags right away today. It really means a lot to me. I've also taken Dad's Bible along every trip. I love you. "Hymie Goldfarb"

October 14

Today I had my second to the last backseat ride. That was at 0720 this A.M. I also had my last backseat ride one hour after my 2nd to last. That is to say 9 hours almost straight strapped in a seat. I also have the 0720 launch in the morning....I just can't believe how beautiful this place is. Today I really noticed a lot of big mountain waterfalls. And then there's this island about 10 miles off the coast, completely untouched by the war. You can see all the colored coral formations just like out of a travel book....Tonight at the club at dinner somebody said, "Hey, did you guys hear somebody playing the harmonica on Woodencrest's (control) frequency?" "Yes, who was that? I heard them on Bluebird's (command post) frequency, too." Need I write further on this subject?

October 24

I'm working nights now. Don't know if you're keeping up with the war, i.e. # of air strikes in N. Viet Nam and number in the south (ones we control), but the strategy is changing somewhat with upcoming elections and hints to the cease fire. We now cover more areas plus 24-hour coverage. If it hadn't been for the weather, I'd really be tired instead of just tired...I just came back from the TASS Hole (our club house in the squadron building). I started off with 25 cents and left $20 richer playing dice.

November 5

What did you do today? Here's another Sunday past and I still haven't been able to make it to church. I had the 0620 launch this morning.

November 9

Dear Girlfriend, Since I'm going to Trail tomorrow, I think it's time to put in a request for a package — food mainly. The cans of pudding are an excellent idea, as are brownies, jerky, dinky twinkies, etc. If you think you can handle it, try for a 14 pound turkey and cranberry sauce, mashed potatoes (not fake), peas, corn on cob and hot buttered rolls. I do have a personal invitation to a party given by some Vietnamese generals while I'm at Trail.

November 11

This morning, I got up and caught the Chinook (helicopter) to bring me here. This place doesn't even have a landing pad — they just landed on a dirt road and pushed me off. I really expected the worst, but this is worse than I expected. I'll sleep in the same room where I work. (Actually there is a wall of sandbags between us.) My room is 5 ft. by 20 ft. with a cot and a mosquito net. The roof leaks so my poncho is nearby. It is well fortified, and they don't take any fire from anywhere. There are about six of us here. It is my job to coordinate air strikes and naval and ground artillery, also to post arc-light (B-52) strikes. I work a 12 hour shift- probably from 7 p.m. to 7 a.m. — the night shift. It costs 25 cents a day to eat here, mostly C-rations and at night hamburgers. For three weeks I'm supposed to be here. There's really nothing to do here except play "You're Still My Favorite Girlfriend Alice Long" on my harmonica and paint and maybe take some pictures...What would you do if I sang out of tune? Would you stand up and walk out on me? Hey! I always have to remind you. Did I tell you there's no running water here! They do have a 50 gallon oil drum with a nozzle attached for a shower...Just some more love from your dude. "Bastogne Germaine"

Trail Control

Trail Control was part of a Tactical Air Control Party or TACP, a small team of Air Force personnel, two FACs and two enlisted radio operators who de-conflicted the airspace, coordinated the assets for close air support, and advised airborne FACs of weather and other conditions pertinent to the mission. Trail was located 30 miles south of the DMZ in a small compound occupied by 400 ARVN troops and 10 U.S. Marine advisors. For the FACs, it was normally a three week tour. Missing three weeks of flying was not considered a good deal. However, my tour occurred during the monsoon season where flying was hampered by bad weather so I didn't miss much. I still complained. Missing any flying justified it.

November 16
Dear little weasel, I'm getting anxious to go somewhere. I want to FLY! Two of our ratty roommates were killed yesterday when the spring on the trap quickly broke their necks...Your boyfriend of the week, "Murphy Benson"

November 18
Steve's dad is a preacher from North Carolina — he's alright and we've made this place almost tolerable.

November 20
Steve (my roommate) and I are getting good so we will make a tape and send you a harmonica/guitar arrangement....P.S. My promotion party is tomorrow and you're invited. I brought a

fifth of Seagram's 7 just for the occasion— haven't touched it yet. Almost 1st LT.

December 7

Dear Favorite Girlfriend, Situation: San Juan Hill — base camp near Ba To. These guys (Americans too) haven't had air support for at least three weeks due to bad weather. Covey 25 (me) comes on the scene and puts three sets of air on the .51 caliber gun sites, reported two enemy battalions in the area surrounding the camp. I had two flights of UNAF A-37's and a flight of Navy A-7's all working under the overcast. Five or six big cargo helicopters land and resupply San Juan Hill. Ground commanders (American advisors) like me — the first air support in weeks....I've been playing my harmonica a lot. I get a lot of volume out of that thing. I was in Laos today and they heard me at Da Nang. I practice Christmas carols so the guys on the ground will feel better. The big harmonica sounds great — like a small organ with all the chords...Your boyfriend, "Nelson Algren"

December 12

Girfriendly, Over at intelligence the guy made me feel real good. He said that he had read a lot of reports with my name (Covey 25) on them. There were all the reports from the ground commanders in the field. The deal down at San Juan Hill was really something to them. And those big bunker complexes I found the other day impressed them. I borrowed a tape recorder and took it up. The tape starts like a typical mission, right from taxi and take-off and includes several conversations with the ground commanders so it's a real good example of what I do every day. Anyway, we destroyed thirteen bunkers at least and had three medium secondaries that the ground commander reported. I had a new guy in the back seat. "Clark Kent"

2nd Lt. Charlie Yates in front of his OV-10,
Da Nang, South Vietnam (1972)

December 14

Dear D'Girlfriend, Exactly three months down, only 9 to go. So far for me, it has gone by fast...Here are some more rumors – if and when there's a cease fire, the OV-10's will go to Thailand –either NKP or Ubon...You're right- the experience I'm getting here is outstanding. Girlfriend, I'm glad you talk to God about me – He's been doing a good job with your boyfriend.... I love you all day. "Sherman Kelp"

December 19

Dear Girlfriend, Well, I guess you've already heard by now that we lost another OV-10 from here. I sure hate this part of being over here. The guy who replaced me at Hue', Frank Eagan, was shot down over Quang Tri. They were hit by an SA-7 (missile).

They started making it toward the water and had to punch out prior. I think Frank was killed after ejection. The marine made it all right. I hate to tell you about things like this, but I want you to know that I'm flying high up there near the DMZ (demilitarized zone between North and South Vietnam) and don't want you to worry about it at all. I think ol' Tricky Dick (President Nixon) is through messing around up there with the talks. He never should have made the goodwill bombing halt above the 20th (latitude)...A bunch of love from your boyfriend, "Marvin Kaputinski" ...P.S. I talked to Chaplain Swaffer in church Sunday – sends his best to your dad.

December 26

Christmas Eve, I went to the candlelight service – probably the best I've ever been to. Then I went over to the Officer's club and the Coveys took over from there on out. They had a real good band and during band breaks we provided the entertainment. It was great. We were loud and obnoxious (probably due to the consumption of wine). We sang good songs. The guys that really shined were a couple of ATOs. I played the harmonica, of course, with the band as my backup. One of the selections was a requested "Turkey in the Straw." The whole place came apart. Everybody was dancing and really having a great time. We all got to sleep in on Christmas morning. We went to the chow hall about 1200. Wow, what a feast! There was plenty of turkey and eggnog and everything. Then after lunch, four of us got together in Steve's room and opened all of our presents. We handed each other presents and oohed and aahed. I just want you to know that I love you and think you're swell and neat. And also I think you have a neat mom and dad and brothers and sisters (whose idea to get a wooden prop-great!) and also your in-laws are swell and your boyfriend is the greatest, too. He's also very happy but sad cause he's not with all the ones he loves most, but next year girlfriend, next year.

December 29

Dear Girlfriend and wife of two years, It seems a lot longer than that (had to throw that in). Hope you like all the neat junk I sent....Girlfriend, I love you just a whole, whole bunch and the last two years have been all right. Hey! I can't wait until we get to go to Hawaii so we can .....Love from your boyfriend, "Henry Springer III"

January 6

I just gotta tell you about yesterday's mission. I had the 1445 go to Pleiku. A flight of 3 A-7s checked in with me when I got to the area. So I put them in and got a truck and some secondary explosions. The ground commander called and said he had a big troops-in-contact (TIC) going over at his fire base...A flight of F-4's diverted from the north especially for me and checked in about 1840, almost dark...BDA: 3 small secondaries, 2 medium secondaries, 2 recoilless rifles destroyed (big guns), one .51 cal destroyed one .51 cal/14.5 mm silenced and X KBA....What a day. It really makes you feel good just knowing you helped the poor guy out like that. He thought we were the greatest guys in the world. He threatened us with riches, wine, women and song. Well I get to go down there again this afternoon, same time.

Troops in Combat

The mission of January 6th was particularly memorable. I was in the process of directing Navy A-7s on a group of trucks parked on the HO Chi Minh Trail in the tri-border area where Vietnam, Laos, and Cambodia come together. As I was debriefing my fighters, I received an urgent call from Fire Support Base Hotel north of Kontum in the Central Highlands only ten miles from my position. He was taking mortar and recoilless rifle fire from an adjacent ridgeline a little over one mile east of his firebase, a precursor to being overrun by the Gomers. I requested Tac Air from Carbon

Outlaw, the local TACP, as I overflew the base. I could see that he was taking a lot of fire but locating the source proved difficult. Methodically, I scanned the ridgeline and noticed light smoke or dust coming through the trees on the ridgeline. That was where the guns were located! Carbon Outlaw informed me that there was no Tac Air available so I declared a Tactical Emergency. Carbon Outlaw was then able to divert two F-4's fragged for a strike on Hanoi.

I continued to roll in on the target, firing rockets until the F-4s arrived. They checked in with MK-82s, CBU-24 (flak suppression cluster bomb units), and 2000 rounds of 20mm to strafe with. I saved two rockets to mark the targets with--they had to be good marks if this was going to work. As it started to get dark, some of the target locations were clearly evident--just follow the source of the tracer rounds as they came up toward you!

My roommate Adam West joined me in another OV-10 and began working a AAA site that came up on the west side of the base camp. I had the F-4-s drop CBU-24 on the ridgeline first. It's a great area weapon with delayed explosions for 30 minutes. This keeps the gunners from shooting at us. Next, I had them drop the Mk-82s on the mortar and recoilless rifle positions I had located earlier. We finished up by strafing the ridgeline and the AAA site Adam located on the other side of Fire Base Hotel. And then it was dark--and quiet.

The excitement and adventure was not over, however. I was out of fuel. This was not something I had missed. On the right side of my canopy written in big letters with grease pencil was "CHECK GAS." When the F-4s checked in, I knew I was not going to be able to work the target *and* return to Da Nang. My plan was to divert to Pleiku, 20 miles south. The O-2s from Da Nang used Pleiku as a forward operating base. Adam was in the same situation. When we checked in with Pleiku tower, they informed us that they had shut down operations and turned off the runway lights because they were under a rocket attack. We had no place else to go. Two things came to mind--*The Big Sky Theory* in which the odds of two objects colliding in the air is slim, and the 122mm rocket is not all that accurate. *"Covey 25, land at your own risk."* *"Roger, cleared to land."*

One more minor issue--my landing light was out, the runway lights were out, and it was dark. No problem. I followed Adam down to the runway and used his lights to illuminate the touchdown zone. We quickly taxied to a protected aircraft revetment, shut down, egressed, and scurried into a bunker. After the attack was over, the maintenance guys found a landing light from an O-2 that "sorta" fit and the light came on. With a full tank of gas and a full load of Willy Petes, I was on my way back to Da Nang.

Vietnam at night is really, really dark. Black as the ace of spades is a good comparison. *"Covey 25 is RTB Channel 77!"* Translation: I am returning to Da Nang, TACAN (navigation aid) identifier Channel 77. I'm feeling pretty good. It's been a great day and no one died. I thought I'd give the fire base commander Bravo at BaTo a call. I had worked his AO for about three weeks and built up a good rapport. I switched to his frequency, pulled out the harmonica and began playing "Wabash Cannonball," his favorite. *"Covey 25, Delta. Is that you?! Buddy am I glad to hear you! We're taking incoming from Charlie!"* I can hear the explosions in the background of his radio transmissions. I'm about ten miles from his general location. *"Roger that Bravo! It seems like everybody is taking incoming today. Got some coordinates?"*

"Roger standby. Bravo Sierra 455, 344, over." I can't pinpoint his exact location because of the darkness. There are no flashes of gunfire or rounds impacting the firebase. As soon as the Gomers hear me overhead they stop shooting, knowing I'll be able to spot their location. Darkness is their ally. Bravo comes out of his bunker and vectors me overhead his position. *"Covey 25 you're overhead now, turn to a heading of about 240 and about 1 click is where they were firing from."* *"Covey 25, roger, rollin' in hot!"* I roll inverted, pull my nose down toward the pitch black nothingness, and roll back over and from a 60 degree dive. I hit the pickle button seven times. One of three pods

of rockets expended. Man those things are bright when you shoot them at night. Five G pull off the target and I set up for another pass.

"Covey 25, Bravo, that's where they are!" "Roger! In hot!" I empty the second pod of rockets, spreading them around. With nothing specific to aim at, you hope to hit something significant and get a secondary explosion. One more pass and I'm "Winchester"--out of ordnance. There are no secondaries. I really am going to RTB (return to base) this time. Bravo, the ground commander, thanks me profusely for showing up when I did. Yep, it was a good day.

January 9, 1973

I guess I'd better write this letter before the swelling in my head goes down. I got cussed by the FAC Control Center (Carbon Outlaw) today. They're the ones that we put in the request for air with. It seems that Powerhouse 301 flight of Navy A-7s really were glad to hear that they'd be working with Covey 25, so Carbon Outlaw asked me what kind of lies I'd been feeding them etc., etc. Here comes the best part. Remember the air strike I had just the other day? Well, the ground commanders down there at Kontoom (north of Pleiku) sent me, personally, a well- used by the original owner, North Vietnamese battle flag, captured by the good guys. Actually, it was a gift from the Vietnamese army unit that I helped out that day.

January 18

Dear Girly friend, Another short letter cause I'm still behind. You'll be getting a tape soon followed by another within a couple of days. When you get toward the end, I don't want you to worry because it's really not as bad as it sounds. I do hold the record for the most SA-7s (missiles) shot (at me) at one time at night. That's confirmed firings. You always want me to tell you how safe it is so you won't worry. Well, it's still safe just so long as you are on your toes and keep your cool. I do, so you don't have anything to worry about. Love from "Miles Hespin"

Two Bravo Arty Go

The Two Bravo Arty Go Linebacker II was implemented to put pressure on North Vietnam to resume the Paris peace talks. The intensity of the war increased in South Vietnam. If the peace talks failed, it appeared the North was preparing to initiate a new offensive in the South. The NVA poured men and equipment, including tanks, across the DMZ now heavily defended by AAA (Called Triple A, anti-aircraft artillery) and SAMs (surface-to-air missiles).

One of the most exciting missions for the FAC was the *Two Bravo Arty Go.* The area just below the DMZ was divided into two sectors, 2 Alpha and 2 Bravo. A contingency of U.S. Marines occupied fire support bases in 2 Bravo. A detachment of Marine Aerial Observers (AOs) were assigned to the 20th TASS and flew in our backseats under the call sign *Wolfman,* specifically to fly in 2 Bravo. Their mission was to coordinate and direct naval gunfire from U.S. Navy destroyers anchored off the coast. When you looked on the scheduling board and saw that you had the *2 Bravo Arty Go,* your stomach tightened and your palms began to sweat.

My mission January 16 was the Two Bravo Arty Go. My back seater was Wolfman 22, a Marine Warrant Officer named Lee Nelson. We took off after dark and proceeded toward the DMZ and the South Vietnamese town of Dong Ha. The preflight intelligence briefing had indicated a target rich environment that included tanks protected by 23mm, 37mm, 57mm, and 85mm triple-A sites, SA-7 heat-seeking missiles. An SA-2 site located just above the DMZ was under construction. Our OV-10 had no Radar Homing and Warning gear to warn us of radar guided weapons and no self-defense flares to protect us from heat seeking missiles.

Arriving on station, we witnessed an RF-4C reconnaissance aircraft fly across the DMZ being hosed by 23mm. He escaped unscathed. Soon after, we watched as an *Arc Light* unleashed its devastating bomb load on the DMZ. There were numerous secondary explosions and sustained fires. I'm sure our arrival was announced by the sound of the twin turbo-prop engines running slightly out of sync to mask our exact location in the sky. All exterior lights had long since been extinguished. The *Master Arm Switch* was on. We were ready for action, and it didn't take long for it to begin. We received targets from the Marines at the firebase camp who were receiving incoming from enemy artillery positions. I put in a request with Trail Control for some "air" and Wolfman 22 began his work coordinating for naval gunfire. *War Rocket, Stud Poker,* and *Lakewood* were the call signs of 3 destroyers off the coast of Dong Ha. Lee made the adjustments and called, *"Fire for effect, over!"* It was effective. The Gomers responded. Sporadic tracers of triple-A arced slowly toward us. They were easy to evade. Suddenly, one lone "tracer" headed our way with incredible closure. Triple-A doesn't travel *that* fast. As I turned, the bright red ball started pulling lead; it was tracking us! *"SA-7! SA-7!"* I called out to Lee over the intercom.

"I got him!" And I think I got the grid!" he yelled as I broke hard into the oncoming missile. At the last second, just before impact, I unloaded, rolled away from the missile and pulled back on the stick, causing the missile to overshoot and explode harmlessly beyond us. As I recovered the aircraft back to some semblance of level flight, Lee plotted the coordinates. More triple-A.

"Here comes another SA-7!" I shouted. *"Which? Where? It's coming from our six! It came from right across the river!"*

"Lakewood, Grid two-six-niner-six-two-two! Altitude two-five feet. Description: Active SA-7 site. Request one gun, fifteen salvoes, high explosive, fuse: time. Fire for effect, over! Sierra Three (Marine fire base camp) you copy?"

"That's affirm! Standing by for air warning data."

"OK, Here come two more!" I sounded while simultaneously performing a high G break into the two missiles followed by a roll and pull out of the missile flight path. Again, they couldn't hack the turn. *"Sierra Three, we just took two more out of there. I need a clearance and I need it fast!"* Lee barked. My buddy Captain Manny Montes was

monitoring the action at Trail Control. He immediately comes on the frequency and transmits "words of encouragement" to get us to go "feet wet" where it's safer. But we've got a job to do. *"Get off the radio Manny, here comes two more!"* - More hard maneuvering, more high G's, more triple-A. Then Lee spots yet another missile headed our way, *"Here comes another SA-7! OK Lakewood fire for effect, over!"* I'm inverted, pulling hard, as our naval artillery begins pounding the SA-7 site. Explosions covered the entire area. There were no more missiles fired that night. Manny tells me he has tactical air headed our way. Lee turns off the naval gunfire as I direct several flights of F-4s and A-6s on and around the bridges at Dong Ha, resulting in numerous secondary explosions and sustained fires-all in a night's work.

I brought my portable tape recorder that night and thought it would be a great idea to send a copy of the mission home to Diane and my folks. Why should I have all the excitement? I mailed the tape two days later after I sanitized the recording. Some of the "words of encouragement," adverbs and adjectives were not words you wanted your mom to hear.

January 24

Well how 'bout that — I ended it — must have been the big strike I put in yesterday that was the deciding factor. I moved yesterday and it looks like I'll be moving again. No word as yet where but you'll be the 124,763rd to know about it...The peace treaty thing may mess up our plans for R&R (rest and recreation/vacation).

January 31

Dear Girlfriend, Let me start at X minus 48 hours. I figured the next 2 days would be bad and they were. I was scheduled for the north go at 0400 on the 27th. Weather canceled the flight which is just as well because we really took a hosing the day before — much AAA (anti-aircraft artillery). So I got back to bed, wondering how come the rockets hadn't hit yet. We took a few that afternoon and I was caught outside. I set up the tape recorder and put a blanket on the floor. At 0500 we got it bad. The tape is good until one hit real close to the barracks which knocked the light fixtures off the ceiling and put the power off. The barracks in the picture is about ¼ mile away. One guy was killed, 4 injured, and one-half of the barracks leveled. Four or five rockets hit within 100 yards of us. All day long, everybody wore their flak vests and helmets. I was busy packing to leave. That afternoon, the last day of the war, this happened — an F-4 and an OV-10 were shot down over enemy territory....Well at X minus 12 hours, intelligence tells us to expect between 60 and 600 rockets between 0600 and 0800 on X day (our last day at Da Nang). We only took 25 the night before. Imagine what that does to your nerves, especially after seeing the barracks. Since I was pulling alert that night, I thought I'd sleep by the plane in one of the hangars. That was more secure than the room. I was preflighting the plane and had just got there about midnight when the first attack came. Sure enough, at 0715 the big attack came. It sounded like an arc light (flight of 3 B-52's dropping 105 500 lb bombs each over a wide area). About 250 hit and another 150 were destroyed before launch. All but about 5 hit off base in the refugee camp. At 1500, I had my OV-10 packed with all my stuff and 8 of us took off for NKP, Thailand. It was great — one to an airplane — 2 formations of 3 planes. I took movies as we buzzed Da Nang. Here I am at NKP. It looks like I will stay here and be a Nail instead of a Covey. The place isn't bad. It's like a real base and best of all — no rockets! Love you all the time. Your favorite, "Merv Jesternid"

A New Mission

The Paris Peace Accords of 1973 was signed and beginning on 28 January 1973 at 0800 Saigon time, there would be an in-place ceasefire. North and South Vietnamese forces were to hold their locations. U.S. troops would begin to withdraw. The agreement stipulated that the withdrawal would be completed within sixty days. U.S. prisoners of war would be released and allowed to return home. Later that morning, the 20th TASS flew eight OV-10s to NKP (Nakhon Phanom, Thailand) to join the 23rd TASS--the Nails. We would continue to fly interdiction missions on the Ho Chi Minh Trail. The North Vietnamese had no intention of stopping the flow of men and supplies into South Vietnam until they had accomplished their objective of taking the South. Our only avenue was to stop the flow on the Trail, a virtual highway in Laos along the border with South Vietnam.

Distinguished Flying Cross
Citation to Accompany the Award of
The Distinguished Flying Cross
(First Oak Leaf Cluster)
To
Charles D. Yates

First Lieutenant Charles D. Yates distinguished himself by extraordinary achievement while participating in aerial flight as a Forward Air Controller in Southeast Asia on 16 January 1973. On that date, Lieutenant Yates flew his lightly armed reconnaissance aircraft in support of an American ground advisor. Despite total darkness, deteriorating weather, intense and accurate antiaircraft artillery fire, and surface-to-air missiles, he successfully directed naval gunfire and tactical aircraft on a hostile storage complex, resulting in numerous secondary explosions and silencing of the hostile fire. The professional competence, aerial skill, and devotion to duty displayed by Lieutenant Yates reflect great credit upon himself and the United States Air Force.

CHAPTER 5

Lt. Charlie Yates Goes to War

Part 2

1973

Nail 50

*"I'm a Nail, fly the Trail
I drop bombs on Nguyen's tail,
Can anybody hit my smoke?"*

Or so the song goes. After 48 hours of tension filled, sleepless nights, the Coveys arrived at NKP with a warm greeting from the 23rd TASS Nails. We were met at the aircraft, handed a "cold one," and presented with a purple MR scarf affirming our status as Mission Ready pilots. I became Nail 50 and Nakhon Phanom a.k.a. *NKP* or *Naked Fanny* was my new home. I was reunited with my classmates from Hurlburt.

After a quick local orientation flight, we were soon flying in two sectors on the Trail, Barrel Roll in the northern half and Steel Tiger in the southern half of Laos. The Barrel Roll was a particularly "hot" area. My roommate, Leroy Barnadge, was tasked for a mission to the Barrel Roll so I asked, *"Hey Leroy, if you don't make it back, can I have your stereo?"* (gallows humor). Naturally there was a rivalry between the Coveys of Da Nang and the Nails of NKP. We weren't true "new guys" since we were all combat ready with as much or more experience as some of the "original" Nails. Still, we were new to this squadron and took some good-natured ribbing. First order of business: we all had to be "hammered," a revered tradition of the Nails. Stand before the squadron members, answer some direct questions about our background and character, show the color of our socks, and then consume the Hammer - three parts vodka, one part *crème de menthe*, for color of course. The real reason for our assignment as Nails is depicted in the patch I designed for our Covey party suits: the patch depicts Snoopy (Peanuts cartoon beagle) with a flight helmet and scarf, sharpening a nail with a file. The patch slogan read "Covey's Nail Sharpening Team."

February 4

Today is Sunday and even a day off. I went to church, ate at the club and am now sitting out in the sun. Is there really a war going on? At least in Da Nang, you knew there was. The flying over here is just not the same. Flying the Ho Chi Minh Trail gets old because there's really no feeling of accomplishment that you get by working for a ground commander.

February 12

I'm glad I went to Bangkok, but now I'm more glad that we're going to Hawaii. We stayed one night in Bangkok (4 of us). That's when I played my harmonica in a bar. The next day we went to the shops...The flying is still good but not as good as at Da Nang. I got a tank today with F-4s even. Only 3 more days of war?

February 14

I've been taking my camera up on just about every mission. Each cassette is 90 minutes long and I'll VR (visual reconnaissance) and put in air strikes to the tune of "Hand Me Down the Can of Beans" or shoot rockets to the soundtrack of "Camelot." I rigged up the microphone so it's just like stereo ear phones. Makes the time pass faster and when they shoot at you, you don't care cause the "1812 Overture" is shooting back.

A Highway in Laos

It was an absolutely gorgeous day over the Trail, not a cloud in the sky, visibility unlimited. I was enjoying the scenery when I found a truck park - at least three trucks were off the side of the dirt road, camouflaged with foliage. What aroused my interest was that the camouflaged foliage didn't match the surrounding trees. A closer look with the binoculars confirmed my suspicion.

I put a request for Tac Air in with *Cricket*, a C-130 Airborne Battlefield Command and Control Center (ABCCC). Thirty minutes later, a flight of two Air Force F-4s checked in with 12 MK 82s. I briefed them on the target, safest bailout, and how I wanted them to make their passes. *"FACs in to mark!"*

I rolled in *"with my smoke to mark, exactly where that truck was parked..."* I thought, it's been a very quiet day, no AAA, so I'm going to sweeten up this shot, just take my time and put my Willy Pete right into the cab of the truck. In my mind's eye, I saw the truck blow sky high with massive secondary explosions that engulfed the other two trucks. I would have to tell the F-4 jocks, *"Sorry guys, I just blew up the trucks, you can go home now."* Instead I heard, *"You better start jinking Nail, you're taking 37mm at your 6 o'clock!"* A quick glance at my mirrors confirmed his call. Flak bursts were going off right behind me. Thankfully the gunner was aiming at me and *not* leading me. Before he could figure that out, I hit the pickle button firing a rocket. Forget about accuracy, I just wanted the thing to hit the earth. That's what corrections are for. Pickle, 5G pull, roll right, hold for three seconds, roll left, 5G pull, hold for three seconds, unload for energy, climb, jink right, and call: *"OK, 100 meters west of my smoke, where the trees have turned brownish, green, Lead put your first bomb there. If you need another mark, that's what I'm here for! By the way did you get a location on that gun?" "Sorry Nail 50, we were too busy watching the flak bursts around you."* The next marks were good enough to eventually destroy three trucks on the Trail.

DEAR MOM
The FAC Theme Song (sung to the tune, *Milord*)

Dear Mom, your son is dead,
He bought the farm today.
He crashed his OV-10 on Ho Chi Minh's highway.
He made a rocket pass
And he busted his ____.
Hmmm, hmmm, hmmmmmmmm.
He went across the fence to see what he could see.
There it was as plain as it could be.
There was a truck in the road, with a big, heavy load.
Hmmm, hmmm, hmmmmmmmm.

He got right on the horn
And gave ol' Big a call.
Send me some air, I've got a truck that's stalled.
And Big he said alright, I'll send you Litter Flight
For I am the power!

The fighters checked right in, gunfighters two by two,
Low on gas and tanker overdue.
They asked the FAC to mark,
Just where that truck was parked.
Hmmm, hmmm, hmmmmmmmm.

The FAC he rolled right in
With his smoke to mark,
Exactly where that truck was parked.
The rest is still in doubt

For he never pulled out.
Hmmm, hmmm, hmmmmmmm.

Dear Mom, your son is dead,
He bought the farm today.
He crashed his OV-10 on Ho Chi Minh's highway.
He made a rocket pass
And he busted his___.
Hmmm, hmmm, hmmmmmmm.

February 18

Dear Wench who is my most favorite, I'm painting today and avoiding the generals 'cause my moustache is way out of limits. My clouds look good in this painting. 30" x 24" is my biggest yet. Your hero and lover, "Buck A. Roo"

February 26

We received quick briefings on the Cambodia situation and then flew the next morning (0500). It was really neat — the minimum altitudes are lower. We flew cover for a convoy coming up the Mekong River. I did get to land, refuel and re-arm at Phnom Penh (P.P.), the capital.

February 28

I went out to one of the village schools this morning and helped teach an English class to 9 and 11 year olds. We taught them a song accompanied by the harmonica, of course.

March 4

Dear favorite of all the girlfriends, ...Guess where your favorite boyfriend is going tomorrow? Thass right! I get to go out to the ship, the USS Constellation. I'll be going out in an A-6 and stay for a couple of days....I love you today, Your Hero

The "Connie"

I was the project officer for a Navy Exchange program that the 23rd TASS initiated with the pilots assigned to the USS Constellation stationed in the Gulf of Tonkin. Their pilots began by flying in our back seats on missions over the Trail. In turn, we were to send our pilots out to the "Connie" for orientation flights. Two of us flew out to the Connie in an EA-6 Prowler (top left) and spent three days experiencing life on an aircraft carrier. I viewed the launch and recovery from every aspect possible, from the bridge to riding in the Sea King rescue helicopter flying abeam the boat. The disappointing part was being recalled before I flew in the F-4 scheduled for a combat air patrol off the coast of North Vietnam. It would be the first and last visit to the "Connie" by the 23rd TASS pilots. Our push into Cambodia cancelled the exchange program.

Commando Clean

Morale for the ex-Coveys was at an all-time low. Not unusual when you attempt to blend two close knit squadrons into one and you're considered to be the red-headed stepchild. Add to that an influx of 12 lieutenant colonels into the 23rd TASS (normally only two assigned) and you have the makings of a miserable assignment with little opportunity for advancement as a young lieutenant.

One of those lieutenant colonels was the new squadron commander, Howard Pierson, a.k.a. Nail 01, CINC Nail, Commando Clean--for his uncanny resemblance to Mr. Clean the "household cleaner guy".

Traditions

As the airmen completed their "365 days and a wake up tour of duty" and were replaced by the new guys, there were parties to send off the old and initiate the new (called "sawadees"). Behind "Top

Secret" closed doors, every NAIL was hammered. The ceremony consisted of lots of harassment, including the requirement to answer personal and absurd questions, a sock check and the "Hammer." For those who preferred not to drink the green-tinted vodka, there was the option of pouring it on top of your head. I remember two men who abstained. One man, who did not drink because of his Christian beliefs, poured the drink on his head. The other refused to drink or pour it on his head, and he was quickly transferred to another unit.

Another great NAIL tradition was "Blow Hockey." Squadron championship teams were formed and challenged. Large amounts of cash were wagered on the favorites and the long shots as well. The game consisted of a playing table which was a shallow lunchroom tray filled with water. The players were corks tagged with team flags. The contestants were to crouch down, mouths at tray level and blow their team corks to the other side. There was a lot of cheering and excitement, to the delight of the old heads. The FNGs (Funky New Guys) were quick to challenge the reigning champs. The FNGs took the bait; they had been set up for the great deluge. As soon as both FNG teams were down low blowing air across the water, someone slaps an open hand in the middle of the water-filled tray and from behind, the old guys drench the FNGs with buckets of water. One memorable night, Lt. Col. Pierson's wife (who was there working with the Red Cross) came to be initiated as an honorary NAIL. She wanted in on the hockey game. She was dressed up and her hair was fixed really nice. Some of the guys looked at Howie and discreetly said, "Boss....?" He shrugged his shoulders and smiled. They let her play. The "boss" didn't have a good night.

"Carrier landings" became a favorite party activity. After lecturing the squadron on the hazards of flying combat and how we were valuable assets to the war effort and that we should not endanger our bodies during extracurricular activities, Nail 01 (Pierson) proudly led the squadron for the first carrier landing on the newly commissioned USS NAILFAC. A waist high platform was constructed that was about four feet wide and eighteen feet long.

It was covered in plastic then watered and soaped down. Shirtless pilots would take a running leap, land on their stomachs and slide down the carrier. If they had their legs in proper position, bent at the knee with calves and feet in the air, their buddies, one on each side holding the end of nylon strapping, would stop the landing. This was to simulate an aircraft catching the cable with a hook on an aircraft carrier. If the legs were not in proper position, the "plane" would slide off the carrier into a carefully prepared mud hole. Sometimes the cable operators failed in their duties, especially after consumption of quantities of brew.

Some of the NAILS - Charlie front row left (1973)

March 15

It looks like we'll be here (Ubon) about 2 weeks TDY or until the Cambodia deal is over. I'm flying with Rustic 12 alias Woodrow Baker. Today we'll be down around the Parrot's Beak and An Loc (Saigon is 40 miles away). The haze is so bad now that we may not see anything. Also they have SA-7s here....WOW! We were just toolen' along. I was singing. All of a sudden I catch a glimpse of an F-4 coming at us, our altitude, etc. Woody didn't see it so I grabbed the stick and pulled up and over...Yea me! Saved the day. We landed at P.P., ate lunch and were off again. I just put some CBU (cluster bomb units) on a truck — damaged only. We're now on our way to blow up a big ferry/barge. If they hit it, it will go up like a Roman candle.

March 16
That was sure some scare yesterday..............

March 22
Dear Girlyfriend, I found out yesterday that I have to have a passport to go on R&R. This is a new "thing" as of yesterday. I got the forms and had my picture taken. It takes two to three weeks to be processed unless you take it to the embassy in Bangkok yourself, and then it only takes one day. So, I'll be leaving here on the 27th for NKP and on the 28th for Bangkok. That will give me a full day to take care of that before I leave for Hawaii. Okay wenchly, you can be my favorite for today and ....I love you lots, "Porky Beans"

April 9
Dear most favorite Girlfriend in the whole-wide world, I just thought I'd write you this letter to tell you I think you're the most wonderful girl in the world and that I love you a whole bunches. I liked being with my girlfriend more than anything and I really can't wait to get home so we can live normal again in our own house. Did you enjoy R&R as much as I did – I don't think so...When I got into Bangkok a guy from NKP told me we'd lost an OV-10 over Cambodia but he didn't know who. I found out later it was Joe Gambino. I don't know if you remember him- he was in our class at Hurlburt. He got hit by .51 cal. They estimate he was about 100 feet when he took the hit. He ejected but was too low and his chute didn't work.......I've been recommended to be upgraded to IP (instructor pilot). That's good but it just means more back seat rides. I just want you to know that I'll be careful and won't pull any really dumb stunts – that's a guarantee. Your Hero, "Alfonce LaRue"

After R&R

It was an idyllic getaway with the love of your life in an all too short recess from the war. There couldn't possibly be one going on, could there? And if there was, why? Then immediately a grim reminder that there is indeed a war going on and you were part of it as you are met with the news that a good friend just paid the ultimate price. Joe was operating out of Ubon Air Base Thailand and flying a mission north of Phnom Penh, Cambodia. He was directing a strike on mortar positions when his aircraft was struck by .51 caliber gunfire from Khmer Rouge soldiers and crashed in flames. Losses in the squadron always had an effect--you were forced to think of your own mortality. Joe, like all of us lieutenants, thought he was invincible.

April 16

It's the same old thing here. Yesterday's mission was kinda neat. I was in the convoy escort. I was to meet the convoy as it came up the Mekong and crossed the Vietnam border, since we can't overfly the border. When I got there, it was under heavy fire on the other side. I put in air strikes 100 meters from the border while it was crossing. The last barge was an ammo barge. It took a direct hit and blew up. That was the biggest explosion I've ever seen — big fireball and secondaries and ammo cooking off. The smoke went up around 5000 feet or so. From when I took the convoy, we didn't take any hits because I pounded the banks with A-7s. They would hold overhead until we needed them so it was all instantaneous.....I got a letter from Bob and he said his squadron commander called down to personnel and requested that I be assigned to a T-38 to Reese, AFB. I hope it worked. It may not have been in time. Good old Bob.

Rules of Engagement (ROE)

With the signing of the *Agreement on Ending the War and Restoring Peace in Vietnam* on January 27, 1973, the United States withdrew its ground and air forces from South Vietnam. The U.S. intensified its support for the government of Cambodia (known as Kampuchea) by providing massive air support. The justification for this action is somewhat complicated. In 1970 the Communist Party of Kampuchea known as the Khmer Rouge staged a coup against the Prime Minister, Lon Nol, who had succeeded Prince Norodom Sihanouk in Cambodia's first national election. The Khmer Rouge was supported by the North Vietnamese who were using eastern Cambodia as sanctuaries from U.S. bombing while infiltrating South Vietnam. With the start of the coup in 1970, North Vietnam attempted to overrun and take all of Cambodia. The U.S. was motivated to help Lon Nol's government prevent a communist takeover of Cambodia.

From March until August 15, 1973, the U.S. would provide massive air support for government forces. No ground troops would be committed. By U.S. congressional mandate, only a fixed number of U.S. forces could be on the ground in Cambodia at any one time. That number included pilots who landed at Phnom Penh. The Nails would stage out of Ubon, Thailand, our closest base to Cambodia. There we would augment the Rustic FACs supplying close air support for Cambodian ground commanders. It would prove to be both a tense and frustrating experience. Logging 10 hours of flying was common as we flew two combat missions a day.

The Khmer Rouge dominated the countryside and was a serious threat to the populace. Burning, looting, and massacres were all too common. Government forces occupied the major cities but were reluctant to engage and eliminate the enemy even under the cover of very effective airpower. During the summer of 1973, the Khmer Rouge began to surround the capital city of Phnom Penh, already overcrowded with refugees. Located on the banks of the Mekong

River, it was the major port city and lifeline of Cambodia. Convoys of large merchant ships escorted by gunboats brought their much needed food and war supplies to the city. The Khmer Rouge set up ambushes by digging into the river bank and shelling the convoys with mortar and recoilless rifle fire. Several container ships were blown out of the water. Our mission was to keep the Mekong and the highways open or Phnom Penh would fall. Air cover was provided around the clock. The Nails and Rustics worked over the enemy with F-4 Phantoms and A-7 Corsairs during the day, and the AC-130 Spectre gunships ruled the night. It was not uncommon during convoy escort missions to have four or five flights of fighters stacked in orbits above the convoy ready to strike on the FACs' direction.

The Rules of Engagement (ROE) were a source of huge frustration for us. They seemed to favor the bad guys who had no rules. To get permission to conduct an airstrike you had to satisfy a litany of conditions before dropping a single bomb. A foreign national (i.e., a Cambodian) representative in the chain of command had to give approval to strike any target in the vicinity of a village, hamlet, or civilian structure. If a religious shrine or pagoda was in the area no clearance would be given even if you or the friendlies were taking fire from that location. Needless to say, fleeting targets were impossible to strike. But the situation on the Mekong was so dire that the ROE were relaxed to give the FAC the authority to strike targets without seeking approval from the 7th Air Force commander.

When the Nails took over the Mekong convoy escort mission, not a single ship was lost--on the Cambodian side of the border. The mission on April 16 illustrates the frustration we had with the ROE.

April 22

The day before yesterday I worked for a Hotel 45 Cambodian ground commander. When I flew over I could see him out there in a field. He had a couple of targets for me about 500 meters away. He told me how glad he was that I was there, and I offered to do an air show for him over his position. I went thru a whole series of maneuvers with the smoke generator on. The guy went wild – thought it was the neatest thing. I put 5 sets of A-7s/F-4s on his target. He was the most enthusiastic guy – just like a kid on the fourth of July. An A-7 driver asked me to play "Turkey in the Straw" – must have heard about me.... Yesterday was even neater. I was sent down to VR an area in southern Cambodia along the Gulf. I got to buzz some fishermen. After I finished, I was supposed to land at this airfield and see if I could get out again (very short runway!) (Forget I said that!!!!) On the way back, Arch and I flew formation thru a maze of cumulus towers and thunderstorms. It was right at sunset and had to be the prettiest, most awe-inspiring flying I've ever done. I really wish you'd been there, but mostly I wished I had film and a 35mm camera. The colors were fantastic......I'm back at NKP but not especially glad. I had to brief General Vogt (4 stars) and his aid General Hudson (only 2 stars). I briefed him on the situation near Kampot and some arc light boxes I had recommended and a few other things that went on.

April 25

...I fixed up the Hawaii movie and have been showing it around. Lots of guys wanted to see it. People call me Cecil (B. Demill the famous movie director).

May 10

Still not much going on-still the same old thing. I flew 9.6 hours yesterday and put in six sets of air along the banks of the Mekong River. I also took a couple of rolls of movies. I guess by the time I get back to NKP from this trip I ought to be able to start on the editing of the (OV-10) movie......Just think Girlfriend, only four more months...On the 15th of this month I go over two years which means a pretty good raise so let's watch for it in the check this month for a slight rise and next month for a bigger increase.

May 17

I told you I had talked to Steve Knight the other day. I put him in on a target. That was a real good/fun day. I was on a special VR mission and found this enemy camp/concentration of supplies and bunkers etc. I even saw a bunch of guys walking around. I put 3 F-4s and 2 A-7s down and then the next set of 2 F-4s checked in with "Hey Covey 25, this is your old Texas Tech buddy." They asked me to play a little "Turkey in the Straw." I told them I had something else. I briefed them on the target and told them to listen up for some inspiring music — something to make them hit the target by. I had my tape recorder with me and played the "Air Force Song" (Up we go...!) by Henry Mancini over the air. Outstanding — really did the trick, came out real clear over the radio. I'm probably not the ordinary FAC (forward air controller). When you work with me you can expect the unexpected and still get the job done right. One flight of fighters had asked the ABCCC, the guys who assign the FACs, if they could work with me.

Medal Ceremony - Lt. Col. Howard ("Howie") Pierson center, Charlie 2nd from right

May 19

Dear girlfriend, I guess since R&R I think about you more and more. (I didn't do that before 'cause it would only make the time go slower.) I love you, "Pete Rejinski"

May 30

I'm here at Ubon fixin' to go back to NKP to work on that party and the skits. I'll be back here on Saturday and stay about five more days. I had the Mekong convoy escort the other day and all the ships made it thru. Then yesterday, I worked around the Gulf of Siam near the town of Kampot. I got to do a lot of low flying — at least 10 feet off the ground. This tower control guy at the little airfield requested several low passes across the field. You should have seen those guys on the ground. (I could real easy.) They thought it was neat.

Charlie on the harmonica

The Harmonica Hold Down!

Charlie Yates, a young Nail FAC deployed to Ubon, was a popular addition to the Rustics as well as being a top-notch pilot. He created a certain amount of notoriety for himself with a slightly unusual habit while flying: when his fighters approached the area and asked for a hold-down (radio communication), Charlie obliged by dragging out his trusty harmonica and playing a rousing rendition of "Turkey in the Straw." The fighter pilots loved it! Once word got around, whenever a strike flight drew Charlie as their FAC, they automatically asked for a hold-down--just to hear Charlie play. As bureaucratic luck would have it, the young Mr. Yates had drawn the attention of the "Brass." As a result I was tasked with giving the young lieutenant a no-notice check ride. The next day as Charlie and I walked across the Rustic ramp to our aircraft, it occurred to me that a check ride for a proven combat veteran like Charlie was pretty lame. We pressed on anyway. Once on station we drew a flight of A-7s for a target near Kampong Cham. As we waited for the fighters to check in, the solution to this awkward situation broke over us like a bolt from the blue. Charlie was a big-time movie buff and used his camera to film some of his air strikes (later showcased in his legendary film, Nguyen's Shadow). It was so obvious! When the fighters checked in asking for a hold down, Charlie played "Turkey in the Straw," briefed them, then turned the controls over to me. I ran the entire airstrike while Charlie filmed it! When we got back to Ubon, I filled out a glowing Form 8 on Lt. Yates, let the boss see it, and smiled to myself when he signed off on the check ride. But there was one more administrative loose end to tie up. I got together with my roommate, Rustic 14, Shell Storer, the Rustic scheduling officer. Shell made sure that Charlie and the top brass never flew at the same time. As a result, Charlie Yates continued to play harmonica hold downs for the remainder of the war! ---Capt. Tom Yarborough (Rustic 22) 1973

June 3

Well, now I'm back at Ubon. The skit was great — it was 12 times as good as the slide presentation I did last year. We had to get all the actors plus a live pig and all the props. No girlfriend, I wasn't the actor. I was the producer, director, tape editor and maker, writer, choreographer, and acting coach plus the sound engineer during the performance. The next morning, I came back down here at 0700 and started flying.

June 7

I guess you've heard that we lost another OV-10. The pilot was killed. He lost an engine taking off from Phnom Penh. He had his gear already up when he touched back on the runway, slid 2000 feet and burst into flames. If he had done things differently, he would have made it. I only tell you these things so you don't worry....I know this is short but I'm "getting short." (The expression means only 99 more days and a wake up to go!)

June 9, Saturday

I finished my movie and had the premiere last night in the Nail Hole. Terrific, magnificent, "colosso," stupendously superb! All day long today nothing but good remarks and "Are you going to make copies?" It ran about one hour exactly. I go to Ubon Monday and will show it down there. Remember these guys are real critics! I sure can't wait to show it to you — it really gives you a good idea on exactly what I did over here.

June 13

I've been reading "Making of a Surgeon"- not bad and tells a little about what my smart girlfriend does — the needle jabbing and all. I can really see why they have medical technologists now. I had to read something like that since I'm not home and you only tell me a little about what you do. I can pick around the part about being a surgeon and see your job. You know that

I think you're real smart and I'm always bragging — believe it or not — to the guys that you are the smartest in your class.

June 15
Yesterday was my celebration of being here nine months; actually it was really my celebration for having only three months/92 days to go. I celebrated by eating and going to bed at 1930.

June 21
Did I tell you that Ron Rounce (IP in T–38s) was over here as an advisor to the Thai's flying T–28s? Well, he is and he went up with me today on a double bang. He flew A–1s out of NKP before he was at Reese. What a time he picked to ride; I had a really good mission- put in 7 sets of air. At one time, I had about 50 gooks running out in the open. They had just cut Highway 5 and stopped the convoy carrying supplies and wounded. They were giving the good guys a hard time. This wasn't like catching them in the open and not being able to do anything about it. I had a set of A–7s overhead. We had just bombed a bunker position when I noticed these guys running. The rest of the work was easy.

July 6
This letter is coming to you really air mail. I'm at 11,500 feet over the "Fingertip Karat," Cambodia. I'm in the backseat flying an IP ride. We're headed for Route 4 and the Route 26 intersection. The bad guys have cut the road and we're going to support the ground commanders to try and reopen it. The weather is really bad in the area with a lot of thunderstorms and rain showers. I just ate part of my flight lunch — 4 pieces of fried chicken, 2 sandwiches, 2 hard-boiled eggs, 2 cookies and an apple. The fourth of July party was a huge success. I took 7 rolls of film. We got permission to reopen the carrier landings

(stomach slide on a wet table to a landing in a mud puddle) and it was really neat. I still have mud in my ears. We had no major injuries.

July 11

Dear most favorite Girlfriend in the whole wide world who I love the most, I got the birthday package...The best thing was the projector bulb. I showed the movie again last night – some of the guys hadn't seen it because of the rotation. This time, I spent a couple of hours at the tape center making a sound track. The movie gets better every time I show it....I bought a plaque to hang with all my flying paraphernalia – probably in a den/study when we get a house. It is engraved with a top and side shot of the OV-10. The quote is by Winston Churchill, "There is nothing more exhilarating than being shot at without effect."

July 14

Happy birthday to me but I'd rather be with my girlfriend on my birthday, cooking steaks, eating corn on the cob with an avocado salad and angel food birthday cake and... (left out the hot rolls and baked potato.)

July 19

The last two days have really been hard. Two double bangs in a row. Yesterday, I was working the Mekong Convoy – that mission has more priority than any other. I had my hands full from the time I got there until I left. I put in 8 sets (or 16 sorties) of air strikes. The convoy took no hits while I was providing cover. There is a lot of coordination involved.....Col. Pierson told me yesterday that he would try to help me out and get my assignment changed to Reese. Also, he said if I didn't get a roll back that he would see if the squadron would release me two weeks early and I'd come back space available.

July 24

The target we had was just outstanding. If you've been reading you might know that Phnom Penh is surrounded – really in a bad situation. I was working just 10 miles away. I could actually see the guys running on the ground. The lead F-4 put down 4 cans of CBU and got 4 real good secondaries.

August 6

Dear Girlfriend, Only eight and a half more days of combat and then we'll have the biggest party yet. Looks like all the Nails and Rustics will be here at Ubon. We plan on getting kicked out of the club. If it's approved, we'll be going back in a 32 ship formation...Here's another good deal on my movie. Col. Goodwin is the wing DO (that's the number two man on the base). He likes me and he told me to stop by his office when I get back to NKP and work out the details. He saw the movie and was really impressed. He wants to send me TDY to Headquarters TAC at Langley, Virginia and show my film to General Knight, Steve Knight's dad. There, we'd work out a deal in conjunction with Hurlburt and make this into a 16 mm training film. This would probably involve going to Norton AFB in California, maybe. The era of the OV-10 and this type of FAC work is almost over. I don't think they've made any kind of combat film on the OV-10 to any great extent. Like I say – the details aren't worked out yet but it looks like some good possibilities. We'll see, girlfriend, we'll see....The war situation isn't much better for those guys. Phnom Penh is surrounded. The air support is fantastic – the bad guys are really taking a loss but they keep coming. If the good guys only had that determination they wouldn't be in this mess. I love you today and you're even my favorite, "Art Baker"

The Inevitable

The war in Cambodia was an air war. The United States did not have ground forces committed to support the Cambodian forces as they fought the Khmer Rouge. The Nails would stage out of Ubon, Thailand, the closest U.S. base to the Cambodian border. The Nails and the Rustic FACs (based in Ubon) provided close air support for the allies Refugees flooded the already crowded capital city of Phnom Penh. Government forces occupied the cities and towns and were reluctant to sweep the surrounding areas to eliminate the enemy, even under the cover of very effective air power. They were content to watch the fireworks but not aggressive enough to fight and take territory. During the summer of '73, the Khmer Rouge forces surrounded Phnom Penh. They set up ambushes of truck convoys along the major highways, which impeded the influx of much needed food and war supplies. The main supply line of the city became the Mekong River where the convoys of ships, boats, and their armed escorts made their way through the jungle-lined winding waters. Communist gunners hidden along the banks of the river were deadly. Our commitment was to provide close air support to the Cambodian ground commanders and keep the Mekong open, and that we did. The pressure was applied from fighter forces out of Ubon, Udorn, and Korat. At "bingo" (empty) fuel, we would RTB (return to base) to Phnom Penh to rearm, refuel, rest, eat a questionable lunch, and watch our "Buds" put in airstrikes across town.

We swapped lies with the Cambodian fighter pilots and threw tidbits to old Fido, the squadron mascot. That dog was a lone ranger since he was considered a delicacy by the locals. I suspect the open sores and noticeable limp kept Fido from becoming dinner. After lunch, it was back to the war. Air operations sometimes took us over the jungles of Cambodia as we protected the highways. Overrun by jungle, the temples of Angkor Wat were the only remaining evidence of the flourishing Khmer Empire that ruled all of Southeast Asia for six centuries until it fell in the early 1400s. The communist forces controlled this territory and inevitably would establish a new, though smaller, empire. The "temple tour" gave us a glimpse into the past; our daily missions gave us insight into the future of this beleaguered country.

August 10

Remember the stuff about my film — well, it's starting to take shape. Instead of chopping up mine and reproducing it in 16 mm, they're going to make another. Col. Goodwin assigned me as project officer. I've been given 3 movie photographers from the 601st. (they've taken all the combat films over here) plus special consideration on the schedule. I had to come up with a format, and I'm using pretty much the same as in mine-same angle shots etc.

August 16

Dear Girlfriend, The war is finally over- the last bomb was dropped at 10:44. The last two days were really pretty neat. The 14th, I had the Ream go — fly a mission, land at Ream, refuel and go home. I had a navigator in the backseat — his first time into Ream. It gave me one last chance to do some "flathatting." The beaches down there are just beautiful. We'd get right down on the deck along the beach and pull up to go over the trees......Only the old heads were scheduled to fly the last day. Every backseat was filled. Woody and I flew together- me in the front, him in the back. Before we took off, we briefed with Col Pierson, Powers, and another guy for a four-ship, five-flight fly by — the last FAC combat mission. We were the last ones out of the war zone...... The party that night was okay- we only got kicked out of the club 3 times. I'll be telling you more about the festivities when I get home. I'm still working on getting out of here around the first. I don't have a port call yet, should be within the next couple of days. Can't wait to see my most *favorite girl in the world and to love her and squeeze her. You're swell. Love, Boyfriend*

The War Ends

NEWSPAPER CLIPPING – "One weary American pilot sang over his microphone, "after today, we'll be gone, but the work will go on." Another pilot radioed there was only 15 minutes to go and asked if he should drop his bombs anyway. "Negative," the air controller replied. "Do not expend any more. Cease air activities." Then someone came on the air playing a harmonica - snatches of an old vaudeville exit theme. Five minutes before the cutoff, somebody whistled the theme of "Turkey in the Straw." The harmonica chimed in as an accompaniment. "I'm on the way home," a pilot radioed. An OV-10 spotter plane did a victory roll over Phnom Penh, trailing smoke like a sky-writer. The bombing halt was in effect 15 minutes before the deadline set by the U.S. Congress."

August 19

One of these days the true story of the FAC is going to come out. If it wasn't for us none of those A-7s or F-4s could have dropped the 'last bomb.' Just being in on the 3 last days this year really made me glad I didn't take an F-4. I probably would never have had a commander like I have now. There's not a guy in the squadron that wouldn't follow Col. Howard (Howie) Pierson, "Blue Suiter," anywhere. He's going to the FAC reunion so you will get to meet him. Only 25 and a wake up 'til I get to see my girlfriend.

August 22

I leave here on the 15th and Clark AFB, Philippines on the 14th which means I'll get there on the 14th (Friday). When I leave here, I don't want to waste any time just sitting around in some airport. I want to be with my girl. Only three weeks to go — each day I get more and more ready to be home.

August 30

My "Sawadee Party" was the other night. Col. Pierson really had a lot of great things to say about me. You would have been proud. We need to start thinking about what we're going to do when I get home. I've accrued about 45 days of leave. We do know that the first couple of days we will be in Dallas at the Royal Coach, right? (Don't forget to bring the projector and new film– I'll probably remind you again.)

The "Fini" Flight

Your combat tour was not officially over until your "fini" flight. It signified that you were finally going home and in the post flight ceremony you would be honored by your Buds, your comrades-in-arm. It officially started with your arrival overhead the field as you beat up the pattern with the smoke generator on. There was great probability that the departing pilot would be drenched with the fire hose. As a precaution against drowning, I inflated my survival life vests upon egress of my plane. As I stood there next to my "Bronco," dripping wet, the boss handed me a bottle of champagne. I hopped on the maintenance cart for the "Last Nail's Ride" down the line of parked OV-10s. Those Bronco's had brought me through 200 combat missions in SEA. I couldn't help but think of the guys I knew who didn't make it to the "fini."

September 4

Dear Girlfriend, I've got my "fini" flight this afternoon....Okay wench....it's after the flight. What a great Finale! I did it in a pave-nail (no stick in back.) so Harry didn't get to fly it. I did a lot of tree-top flying and came in and shot some GCAs. Then I entered on initial and out for a low pass on the field and pulled up for a closed full stop. Harry had already taken off his flying suit an hour before and put on his tennis outfit. We taxied into the fini flight area (smoke still going) and I stopped and feathered both engines. Harry jumped out with tennis balls and racket. Howie Pierson shook hands and I jumped out. Just before I hit ground, I popped both APU's (life preservers) and then got drenched. It's over — I made it. Kinda sad- what a good time I had in this airplane. But like I've probably said every letter — I'm ready to come home to my Favorite. I just love you so much and wish I could share all these events, but the movies will put you there with me and you'll get to see a lot more than 98% of the other wives will — you're swell. Your boyfriend, "Irving"

Finally Home

I picked Charlie up at the airport in the lime green Cutlass, almost new; no dents or dings to account for. We went to the same hotel where we spent the first night of our honeymoon, The Royal Coach Inn, on Northwest Highway in Dallas. He brought gifts, including a double strand of Mikimoto pearls he purchased in Japan on his way home. He also brought stories and the movie he talked so much about. I brought the projector he shipped to me. Before 24 hours had passed, we had watched the entire movie together.

After a couple of days in the hotel we had to go somewhere and get on with life. I graduated from medical technology school the week of his return. My parents had moved to Taiwan a month earlier. His parents were transferred to Loring AFB, Maine, a few months before that. Our household goods had already been shipped to Webb Air Force Base, Big Spring, Texas. We flew to Maine to spend a week with Charlie's folks, and upon our return we headed for West Texas.

Charlie still wanted to go back to Reese AFB in Lubbock, so we drove to Lubbock and he personally went in to talk to the squadron commander to ask if he could work for him. The commander made a few calls and then told Charlie not to check in at Webb because the paperwork would come through in a few days. We started house hunting in Lubbock.

"All Gave Some, Some Gave All"

FACs were U.S. and Allied airmen who principally flew small, slow-flying, lightly-armed aircraft such as the O-1, O-2 and OV-10 throughout Southeast Asia (SEA) from 1962-1975. Serving alongside them were maintenance and munitions personnel who ensured that the airplanes were kept operational, fueled, and armed. Additionally, radio operators maintained and helped operate the FACs' radios and performed their duties alongside those FACs who deployed with ground forces in the field. FACs flew day and night at low altitude in every sort of weather, and they also served in the field with U.S. ground forces. They probed targets, directed air strikes to support embattled U.S. and Allied ground units, interdicted enemy infiltration routes, and coordinated rescue operations for downed airmen. Using smoke rockets and smoke grenades to mark targets, FACs controlled air strikes, naval gunfire and artillery fire against enemy positions. Fighter aircraft know where to drop their weapons when they heard the FACs trademark radio call directing them to "Hit my smoke!" FACs were the eyes, ears, and voices above the battlefield. They were gallant airmen who provided the vital link between troops in the field, the various command and control agencies, and the U.S. and Allied war planes. Captain Hilliard A. Wilbanks (O-1) and Captain Steve L. Bennett (OV-10) were two of the 220 FACs who perished in SEA. Both were posthumously awarded the Medal of Honor. – Forward Air Controllers Association

CHAPTER 6

Back in the USA

1973-1982

"I liked being with my girlfriend more than anything and I really can't wait to get home so we can live <u>normal</u> again in our own house." - Charlie, April 9, 1973, Thailand

New Rules of Engagement (ROE)

Charlie had a new assignment, and we had a new house, but what was "normal?" I received this letter from Lt. Col. Howard Pierson, Charlie's squadron commander, in early September, 1973, a few days before Charlie returned home from the war. The letter was enlightening to say the least. It was several months before I fully understood the meaning of much of the advice.

FROM: 23rd TASS/CC SUBJECT: Return for Rehabilitation

TO: MRS. DIANE YATES

1. 1/LT CHARLES YATES, having completed a tour of duty in the southeastern paradise of Asia, is being returned

to the Continental United States for rest, recuperation, and refinishment. Soon he will be in your midst, de-Americanized, demoralized, and dehumanized. He must once again assume his rightful position as a civilized member of American society, a task which could require supreme sacrifice and understanding on your part.

2. As a combat aircrew member, your husband has been subjected to extremely severe psychological traumas, the least of these involving actual combat. Please consider it your single duty to assist in every possible way with his rehabilitation.

3. Aside from the most obvious measure of bestowing inordinate quantities of affection, there are a few specific measures which should be taken. This will insure his complete recovery and prevent occurrences of Asiaticus Fanaticus. A sampling of these measures are included in Attachment one (1).

4. I sincerely thank you for the loan of your hero. We appreciated his service almost as much as you missed him.

HOWARD J. PIERSON, Lt. Col, USAF 1 Atch
Commander

HINTS FOR REHABILITATION

1. In making your preparations to welcome him home and return him to respectable society, you must make allowances for the crude environment in which he has lived for the past year. His language will be profane, his manners non-existent, his eating, sleeping, and drinking habits impossible.

2. Inform all relatives, friends, and neighbors to stay away from the premises for the first 48 hours. (I'm sure <u>you</u> will not want any visitors anyway.) This is the DANGER PERIOD! We have absolutely no idea as to what he may do. Be prepared for anything.

3. For the first few months (until he is housebroken), be especially watchful when he is in the company of young, beautiful women. The few American girls he may have seen since arriving here were either 13 years old or married to civilian personnel. His initial reaction upon meeting an attractive ROUND EYE may be to stare. Take advantage of this momentary state of shock to move the young lady out of his way.

4. There are definitely some things he must not be exposed to. Do not mention the words McGovern, Fonda, burnt draft cards, student protests, or dead bugs. Do not expose him to any loud noise that may be construed as a rocket explosion. (Otherwise he may dive under the closest article of furniture offering protection.) Do not feed him rice and be especially careful not to offer him iced tea for lunch. Never ask him to go out and look for something "over the fence."

5. Some of his characteristics have changed. That vacant stare will disappear in a few days. His language will gradually improve. (By the way, SH___ HOT is not a cuss word.) He will start wearing an undershirt as soon as he realizes it won't be torn from his back. Phrases like "hit my smoke, "nitnoy," "secondary explosion." "numba-ten," and "suspected tree park" will gradually disappear from his vocabulary.

6. Such words as CTO, 7&&, DEROS, and "SHORT" may still bring a smile to his face. Others such as frag, words, QRF, and double bang will produce a seemingly unjustified

quantity of hate and profanity. If he says your "sierra" is weak and you'd better get it together, just smile and say, "yes dear."

7. If you intend to meet him at a public place, take enough money to pay for the damaged property. Also you might have sufficient reserve to pay fines for slander, drunk and disorderly conduct, and other offenses he has become accustomed to committing over here.

8. He may have an uncontrollable desire to burn hats. This is a natural reaction and should pass in time. However, upon seeing an unattended hat, don't be surprised if he jumps up and screams, "Nape the S___." It would probably be best at this time to ignore him and call the fire department.

9. After a SEA tour, it appears that all Nails have become addicted to bathing with their clothes on. This ritual is so ingrained that the sudden withdrawal could put undue stress on the returning hero. To ease the withdrawal pains, he should be soaked at declining intervals. This is known as the Nail Hosing Plan.

T-38 Instructor Pilot (IP)

All USAF officers selected for pilot training were initially trained in the T-37, followed by more advanced training in the T-38. Charlie was assigned to be a T-38 instructor in the 54th Flight Training Squadron, "F" Flight. He had flown the "white rocket" as a student and loved every minute that he spent in the high performance jet. Before he could teach students, however, he had to go to Instructor Pilot Training at Randolph AFB in San Antonio, Texas. Our "normal" life was another separation as he spent three months at IP School, and I began work as a medical technologist at Methodist Hospital in Lubbock. His best friend, Bob Fleer, was still a T-38 IP at Reese

AFB, and on one occasion he took a T-38 to Randolph and visited Charlie. One night while they were at the Officers' Club bar, they ran into Lt. Col. Pierson in his "blues." The Air Force is a small world. Bob was a bellman at Green Oaks Inn when he first saw Howie Pierson. Howie was a tall man and quite an imposing fellow. At that time, he was a major, dressed in his blue uniform, with all the fruit salad (ribbons representing his medals), and a clean-shaven head. Pierson chatted with Bob at the bell stand for a while. Later, when Bob was in pilot training, he recognized the impressive warrior in a training film. Bob and Howie were two of the most influential men in Charlie's life, and on the occasion of their meeting at the Randolph O-Club, their three paths intersected. Meanwhile, back in Lubbock, in our recently purchased house in a new development called "West Wind," planted in a cotton field off 4th Street, I waited for a new "normal."

T-38 four ship formation near Lubbock, Texas

Buddy IP

At the end of IP training when Charlie reported back to Reese AFB to begin his instructor duties, he was assigned a "buddy IP." It was the responsibility of the buddy IP to make sure he knew the ropes. The buddy system was akin to having a big brother in a fraternity. He was someone in your flight who could answer any questions and who made sure you were ready for your check rides. When an Air Training Command (ATC) IP returned from Pilot Instructor Training (PIT), he flew numerous check rides over the next year. There was a contact IP check, a formation IP check, an instrument IP check, and an instrument check under the hood, a wing touch and go ride, and a four-ship formation check. He was also subjected to a no-notice check in one of these areas. It was a grueling year of check rides, considering he had just been given three check rides during his PIT course in the previous three months. His buddy IP made sure he was prepared for everything that first several months to a year. After all, he was an instructor, and the commanders wanted instructors to perform well on their own check rides. Following that first year break-in period, the now thoroughly "checked out" IP became a buddy IP for an incoming new IP.

Charlie's buddy IP was Lt. Bruce Crimin. In future assignments they flew fighters. When Bruce became an F-16 pilot, his call sign was "Criminal." When Charlie became an F-15 pilot, his call sign was "Rowdy." They were quite the pair. His wife, Jan, was a nurse at St. Mary's Hospital, and we became friends. The four of us had a lifetime of adventures which began in our years together in Lubbock. In the mid-seventies we did a lot of backpacking and snow skiing together in the mountains of New Mexico. In time, Bruce and Jan became "Uncle Bruce" and "Aunt Jan" to our two children.

IP Plane Talk for Civilians - Bob Fleer

In the T-38, the hood was a curtain on rope stringers that ran from the back to the front of the rear cockpit. The curtain was white canvas, and it let in a small amount of light, but the pilot could not see through it. So, he flew blind under the hood with nothing but the instruments for the entire ride. At some point in the ride, everyone got a little vertigo because light would seep into the cockpit from tiny translucent cracks in the canvas. The pilot pulled the hood over immediately after gear up and was allowed to pull it back on short final, at decision height on the final hand flown Ground Control Approach (GCA). Those GCA minimums are the exact same minimums that civilian airline pilots fly to on a Category 2 (CAT II). The CAT II is an auto pilot engaged ILS approach (Instrument Landing System) that guides the pilot to 100 feet AGL (Above Ground Level). The T-38s had no auto pilots.

The Contact "Talkie" check included a heavy-weight, single engine pattern to a touch and go immediately after take-off, then multiple aerobatics: loop, barrel roll, aileron roll, clover leaf, Cuban eight, and a full aft stick stall in the area. Then the pilot returned to demonstrate no flap emergency overhead patterns from initial and normal overhead patterns.

The IP checks in contact, formation and instruments involved two grades. The grade sheet had parallel columns with a "talkie" grade on one side and a performance grade on the other. The instructor was graded: Unsat (U); Fair (F); Good (G) and Excellent (E) on both parts and could bust a check simply on the instructional part. So, flying well and talking articulately through the maneuvers, simultaneously, was the double challenge. Of course, all of this was demonstrated from the rear cockpit. On the heavy weights and the no flaps (types of landings), one could not actually see the runway on final until in the flare to touchdown, so the pilot flew looking out the side at peripheral references. Crosswinds were a God-send. Nevertheless, the instructor had to demonstrate what the perfect landing should look like.

Fingertip does not refer to how close the planes fly. It refers to what the formation should look like from above. A two ship looks like the middle and index fingers laid flat. A four-ship looks like the four fingers laid flat. Close formation position was correct, they said, when it had three foot wing separation. That is a very misleading term with which students took large liberties when talking to their girlfriends. The three feet is not how far apart the airplanes are. It refers to wing overlap. There is none. It is a negative overlap of three feet. The vectors of the wing tips are separated by about three feet. The metal to metal is actually separated, counting the back and down position of the wingman, by about 20 feet. Of course, the little T-38 is 46 feet long, twenty feet longer than a Cessna 172, so that still looks and feels pretty close. Formation "talkie" checks included a wing take-off, close (fingertip) ATC formation, 90 degree wing-overs, nonverbal formation signals with hands, fingers and the airplane, crossovers, close trail, and pitchouts and rejoins. Then, the ride returned for a formation approach and go around, followed by another approach and wing landing.

Mad Dog

Charlie and Bruce were friendly guys and cultivated relationships with the crew chiefs who worked on the airplanes. Ordinarily, the enlisted men and the officers didn't spend off-duty hours together; however, the crew chiefs invited the two lieutenants to join them for a party at a sports bar in Lubbock. Charlie and Bruce thought they should drop in and buy the guys a couple of pitchers of beer. There happened to be a "wet T-shirt" contest at the bar that night.

There also happened to be another officer at the party. That major was a section commander of four flights in the squadron, one of which was "F" Flight, Charlie and Bruce's flight. His nickname was "Mad Dog." You would think that two grown men would know not to mess with the boss, especially if his name was Mad Dog. They called in a page over the public address system. "Mad Dog, please call your mother." Charlie and Bruce thought they got away with it, but early Monday morning, they heard the booming voice of Mad Dog, echoing down the hallway of the flight instruction building. He commanded Lt. Yates and Lt. Crimin to report to his office immediately. "Attention! Growl, bark, bark, bark, growl, bark. Dismissed!"

Capt. Charlie Yates in front of T-38 (1976)

Risky Business

Teaching inexperienced pilots to fly high performance jets is not as risky as flying in the combat arena, but there were some adrenalin pumping moments. In the T-38, the instructor and student sat tandem, one behind the other, with the IP in the rear. The instructor had to be constantly on guard, ready to take control of the aircraft. Crosswind landings and formation flying required special vigilance on the part of the IP. Charlie didn't talk about his day-to-day flying much except when a student made a bad move that put student and instructor at risk. Whenever there was an accident at one of the training bases, there was always a lot of discussion among the pilots regarding the cause. Most pilots believed that they were good enough to get out of a tough situation, but they wanted to know all the particulars of a crash. Was fault due to pilot error or to some mechanical malfunction of the aircraft? During the four years of Charlie's IP assignment, there were five accidents involving Reese T-38s. Some of the fliers parachuted to safety, but two solo students died; another student and his IP were killed; and a fourth student died while his IP was severely injured.

The danger wasn't always the inexperienced student. On several occasions, the weather proved to be a great cause for concern. Sometimes it was a dust storm or reduced visibility due to fog or low clouds. If Charlie told me about how difficult a landing was under minimum ceilings and low fuel, I knew that it truly was a critical situation in that he shared the experience with me.

It was rare that the instructors had a chance to fly without students. One July weekend, Charlie and Bruce went on a cross-country trip in a T-38 that needed some additional flight hours for maintenance purposes. Charlie wanted to go to Maine to drop in on his parents. However, there was a line of thunderstorms setting up near the Great Lakes with tops to 40,000 feet. Bruce tried to talk him into going west, but Charlie suggested they fly to Richards-Gebaur (nicknamed "Dicky-Goober"), an Air Force Base in Missouri. There they would refuel, check the weather, and then make a decision regarding their destination.

Upon landing, they checked in with the weathermen and found that the storm system had grown in length, height, and breadth. It was nearly a solid line of incredible storms moving east. They plotted a route where they could fly over the tops of the storms and land in a clear area at Wurtsmith AFB in northeastern Michigan.

When they landed at Wurtsmith, it was dark and after hours on Friday, so they had to make the weather check themselves. The radar showed that the immense storm system was east of them, so they decided to go north into Canada, around the storms, and cut across into Maine. They refueled, filed their flight plan and took off into an overcast sky. As they gained altitude through the cloud layer, they experienced the light show and sound effects of "St. Elmo's Fire." St. Erasmus of Formiae, nicknamed St. Elmo, was the patron saint of sailors. The weather phenomenon of St. Elmo's fire was observed on the masts of ships at sea during thunderstorms. The phenomenon has also been observed on sharp objects such as lighting rods, spires and aircraft wings.) The "fire" is a mixture of gas and plasma that has a bright blue or violet glow and can appear like fire in some circumstances, and a distinct hissing or buzzing sound often accompanies the glow. The sound was more like that of explosions to Charlie and Bruce. They weren't watching a fireworks display; their white rocket *was* the display, which made the flight one that they would never forget.

As they entered into Canadian air space, the Canadian Air Force contacted them to determine if they were "friend" or "foe." The Reese pilots had filed their flight plans, but the plans had not been received by the proper authorities. With the identifications made, they continued to their destination, Loring AFB, Maine, arriving late Friday night. Saturday was a gorgeous, sunny day in Maine, and Charlie's parents treated them to a lobster dinner on the St. Lawrence Seaway. The men departed early on Sunday because they needed to get back to base before 4 p.m. The storms had moved out to the Atlantic, but the headwinds for the return trip were extremely strong. They had to make an extra refueling stop, and they arrived at Reese AFB after the base closed at 4 p.m., which meant the plane would not be fueled and ready for routine operations on Monday morning. There would be repercussions.

"Early Monday morning, they heard the booming voice of Mad Dog echoing down the hallway of the flight instruction building. He commanded Lt. Yates and Lt. Crimin to report to his office immediately. "Attention! Growl, bark, bark, bark, growl, bark. Dismissed!"

The Producers

Bob Fleer and his wife, Leslye, lived a couple of streets over in our West Wind neighborhood. The previous friendship of two became a friendship of four. Bob and Les had a four-year-old son, Dean, and in December of 1974, I gave birth to Charlie's son. We named him Andrew. The Fleers and the Yates spent many hours enjoying their mutual interests. We made several backpacking trips together. We waterskied on the pitiful and only lake in Lubbock. And Leslye and I became the cheerleaders, key grips, set crew, and "gofers" when Charlie and Bob became movie producers and actors with the stage names Tully Baskum and Ludwig Bulfusch.

The 54th Squadron parties had been pleasant - dinner then dancing, but they were also very predictable, and attendance was beginning to languish. Late into one party, one of the bachelors had invited a hoard to his house. Later, he put an "inappropriate" black and white movie on the projector, which alienated quite a few people, particularly wives. Couples quickly filed out and the word got back to the squadron commander. That event disturbed the commanders but lit a light bulb over the heads of Charlie and Bob. That was the birth of "Low Rent Productions."

In 1974, there were no DVDs or VHS. If you had any motion pictures in your home at all, they were probably four-minute home movies on 8mm film. In drug and stationery stores, one could occasionally find eight to ten minute 8mm film copies of portions of very old, out of copyright, B westerns, B detective stories, and horror movies. They were all in black and white. Charlie and Bob hatched the idea of buying "The Mummy's Ghost," cutting it up, and splicing themselves in as additional characters "disguised" in "nose- n-glasses." The idea came from a Woody Allen movie in which Allen played a jailed crook whose parents wore "nose-n-glasses" while they were being interviewed about their son.

The consumption of a few Coors beers was a factor in the producers' inspired scriptwriting. Everything seemed funny to them. A life-sized, homemade, often headless "stunt" mannequin named Gort, along with key grips Leslye and myself, rounded out the main production crew. Elaborate sets made with cardboard, toilet paper and magic marker pens; mood lighting using table lamps sans shades, and potentially award winning sound using phonograph records and reel-to-reel tape recorders combined to set the standard for Low Rent Productions (LRP). Special effects such as spinning titles were accomplished by mounting a piece of construction paper with the titling on a spinning phonograph platter. Lapse dissolve and editing made figures appear and disappear.

The first LRP film was appropriately named "Gort's Ghost." At the next squadron party, Charlie and Bob brought the film and projector, unsolicited, and set up the projection equipment as the party predictably began to wind down. The squadron operations officer nervously asked them, "What kind of film is this?" Charlie answered, "black and white," which added to the commander's discomfort. A little later the operations officer asked again what it was about. "It's about twenty minutes." replied Charlie. With that the operations officer sat down beside the projector and told the producers he would turn it off at the slightest suggestion of bad taste. It turns out he was not a man of his word since the entire movie was tasteless, meaning it was full of sight gags, bad acting, and corny jokes. He never even attempted to throw the switch. Instead, he laughed throughout! The squadron commander then directed Charlie and Bob to make another movie and run the next party!

The next Low Rent movie was a western, "The Bad, The Ugly, and Gort." The theme of the party would be "the movies," and the dress, rather than coat and tie, would be costumes. Everyone was to come as their favorite movie personality. Of course, Charlie and Bob came as Tully Baskum and Ludwig Bulfusch, famous directors and co-stars of "Gort's Ghost" and "The Bad, The Ugly, and Gort." Leslye came as Bugs Bunny, and I came as a giant paper mache' carrot, proving that the key grips could be as funny as comedy stars. The carrot costume disguised the fact that I was eight months pregnant. Tickets were sold to buy door prizes of champagne and wine. Charlie and Bob set up movie-related games such as "Name That Show Tune." That particular game was patterned after the 1950s very popular TV game show, "Name That Tune." In the late fifties, John Glenn, a world-speed-record-holding Marine fighter pilot and future first American to orbit the Earth, was a contestant. He and fellow contestant Jimmy Hodges, child actor from the movie Huckleberry Finn, drew record ratings for the program. Charlie and Bob hoped to do the same. They set up a theater with a marque entry in a large room of the Officers' Club. Late in the evening, the new movie premiered. Nobody left the party early this time.

The producers, Charlie and Bob

The following Monday, Colonel Ingram, the producers' beloved squadron commander, was so enthusiastic, he asked them to run the next party as well with a new movie. The tentative plan was a space movie with old Flash Gordon footage. It was to be called, of course, "Flash Gort." It was not to be, however, since Bob had orders to go to F-4 School. Colonel Ingram offered to fly Bob back and forth on weekends in a T-38 from Holloman Air Force Base in New Mexico so the new movie could be completed, but the colonel didn't realize the enormous amount of time required to put together one of the monstrosities. The "gig" was short-lived but the priceless memories live on: through the magic of film, Bob being run over by a bus on a west Texas highway, then jumping up, dusting himself off and continuing to pursue the mummy; Charlie pretending to be a flasher in "nose-n-glasses" and shocking an elderly woman; Charlie and Bob in a couple of my old "hippie peasant" dresses and hairpieces, pretending to be dance hall girls; the two of them playing tough cowboys gambling in a bar, with a deck of Old Maid cards; Charlie trying to repair a broken gun with screwdriver, pliers, and a hammer; Bob dressed up in a sheet and cardboard headpiece representing the statue of liberty. Tully and Ludwig were proof that fun is not necessarily where you find it; it is also very much where you make it.

A New Assignment

In 1978, Charlie received orders for his new assignment. His dream to become a fighter pilot became a reality when he was 29 years old. The assignment included two more training schools. The first was Fighter Lead-In Training at Holloman AFB in Alamogordo, New Mexico. Here Charlie flew the T-38 and received three months of instruction in basic fighter and air combat maneuvers. His next school was at Luke AFB near Glendale, Arizona, where for five months he learned to fly and employ the F15 Eagle. During these eight months of intense training, I stayed in Lubbock, where I was now the lab manager at the South Plains Dialysis Center.

We started building a house in Alamogordo, New Mexico, Charlie's follow-on assignment after training in Arizona. Andrew (Andy) and I traveled to Glendale on several occasions to spend several weeks with Charlie. There we bought an inflatable alligator for three-year-old Andy to play with in the apartment pool. Charlie named the alligator "Smedly." Evidently, Andy had fond memories of playing with his dad and the alligator; eleven years later he gave himself the nickname, Smedly. (Although in the intervening years, Smedly was only one of a number of pet names that Charlie called his son.) The family reunion occurred at the end of Charlie's training when we moved into our new house on Sunrise Drive at the base of the Sacramento Mountains.

F-15 Eagle

F-15 Eagle Primer – Charlie Yates

The United States learned some valuable but painful lessons from Vietnam. US pilots needed electronic methods to identify targets and shoot beyond visual range (BVR). The Air Force needed flying units trained for specific functions and not the "jack-of-all trades" fighter pilot. The US military needed another air superiority fighter like the P51-Mustang (WWII). Most importantly, military leaders recognized the need to improve aerial combat skills through realistic training. In 1970, the designers went back to drawing boards with specific guidance to build an air superiority fighter with superior turning performance, speed, acceleration, and firepower.

The F-15 Eagle has a 43-foot wingspan, which is large for a fighter. With a 1:1 thrust-to-weight ratio, the F-15 has the ability to accelerate straight up or sustain high levels of energy while maintaining high airspeeds in tight turns. At 400 knots in a 5g turn, the Eagle will either climb or accelerate. (This gave the F-15 an enormous advantage over other fighters of the era.) In 1974, "Streak Eagle" set the world's time-to-climb record by climbing to 103,000 feet in less than three and a half minutes. The high thrust generated by the Pratt and Whitney f-100 engines gives the Eagle its excellent turning capabilities but it comes at a price. In afterburner, fuel consumption is high, as much as 23,000 gallons per hour, or 400 gallons per minute at low altitude. This only allows about three to ten minutes of combat time. The most aggressive ride in an amusement park might pull 3 gs for few seconds. In the Eagle, sustained turns of 6gs are common.

The F-15 can pull nine times the force of gravity (9gs). At 9gs, a four-pound helmet weighs 36 pounds so excellent physical conditioning is a must. As the g forces increase in a turning fight, the blood begins to pool in the lower extremities of the body. A fighter pilot wears an anti-g suit that squeezes the calves, thighs, and abdomen to keep the blood in the upper part of the body. The suit could possibly give the pilot an extra 2 gs of tolerance, but it is not enough. While keeping his eyes on the "bandit" (enemy aircraft), employing his weapons, and communicating with his wingman, the pilot is tightening his whole body and "grunting" in an attempt to keep the blood in his head so his vision doesn't "black out." A familiar fighter pilot proverb is, "Lose sight, Lose fight."

The difficult and dangerous part about flying the F-15 is employing the aircraft, which means achieving maximum performance while bringing lethal weapons to bear on the enemy, assuring his destruction. The occupation of flying fighters is not only physically demanding, but it is intellectually demanding as well. Sophisticated weaponry, high speeds, numerically superior enemy forces, constant radio chatter, and the need for continuous situational awareness is mentally draining. Truly this is a "three dimensional, full contact, supersonic chess match" in the sky.

Bunyaps

At Holloman AFB Charlie became a "Bunyap," a member of the 7th Tactical Fighter Squadron of the 49th Tactical Fighter Wing. In WWII, this squadron flew patrols in the Pacific theater. The operations officer, fighter ace Bill Hennon, painted the image of the mythical Java jungle demon on his P-40's vertical tail. The demon, called "Bunyap" typified the fierceness of Hennon in combat, and the squadron soon adopted the image and the title, "Screamin' Demons." The aircraft history of this squadron included P-40s, P-38s, F-100s, F-4s and the F-15 beginning in 1978. The mission of the

7th Squadron (the Bunyaps) and the 8th Squadron (the Black Sheep) was to prepare to fight the Soviet Union in an air battle over Europe. The United States and the Soviet Union were the super powers engaged in the "Cold War." Readiness to fight was the strategy that was considered to be a deterrent of actual hostilities.

One aspect of the training for the mission was to fly the F-15 in Europe. Charlie was the pilot of one of six Holloman Eagles that flew 11 hours from Holloman to Lahr Air Base in the Black Forest in Germany. The flight required six night air-refuelings from a KC-135. Lahr was a Canadian operated North Atlantic Treaty Organization (NATO) base, also known as the combat operating base (COB), for the 7th and 8th Squadrons. The Bunyaps and the Black Sheep would supplement other NATO air forces providing defense of Western Europe against an attack by the Warsaw Pact.

Another aspect of F-15 training was combat practice against aircraft other than the F-15. Much of this training was done periodically at a training exercise called "Red Flag."

Red Flag – Charlie Yates

A Red Flag exercise is the closest thing to actual combat that a fighter pilot can experience, short of going to war. The objective is to provide tactical training against simulated air and ground threats in a realistic environment so that a pilot's first combat mission will be a familiar event. In a typical Red Flag scenario, the Blue Force is tasked to destroy the Red Force industrial complex located deep inside "enemy" territory. There are secondary targets such as airfields, truck convoys, and storage facilities. Surface to air missiles (SAMs), anti-aircraft artillery (AAA), and "MiGs" (fighters flown by the Soviets and their allies) protect the targets. The simulated Soviet aircraft (MiGs) are actually F-5 Aggressors and other fighter types that are not part of the Blue Force strike package flown that day.

This is to distinguish Red Force from Blue Force in air-to-air engagements. Electronic emitters simulate known surface-to-air missile threats while "Smokey SAMs" (large bottle rockets) are launched from the SAM sites to provide a visual threat to the aircrew. Video cameras on the range record the effectiveness of evasive maneuvers by the pilots.

The day prior to the "strike," the Blue Force mission commander breaks out the "air tasking order" (ATO) and meticulously plans and coordinates the mission. Ingress and egress routes of this 80-100 plane strike package will have to be de-conflicted. The inevitable weather and tactical constraints must be considered. Limited tanker resources add to the complexity of getting all the aircraft to their prescribed "time on target" (TOT) as planned. Before the strike package can successfully destroy the target, the SAM, AAA, and MiG threats will have to be eliminated or neutralized. F-4G "Wild Weasels," escorted by F-15s to protect them from the MiGs, will have the responsibility to take out the SAM sites. Other Eagles will perform a "fighter sweep" to establish air superiority over the target area. As the Red Force threats are engaged, the strike package can attack their targets – hopefully, unopposed.

When the mission is completed, it will be painstakingly reconstructed. Lessons will be learned from the things that worked according to plan as well as from the things that did not. What is learned in peace time will help equip the forces for combat. The criticism in the debriefing is not taken lightly. It is a matter of survival.

I'll get the Balloons

War readiness training for pilots was staged out of Nellis AFB, near Las Vegas, Nevada. The exercise was called Red Flag, and many flight squadrons with dissimilar aircraft from all branches of the military participated. There was not enough military housing for the participants so many were housed in the hotels of Las Vegas. My first exposure to the city was in 1976 when Charlie and I went for a 3-day weekend with friends. In the next few years, Charlie would go to Vegas many times so it was helpful for me to be able to picture the place in my mind when he told me stories. Years later, I returned when I attended a job-related convention. I found it interesting but not particularly appealing. My last trip to the "strip" was with Charlie, and we were visiting my brother Mike, who was stationed at Nellis, serving as a chaplain. As we walked down the center of the entertainment mecca, we marveled at all the spectacular, ostentatious, "over-the top," new construction. My brother stopped and then made a 360 degree turn and said, "Look at all this. My Father in heaven owns all of it, and one day He is going to obliterate every bit of it in all-consuming fire." The most disturbing trend in the changes that occurred over the decades is that this city of adult vice began to market itself as "family entertainment." Most certainly judgment is coming.

Some things remained the same from the time of inception of the "wild West" town until the present. As Charlie and some of his pilot buddies walked the streets, they were approached by a group of "girls" who asked, "Do you guys want to party?" Charlie quickly piped up, "Oh yes, I love a party. We'll need some party stuff." He turned to his buds and said, "John, you go find us a cake and chips. Keith, go round up some cokes and paper goods. Rick, come with me and we'll get some balloons and whistles." Charlie then turned to the women and asked, "Where do you want us to meet?" The "party girls" rolled their eyes, and they strutted off.

The Father

The evidence that Charlie did spend some time at the home front was the birth of Angela Jean on January 10, 1980. When Andy was born in 1974, Charlie made a carefully edited "tasteful" 8 mm movie of the experience – complete with soundtrack and sound effects. This was in the day when the film was painstakingly cut and spliced together. Most of the sound was recorded with a small cassette recorder and later added to magnetic tape on the film strip. Before Angela was born, Charlie bought a new movie camera that could also record sound. For Angela's movie, he planned the scenes he would shoot before, during, and after the birth. It was quite a production with Andy also having a part in the movie.

Charlie already had a reputation around the squadron for his photography and movies. In 1979, he won first place in an inter-service photography competition sponsored by the Air Force. He produced a movie about the F-15 mission at Holloman AFB, and he made a training film addressing the problem of foreign object debris on the runways. When the word got out that he also made "baby" movies, soon-to-be parents came knocking on his door. Charlie only had two children of his own, but he was present at the birth of seven babies, with his camera rolling. He didn't just film on the birth day. He had meetings with the parents, and they wrote scripts, planned scenes, and took footage before the birth. One staged scene was of a couple speeding off to the hospital on a motorcycle. The obviously pregnant wife rode on the back of the motorcycle. One arm was wrapped around her husband, and the other held a partially opened suitcase that left a trail of belongings in the street. On each occasion, Charlie's presence in the delivery room was cleared ahead of time with the doctors and the hospitals. One day, the charge nurse didn't get the memo. She adamantly refused to let Charlie into the delivery room. Our dear friends, Keith and Missy, were about to have their first child. The planning and preliminary photography work had already been done. The nurse curtly informed Charlie that only husbands and fathers could be in the delivery room. Charlie immediately retorted, pointing at Keith, "Well, he's the husband, and I'm the father!" The nurse relented. The show must go on.

CHAPTER 7

Forgiven and Transformed

"Amazing grace, how sweet the sound, that saved a wretch like me. I once was lost but now am found, was blind, but now I see." - John Newton

The Letter of Reprimand

1973

In 1973, the official letter of reprimand from the wing commander read as follows: "Lt. Yates recited poetry and played a musical instrument over a combat radio frequency. He, also, did three victory rolls for a Cambodian ground commander." Charlie's sins and trespasses had been found out. His squadron commander, Lt. Col. Howie Pierson, called him into his office and said, "I have a little matter I need to discuss with you." Charlie said, "Yes sir." Pierson held up the document that was neatly typed on official letterhead and read it to his young lieutenant. He asked, "Is this all true?" "Well, not exactly, sir." Charlie explained. "You see, it wasn't poetry. It was a speech that John Wayne made in the movie." The squadron commander needed to follow through with his instructions from above to take care of the matter, so he said, "I guess *that* ground commander won't need to hear the speech again, will he?" "No sir!" answered the lieutenant. Pierson responded, "I'll put this letter in the round file. That's all. Dismissed." (The round file was the one with the discarded paper cups, gum wrappers, and the rest of the trash.)

Charlie was in his element that day he gave the "Alamo" speech. He was flying what the pilots sarcastically called, "the friendly skies of Cambodia." One reason had to do with language barriers. The Cambodian ground commanders were notoriously hard to understand. French was their second language and English a rough third. One day as Charlie flew overhead, he checked in via radio with the Cambodian unit on the ground. Charlie could see that the good guys were periodically receiving fire from the enemy not too far away. The Cambodian commander asked Charlie to get him some air support and get rid of those guys. Charlie made the request and maintained his position overhead. While they were waiting, the Cambodian wanted to have some conversation. He asked if Charlie could speak French. Charlie said, "Ah, yes. I know a little French. Parlez vous Francais?" The ground commander replied, "Velly good." Then the commander rattled off a little diatribe in French. Charlie replied in his best 10th grade, first semester French, "Ou et la biblioteque?" (Where is the library?) After a period of radio silence, the Cambodian said, "Never mind. We speak English."

The commander then expressed his gratitude to Charlie for fighting for the Republic of Cambodia. Charlie responded, *"Republic. I like the sound of the word. It means people can live free, talk free, be drunk or sober however they choose. Some words give you a feeling. Republic is one of those words that make me tight in the throat. The same tightness a man gets when his baby takes his first step or his first baby shaves and makes his first sound like a man. Some words can give you a feeling that makes your heart warm. Republic is one of those words."*

The ground commander was ecstatic. "Velly good, Nail 50. Can you say more poetry?" Charlie gave him another of John Wayne's speeches.

"I'm going to tell you something, Flaca, and I want you to listen tight. It may sound like I'm talking about you, but I'm not; I'm talking about all people everywhere. When I come down here to Texas, I was looking for something. I didn't know what. It seems like I added up my life, and I spent it all either stomping other men or in some cases, getting stomped. I had me some money and I had me some medals, but none of it seemed worth the lifetime of pain of the mother who bore me. It was like I was empty, but I'm not empty anymore. That's what's important, to feel useful in this old world, to hit a lick against what's wrong or to say a word for what's right, even though you get walloped for saying that word. Now I may sound like a Bible beater yelling up a revival at a river-crossing camp meeting, but that don't change the truth none. There's right and there's wrong. You got to do one or the other. You do the one and you're living. You do the other and you may be walking around but you are dead as a beaver hat."

The Cambodian broke out in a flood of Cambodian, French, and mangled-English expressions in admiration of the American pilot keeping watch on the enemy. Not long afterward, a pair of fighters checked in with Charlie and asked for a 'hold down' so they could get a fix on his location. Instead of the usual countdown on their radio frequency, he gave them the Nail 50 special, "Turkey in the Straw," on the harmonica. Once they had a fix and were in the vicinity, Charlie rolled in on the target and dropped a smoke rocket, aware that the enemy had him in their gun sights. "Hit my smoke!" Charlie radioed to the fighters. They put their bombs on target and left the area. There were some secondary explosions. Charlie flew over the target to evaluate the effectiveness of the attack. He recorded equipment and munitions destroyed and the number of enemy killed. He reported back to the Cambodian ground commander that the enemy unit would no longer be a threat.

Charlie played some patriotic music for him and then made three victory rolls in his OV-10 upon leaving the scene.

A Creed of Conduct

1974-1979

Charlie's fascination with the Alamo began in childhood with the toy fort and all the horses and soldiers. What little boy didn't like Davy Crockett? He read Davy Crockett books, watched all the TV episodes, and even went to San Antonio to visit the actual Alamo. When the movie came out, starring John Wayne as Davy, Charlie was there opening night. He was born in Lubbock, Texas, so he was a 'Texan' and this movie was all about Texas heroes. The themes were bravery and sacrifice for a just cause. There was fighting and strategy and soul-searching. The speeches and the music were memorable, so Charlie memorized some of both. He saw himself as a patriot and a fighter, one who aspired *"to hit a lick against what's wrong or to say a word for what's right, even though you get walloped for saying that word."*

A year and a half after *my* 'Davy Crockett' returned from the war, I bought him a shotgun for a Christmas present. He had been asked to go on a bird-hunting trip with some friends on December 14, 1974. I gave him the gun early, and he had purchased hunting supplies and ammunition.

It had been a while since he "shot" anything. He was much more excited about the prospect of hunting than he was about the Lamaze classes that we were required to attend. Our first child was due Christmas Day. I was working the evening shift in the lab at the hospital on Friday the thirteenth. At eight o'clock that night, I called Charlie to tell him the hunting trip was "off." The signs of the impending birth could not be ignored; we were going to have a baby!

And we did. Andrew Edward Yates was born on the 14th of December. We called him 'Andy.' As far as Charlie was concerned, Andy was under the purview of his mother for about six months. From that point on, the father began to teach the son everything he knew. He taught him the rules: no whining, no crying, no fooling around, no coloring on the walls, no talking while others are talking. He taught him to respond with "Yes sir. No sir. Yes ma'am. No ma'am." He taught him how to wrestle, catch a football, tie a slip knot, fish, and build things with Legos (especially airplanes). He taught him songs, jingles, sayings, and he taught him the John Wayne speeches.

When Andy was four, our church had an all-church talent night. Charlie and Andy practiced for the event. On the big night, they both dressed in jeans, button down denim shirts, bandanas and cowboy hats and boots. Andy had a toy gun and holster on his hip. When their turn came, Charlie walked down the side aisle and sat on the steps leading to the stage. He began to play on his harmonica "The Green Leaves of Summer" from the Alamo soundtrack. Andy slowly rode his stick horse with the green plastic head and stringy white mane down the center aisle. He parked his horse at the steps, walked up to the center of the stage, faced the audience, looked them straight in the eyes, and began to speak: *"I'm going to tell you something, Flaca, and I want you to listen tight..."* Staying in character with clear, strong boy-soprano voice, he continued, *"... Now I may sound like a Bible beater yelling up a revival at a river crossing camp meeting, but that don't change the truth none...... There's right and there's wrong. You got to do one or the other. You do the one and you're living. You do the other and you may be walking around but you are dead as a beaver hat."*

You could hear a pin drop. When he finished, he walked down the steps, got on his horse, and rode 'off into the sunset' as his dad played the harmonica. With the last note, the place came apart – laughing, crying, clapping, whistles, 'hoorays.' My boys came home with a blue ribbon.

It turns out that Andy didn't just memorize a speech. He learned an attitude, a principle, and a creed. You never know when you might need a speech in your hip pocket and a plan of attack. Seven months later, we took our first trip to Six Flags over Texas in Arlington. We were at the park with Charlie's parents. The five of us got on the riverboat for the "LaSalle Adventure Ride" which represented the period of time when the French flag flew over Texas. As the boat floated down the winding river through the swamp, an alligator with big teeth stuck his ugly head out of the murky water. Then two Indians with war paint appeared, one with his bow and arrow pointed at the passengers and the other menacingly waving a tomahawk. We barely escaped that threat before hearing an explosive bang and the sound of a cannonball landing in the river. That was it! Andy was white as a sheet, and as the saying goes, "shaking like a leaf." That was enough! Andy stood up in the front of the boat, eyeballed the fifteen or so passengers and began to speak, ""*I'm going to tell you something, Flaca, and I want you to listen tight...*" The riverboat guide was shocked at first but then gave Andy the microphone. There was a shooting war going on in the swamps around us. There was a drowning man in the eddy in the water. But for those of us on the boat, we were safe because we had "Davy Crockett" at the helm.

The Testimony of Charlie Yates

1996

Charlie was one proud dad. He had a lot to be proud of – his family, his accomplishments, and the attainment of his goal to fly a fighter. The one he flew was the premier fighter of the world, the F-15. His job each day was to practice using that lethal weapon to shoot down other planes before they shot him. If you weren't the best at what you did, you died. Some of his fellow F-15 aviators did die – not in combat, but when practicing to be the best. There was a lot of swagger, a lot of drinking, and constant competition among this group of men. Often, when you get to the place where you think you want to be, you find,

"......I was looking for something; I didn't know what. It seems like I added up my life, and I spent it all either stomping other men or in some cases getting stomped. I had me some money and I had me some medals but none of it seemed worth the lifetime of pain of the mother who bore me. It was like I was empty....."

In 1981, by God's grace, Charlie discovered the remedy for the emptiness. In 1996, fifteen years after that discovery – as he accepted the position of deacon at his church – he stood before the congregation and told his story.

"I used to live my life according to the Gospel of John....Wayne. It was that way until I came to understand the Gospel as recorded by John, the beloved apostle of Jesus Christ. I was raised in a good family with wonderful parents. We went to church regularly because that is what good families do. Since we were an Air Force family, we attended the Protestant services at the base chapel wherever my dad was stationed. When I was 12, Mom had me attend confirmation classes with the Methodist chaplain. I remember sitting there listening but not having a clue what he was talking about. At the end of four weeks, I was a confirmed Methodist and therefore a 'Christian.' I believed that Christ died for my sins and as long as I stayed basically good—didn't rob banks or kill anyone—I would go to heaven. So, I didn't do any of those things. I attended Texas Tech University, belonged to a fraternity and enjoyed the camaraderie of like-minded guys—party animals. My goal in life was to get out of college in minimum time and be an Air Force fighter pilot. Diane and I were married during my senior year. After graduation, I entered Air Force pilot training in Lubbock. Once again, I enjoyed the camaraderie of like-minded pilots—party animals. A tour in Vietnam only added to the mystique of this unique brand of camaraderie. I returned from the war as a "hero" in the eyes of the students I instructed in the T-38. My next assignment was the F-15 Eagle, the pinnacle assignment for a fighter pilot. At the time, I truly loved the life of being on top of the pecking order.

However, this was not conducive to a godly family life. Even though we attended church regularly, I was certainly not the true Christian I thought I was.

God used circumstances in my relationship with Diane to get my attention and to show me that He was Lord and in control—not me. He convicted me that I was indeed a vile sinner before Him, and the fact that I thought I was basically a good person was totally false. Unless I repented and became obedient, not only would I lose my family, but I would spend eternity in hell. I thought a loving God would forgive me if I just said, "forgive me of my sins." I said that often. He won't. God demands a changed, repentant life and that's what He graciously gave to me, as well as to my family. When God saved me, He gave me a hunger for His word that I never had before. That was in 1981. As I look back on my early Christian life, I now realize the importance of discipleship. We attended churches where the teaching of Scripture was shallow and even in some cases in error. "Easy believe-ism" seemed to be the norm. For years on the way to work, I listened to the teaching of men like John MacArthur, J. Vernon McGee, and others on the radio. In Redlands, California, we attended our first church where the preaching was expository rather than a 15-minute topical sermon. The pastor taught verse by verse through books of the Bible, explaining the passages in the context of the entirety of Scripture. As I listened to the sermons and read Scripture, I was convicted that my "sprinkling" as a baby was not true baptism. Our church had a baptism service adjacent to a lake. I was baptized in that lake in California in 1990.

My desire is to serve our Lord wherever He leads me, and I am content to serve in any capacity. Certainly, it is an honor to serve as a deacon and it is the type of work that all should desire to perform. I love our church and strongly desire to see it grow in the strength of God's knowledge and in compassion for the lost."

The Salvation of Nail- 01

1983

Two years after God gave Charlie a new heart and a changed life, he received a letter from Howie Pierson (Charlie's squadron commander in Thailand). The letter was dated 15 Aug- 73/83 on the occasion of the 10th anniversary of the end of U.S. involvement in Southeast Asia. It was written in Howie's cryptic style. N-50 is 'short' for Charlie's call sign Nail-50. 'B' (short for Bravo) refers to me, N-50's wife, and C (Charlie) and D (Delta) refer to our two children. Lt. Col. Pierson, the commander, was N-01. (By the way, Charlie was never called "Chuck" – however, it was tolerated from his beloved commander. To others who asked, "What's up Chuck?" he would respond, "Glad you asked. Chuck is the abbreviated form of 'upchuck' which means to hurl, heave, vomit." He did, however, show some discretion with regard to this response. Tully Baskum was a nickname Charlie gave himself.)

Chuck, Dear "Bud"-

"N-50/B/C/D – check in!" – Happy anniversary on our last sortie together Sir. You were there - in the arena - and it was my high honor to serve with you. This time was a grand time for the military aviator and for the young men of your generation. You served well and faithfully in your first war. I pray that it was your last - but be ready! I have written to all I could who made my NAIL tour in Cambodia one of the most significant events in my life. Thank you for your contribution. A decade later we must stand tall and press on Tully - you are my main man out there on point. Cleared hot! Happy Anniversary - check 6, N-01

When Charlie received this letter, he was flying F-15s out of Elmendorf AFB, Anchorage, Alaska. It was the mission of the Hornets of the 43rd Tactical Fighter Squadron to provide top cover for America during the height of the Cold War. This was Howie's reference to "my main man out there on point." It would take on a whole new meaning eighteen years later.

1991

In 1991, Howie was a consultant to American Airlines. He also founded and was a motivational speaker for the "Top Gun and Formation Leadership Seminar." He was a gifted communicator and was often tasked to speak at various functions, military related and otherwise. Ron Knott, a pilot and entrepreneur, first met Howie in June, 1991, at a speaking engagement. He was impressed and wanted to know more about the man so he invited him to a 4th of July lunch at his home. Howie's son, Howard, came with him.

After lunch, they told sea stories and war stories. They had both begun their military careers in the U.S. Navy in World War II. Ron told Howie that he was the only living pilot out of his Navy graduating class. Howie said, "You must be a very good pilot." Ron replied, "No better than the rest; I just had a praying mother." Howie asked Ron about his line of work. Ron told him that he was a businessman and he taught people how to become Christians. Then Howie responded, "Can you tell me? I think I'd like to be one." That statement led into a Bible study with the two Piersons. Ron started at the beginning with the source of good and evil. He stressed the main theme of the Bible, the redemption of man and how it was accomplished through the atoning blood of Jesus Christ. Howie had a lot of questions. Ron carefully and patiently answered his questions with the Word of God. Howie and his son repented of their sins and believed that Jesus, Who was God incarnate, had paid the ransom for those sins. Ron asked if he had been baptized. Howie said, "No, but I would like to have it done." "When?" Ron asked. Howie responded, "Today. I'd like to be baptized today. I'm a patriotic guy and it's the 4th of July. Why not today?" Ron made some calls and found a pastor who would open his church that day. Howie and his son were baptized.

Compassion for the Lost

2001

The Yates family moved to Grapevine, Texas, in 1991. Howie lived in an adjacent suburb and he and Charlie reconnected. At the time, Charlie was flying for Delta Airlines. He would meet up with Howie at a restaurant or Howie would come to our house for dinner. Occasionally Howie would attend worship services with us. Where once the topics of conversation were war stories and the whereabouts of mutual friends, the new conversations were of a spiritual nature. They would share their stories about their efforts to tell the "good news" to others.

Howie was especially interested in reaching out to all the aviators who had served under him. Charlie's compassion for the lost brought him full circle. In May, 2001, he returned to Cambodia.

Charlie and I and several other members of our church joined a mission team put together by Dallas Turner of On Board Ministries. We partnered with an organization in Cambodia called "Kampuchea for Christ," which was headed by Rev. Setan Aaron Lee. Reverend Lee was a Cambodian refugee who had escaped the "killing fields" of the Khmer Rouge during their reign of terror from 1975-1979. He became a Christian in a refugee camp in Thailand. Later, he emigrated to the U.S. and made his home in Colorado.

The Soviet-backed Vietnamese communist regime pushed the Khmer Rouge from power in 1979. It finally left Cambodia in 1989 after the collapse of communism in Europe. This made it possible for Christianity to be formally recognized in Cambodia. Setan Lee returned to his homeland and began a ministry to train pastors and teachers. When Charlie learned of this ministry and that he could take part in it, he was determined to go. He wanted to see with his own eyes what had become of the country that he had risked his life to save. He knew that when the Americans pulled out of Cambodia in April of 1975, the Khmer Rouge marched victoriously into Phnom

Penh. They drove everyone into the countryside and over the next four years between 2-7 million Cambodians were killed or allowed to die of starvation and disease. Virtually all the Christian leaders and ninety percent of the church died. So much death and destruction, and Charlie, himself, contributed to the deaths of many during his missions as a fighter pilot. This time when he came, he would be carrying not the sword than brings death, but he would have the sword of truth, which is the Word of God.

We met with Howie a few days before our departure. Howie discreetly slipped a sealed envelope into my hand. He asked that I give it to Charlie as we approached the Phnom Penh airport. At the appointed time, I gave Charlie the letter. I watched as he read. The tears began to flow as he read the instructions from his former commander. Howie reminded him of the duty before him: He was a soldier for Christ.

We traveled to Battambang in the northwestern region of the country. The last remaining holdouts of the Khmer Rouge had been flushed out of the region in the previous year. Our team held a conference in a community center that had been a military outpost. During the days of the conference, Charlie became acquainted with many of the attendees. His teaching assignment was to present "The Big Picture" – an overview of the whole Bible. After his teaching sessions, the Cambodian men would stand in line to talk to him and ask questions. God told him to "Hit my smoke!", and Charlie was right on target.

The conference ended with the hymn, "Amazing Grace." Charlie was standing on the stage and noticed the three Cambodians on the front row, the former Minister of Information under the notorious Pol Pot, a former Khmer Rouge general, and a former Cambodian government general. Charlie had fought against two of those men and was an ally of the other. He was so overcome with emotion that he couldn't sing.

God had brought the enemies together. They once were "lost" but now were "found."

CHAPTER 8

Top Cover for America

"I guess God still has a purpose for you." - Steve Pritchard

1982-1991

The Next Assignment

When the time came for a change in assignments, Charlie asked me if I would rather go to Germany or Alaska. With no hesitation I said, "Alaska." I had nothing but good memories from my high school years when I lived on Elmendorf AFB in Anchorage. In 1982, there was no base housing available to us so we bought a house 15 miles away in Eagle River. In June, we moved into the split-level, cedar house on Meadow Creek Drive. Meadow Creek was the gurgling trout stream that marked the border of our backyard. We had only been in our new home a few days when late one night, Charlie abruptly woke up. He turned to look at me and noticed that I was awake and staring at him. (Because of the long daylight hours, and the fact we had not yet put up dark shades on our windows, we could see each other.) I said one word, "earthquake." Within in a few moments the house jerked and then rocked and rolled for 15-20 seconds. Charlie asked, "How did you do that?" "What?" I responded. "How did you know an earthquake was coming?" I could only shrug. I had lived in Japan and Alaska as a child and had experienced many quakes. Somehow, I just knew when an earthquake was about to hit. I had neglected to tell him about this part of living in the wilderness paradise.

Flying Top Cover for America

In 2012, a few months before his death, Charlie published a photo journal he called, *Mount Up with Wings as Eagles*. Over the course of eleven years, he flew the F-15 with six different squadrons and accumulated over 2200 hours of flying time. The book chronicles his experiences. He wrote the following about flying top cover for America.

"Alaska's close proximity to the Soviet Union makes it a key strategic location for national defense. Based at Elmendorf AFB in Anchorage, the Hornets of the 43rd Tactical Fighter Squadron of the Alaskan Air Command have the honor of providing "Top Cover for America." In the height of the Cold War, intercepts of Russian bombers, such as the TU-95 Bear H, were routine. In the late'80s the Soviets had the capability with the Bear H to launch cruise missiles on targets in the "Lower 48" states. It was the mission of the 43rd Tactical fighter Squadron to intercept and destroy the Bears before they reached their launch points.

Four F-15s were kept on seven day, 24-hour-alert at two sites, Galena Air Base on the Yukon River in central Alaska, and King Salmon Air Base on the Aleutian Chain. Galena AB is located 250 miles northwest of Anchorage in a horseshoe bend of the Yukon River. No roads lead to Galena. Supplies are either flown in or brought in by barge during the summer when the Yukon is not frozen over. Winter temperatures run -30 degrees F to -40 degrees F. With a 6700 foot runway, the typical F-15 recovery during ice and snow conditions is by a cable engagement – drop the hook and snag the wire.

An E-3A Sentry AWACS participated in a 1985 intercept of a Bear H north of Point Barrow. The AWACS (Airborne Warning and Control System) would enable the Eagles to intercept a Soviet bomber force well before reaching cruise missile launch points. It would also aid in intercepting and destroying a cruise missile after it was launched. For the Russian aircrew, being intercepted by US fighters must be the highlight of the greater than 10-hour mission from their base in the central portion of the Soviet Union. The counter-rotating turboprop engines of the TU-95 Bear give it excellent economy – a 7800 mile range and a top speed of 400 mph. At 1000 feet from the Bear during an intercept, an F-15 pilot could actually hear the engines. At 500 feet, he could distinctly feel the vibration of the props.

Alaska's rugged terrain and vast airspace made it an ideal location for training. During the summer, fighter and tanker units from the Lower 48 deployed to Alaska to provide Dissimilar Aircraft Combat Training (DACT) support for Alaska's Eagles. During the winter, the 43rd would deploy to the Lower 48 for Red Flag and other exercises. If the truth be known, the real squadron motto was "Fishin's the Mission." Why would you leave Alaska in the summer when the fishing was so good?

Alaska's matchless beauty and grandeur provided a spectacular setting for flying the F-15. Flying formation at 550 knots on the deck through the high mountain valleys and glaciers is an unforgettable experience."

Major Charlie Yates (1987)

Shoe clerks

After the movie "Top Gun" starring Tom Cruise became such a big hit, the local news channels and the newspaper did follow up stories with the F-15 squadron at Elmendorf AFB in Anchorage, Alaska. The movie portrayed the pilots as extremely competitive, arrogant, party-loving guys who took their mission seriously, and who were very aware of the dangers inherent in the profession. The television news stories had great footage of F-15s in flight, with short interviews with some of the pilots who were quick to point out the technical shortcomings of the film with regard to air-to-air combat. The more lengthy interviews reported in the newspaper caused a public relations debacle. One of the pilots referred to those who weren't pilots as "shoe clerks," which offended just about everyone, including those who sold shoes for a living. The mission for the F-15 pilots was to "fly and to fight;" the mission for the maintenance people was to keep the planes flying; the mission for the chemical warfare people was to make sure everyone had been trained in using the protective gear; the mission of the social services department was to make sure everyone was trained to treat others without prejudice or abuse; etc. Everybody had a mission, and of course, everyone thought theirs was the most important. One day a "shoe clerk" in the Materials Management Shop thought his job was key to operations in national defense.

Charlie broke a shoe lace on one of his flight boots. The laces were specifically designed for the fire retardant boots. They were elasticized with quick release clips for easy loosening and tightening. The laces were formerly dispensed in the squadron but due to budget tightening in the Defense Department, stricter accounting methods were implemented and the laces had to be requisitioned with specific paperwork from a centralized supply location. The supply building was on the other side of the base, 40 minutes away from the squadron building. Charlie was told that he had to get laces at the supply building, but he was not told that he needed a special form to exchange for the laces. Who knew? This procedure was not in the operating or emergency procedures for the F-15. He approached the counter and told the young airman what he needed. The airman asked him for the request form which also needed to be signed by the squadron commander.

Of course, Charlie was more than a little agitated. He had just driven 40 minutes to pick up a shoe string and was told by an 18-year-old shoe clerk that he needed a signed piece of paper to procure it. Charlie needed the shoe string to go "fly and fight." The airman needed the piece of paper to keep track of every item that left his shop. Charlie drove back to the squadron, asked the administration clerk to find the appropriate form, and then he had it signed by the commander. Two and a half hours later he is back at the supply desk with the form. The airman looked at the form and said, "Ten boxes? Sir, I don't have ten boxes of flight boot laces." There were ten laces in a box. Charlie replied, "I will take what you have and you can order the rest for me. By the way, if anyone comes here looking for boot laces, you can tell them that we have a supply at the squadron building. Thank you for your help." A memo was sent to all the pilots letting them know they could get laces at the squadron front desk. The mission was to "fly and to fight."

Hold the Tapes

The day began like many other days. The sortie for the day was a four ship F-15 combat training flight. The four planes would fly in formation to the training area in a remote mountainous area and set up "2 V 2" (a pilot and his wingman versus a pilot and his wingman). The two pairs would separate, then find each other using their radars, and tactically maneuver in for aerial combat. The four pilots briefed the mission and took off, quickly joining in tight formation with Charlie in the lead. Normally, the lead would contact air traffic control and ask permission to climb to altitude. The F-15 was a "rocket ship" and could shoot through thousands of feet in seconds. On this occasion, the air traffic controller denied speedy ascent and instead kept the formation at a slow steady climb. The flight path took them across the flight pattern of Anchorage International Airport. Part of the ascent to altitude was through a layer of broken clouds. As they neared the top of the cloud layer, the cockpit of a 747 airliner filled Charlie's windscreen. "Break!" Charlie yelled over the radio. Immediately, as a result of intense flight discipline and training, the four F-15 pilots pulled straight back on the stick, full throttled into afterburner and hurled their crafts up into space forming a bomb burst around the 747. Charlie instinctively pulled his legs up expecting impact. When there was none, he firmly believed only the intervening hand of God had prevented a horrible disaster. The altimeter needles spun around like tops as the 4 planes peeled off in 4 different directions. The irate voice of the controller came over the radio, "I told you to maintain altitude until directed otherwise." Charlie calmly but tersely responded, "You nearly ran us into that 747. Hold the tapes and we'll talk when we land." There was silence on the radio. A few long moments later, a controller identified himself as the supervisor and told Charlie he would take care of the matter.

Cabin Fever

Charlie was the assistant operations officer which meant he was responsible for flight operations for the F-15 squadron at Elmendorf AFB. One day he was in his office minding that business when the wing commander walked in and said, "I need the names of the wives who went on the trip to Seattle." Charlie just looked at his commander, not able to process what he just said. "Say again, Sir," Charlie responded. He boss answered tersely, "I need the names of the wives who went to Seattle. That's all." He left the office. Charlie didn't know that "wives went to Seattle." At that time, I worked in the laboratory at a hospital in Anchorage. Charlie called me at work and asked if I knew anything about a wives' trip to Seattle. I told him I didn't have a clue what he was talking about.

It was not easy for some military wives to adjust to living in Alaska. They moved to this distant, northern wilderness, far from family, needing to make new friends, set up house, and help their children in the adjustment. Their husbands knew at least some of the men they worked with because they had been stationed with them or knew them from a training school. They had a support network by nature of their work. The husbands were away from home often. They were either pulling alert duty at one of the remote sites or on training exercises in the "lower 48" (states other than Alaska or Hawaii). "Cabin fever" is a common malady among those who live in Alaska. Six months of the year, daylight hours are short and if you do not enjoy outdoor activities such as ice skating or skiing, you spend much of those months of the year in your "cabin." Discontent grew among some of the pilots' wives, especially when the squadron would go to sunny, exciting Las Vegas to participate in training exercises for several weeks at a time. Some decided it wasn't fair for their husbands to have all the fun, so they went on a shopping trip to Seattle for several days.

Charlie went to the squadron building and started asking questions. Some knew of the trip; others, whose wives did not go, knew nothing. After a lot of digging, he found that about 13 wives took a shopping trip to Seattle. So, why would the higher-ups care that they went shopping in Seattle? None of the pilots seemed to know anything. He took his list of names to his commander and asked him, "Why does anyone care that these women went to Seattle?" The commander replied, "I care because the Base Commander cares, and the Commander of Alaskan Air Command cares, and the CEO of Alaskan Airlines cares, and now we have to figure out how to resolve this problem." Charlie asked, "Problem - what did they do?" "The airline has requested that we make a formal apology to the airline and to several passengers on the plane because a couple of inebriated women wearing squadron t-shirts harassed and insulted passengers and crew members, and were noisy, disruptive, and uncooperative on the flight." Charlie thought to himself, "Does my job title include the words 'marriage counselor'?" Now someone would have to talk to the husbands and wives to discover the culprits; someone would have to write official apology letters, write a policy directive regarding dependent travel and dress codes, draft a memo for personnel files, and someone would need to have a pilot meeting and address the men regarding the mental health of their wives. Charlie was tasked for some of those details. His personal advice to his fellow pilots was for them to take their wives and children, if possible, to Hawaii for two weeks, which is what he did.

Andy, Angela, Charlie, and Diane in Hawaii (1984)

Vegetable Monitor

Charlie made it his goal to quickly establish relationships with those who crossed his path. One of his methods was to ask random questions, for example, a quiz on states and their capitols. Most people learned all the capitols at some time in school, usually late elementary or junior high. Not everyone learned them well enough to remember them in adulthood. He often asked the question of the young men who worked on the airplane that he was about to fly. As a crew chief was assisting Charlie, while strapping into the F-15, the chief would give him a final briefing on the state of the aircraft and would ask if there were any questions. Charlie would reply, "What is the capitol of Connecticut?" Most would guess wrongly, giving the answer in the form of a question, "New Haven?" Charlie would respond, "Wrong answer, wrong information." If the initial response was "New Haven!" Charlie's response would be, "Right answer, wrong information." And if the response was the correct capitol spoken with confidence, Charlie emphatically said, "Right answer, right information!" The word got around and many young men boned up on their state and capitols, so Charlie had to make sure he knew them all.

Another method of harassment (relationship building) was often utilized in the mess hall at the remote alert facility, Galena Air Base. The airmen would be walking along the chow line selecting what they wanted on their plates. If they were picking only meat and potatoes, Charlie would instruct them to get some vegetables. After the men had been eating for a while he would walk around the chow hall and see if they were eating their vegetables. He became known as the "vegetable monitor." An officer cared that they ate their vegetables, just like "Mom." They ate their vegetables. The communication barrier between officer and enlisted was broken and Charlie would engage them in more meaningful conversations. Those men never forgot him, and he remembered most of their names.

Smile for the Camera

On one occasion while pulling F-15 alert duty at Galena, Charlie intercepted a pair of Soviet Bear H bombers. The Bear was an old design, but this particular variant was new off the assembly line. Various intelligence agencies wanted some air-to-air pictures of the planes. So Charlie's job was not only to shadow and monitor the Bears, but also to get some good pictures. When the F-15s intercepted the bombers, the Soviets frequently had their cameras out, too, to take pictures of the US fighters. The Soviet crewmen would pull out large format, mapping cameras. When Charlie saw the camera pointed at him, he immediately pulled out from the wing position and moved right up close beside the rear blister window of the Bear, raised his helmet visor, pulled off his oxygen mask, and donned a pair of "nose-n-glasses." This mission garnered the attention of the press. The local news station interviewed Charlie and the piece was picked up by ABC and shown nationally. The story was about Soviet intrusion of our airspace and the front line of defense. Only the Russians knew about the "nose-n-glasses." In 1996 about 8 years later, Charlie visited a Soviet war museum and spent hours in the aviation section looking for that photograph.

Can I shoot?

The wing commander came into his office and told Charlie that he had been tasked to take a wingman and fly a two ship of F-15's down near the most western island of the Aleutian chain, which was 200 miles from the coastline of the Soviet Union. Charlie asked, "What is the purpose of the mission, Sir?" The commander replied, "We want you to 'show the flag.'" "Show the flag" meant that they were to demonstrate that the U.S. had military assets in the region. Charlie thought about that for a moment and then asked, "Can I shoot?" The commander responded, "Of course, you can't shoot." Charlie said, "Then I'm not going. I don't want to be the headline story on the evening news."

On September 1, 1983, the Soviets sent two fighters to intercept Korean Airlines (KAL) flight 007, which was on the last leg of a flight from New York City to Seoul, with a stopover in Anchorage, Alaska. The airliner began to veer off its normal course as it approached its final destination. In just a short time, the plane flew into Russian airspace and crossed over the Kamchatka Peninsula, where some top-secret Soviet military installations were known to be located. The fighters quickly located the KAL flight and tried to make contact with the passenger jet. Failing to receive a response, one of the fighters fired a heat-seeking missile. The Korean airliner was hit and plummeted into the Sea of Japan. All 269 people on board were killed.

Charlie felt that there was a high probability that the Russians would respond with more than 2 MiGS (Soviet fighters) and either shoot down the F-15s or escort them to a Soviet Air Base. After explaining his concerns to his commander, the commander responded, "I'll get back with you on this." The mission was scuttled.

Call Signs

All of the pilots had a call sign, a short nickname by which they were identified over the radios. Sometimes the nickname was related to their given name, and sometimes they earned the name. Charlie was named after Clint Eastwood's character, Rowdy Yates, in the television series "Rawhide." One young lieutenant earned a name he was desperate to ditch. Several dignitaries were visiting the base, including a high ranking general and his wife. There were no women's restrooms in the squadron so the restroom doors were equipped with a hook on which hung a reversible sign labeled "men" on one side and "women" on the other. The general's wife was directed to the restroom, but she did not realize she needed to flip the sign on the door. Shortly after she entered, the lieutenant, not knowing the facility was womanized, entered also. They occupied stalls, neither realizing the other was there. When the general's wife exited the restroom and the young man followed soon after, there were spectators, some of his fellow aviators. Thereafter, he was known as "Peepers." He hated that name. The moniker was an ever present reminder of that embarrassing situation. Whenever someone new came into the squadron the story was retold. He came in confidence to Charlie one day and asked if there was any way he could change his call sign. Charlie explained to him how difficult it would be to get all the guys to call him by another name, but he told the young man he would think about it and try to come up with a plan.

The squadron was preparing to go to another Red Flag exercise in Las Vegas. During one of the planning sessions, Charlie asked a group of the more senior pilots if they really wanted to have one of their guys to be known as "Peepers." That name would be heard over the radios by many pilots from multiple branches of service, and it would be affiliated with the F-15 pilots from Elmendorf. The pilots agreed to give the young lieutenant a more suitable name.

Combat Practice

The weapons of a knight in the middle ages were the lance, the sword, and the dagger. Charlie compared the weapons of the Eagle to those of the knight. The AIM-7 Sparrow, a radar- guided missile, was the lance. The AIM-9 Sidewinder, a heat-seeking missile was the sword, and the 20mm Gatling gun was the dagger. Most pilots agreed that any fighter pilot worth his salt would choose guns only (the knife) – no missiles. The effective range of the F-15 gun is 2500 feet. The gun provides short-range capability inside a half mile against high "g" maneuvering targets where missiles are restricted because of minimum effective ranges.

There is inherent danger in practicing air-to-air combat maneuvers. Charlie had one close call that was especially unnerving. He and another F-15 pilot were practicing gun shots. The less experienced pilot positioned himself for the shot but became so fixated on gun sight that he exceeded the parameters for "calling off the fight." Charlie watched in horror as the other plane closed in at breakneck speed with the bulls-eye on his cockpit. Charlie was at a point in his maneuver where he had no airspeed; he couldn't get out of the way. Instinctively, he lifted his feet and closed his eyes. Miraculously, there was no impact. Practice was over. Back on the ground, after a tense debriefing, Charlie sought out a friend and senior officer to talk it over. Steve Pritchard calmly said, "I guess God still has a purpose for you."

Double Tragedy

A more experienced pilot was paired with a less experienced one for Red Flag deployments. They practiced before they went to Red Flag, and they were wingmen for the duration of the exercise. They roomed together. Captain Charlie Yates and Lt. Marc Williams both arrived at Elmendorf ABF in 1982. They were wingmen and roommates on several occasions. They became a team and forged a friendship.

Marc and three other pilots from the 43rd Tactical Squadron spent over a year preparing to climb Mt. McKinley, the highest mountain peak in North America. They began their climb in early May, 1985. On May 12,th they set up camp on the mountain's west rib at 16,000 ft. Strong winds came up, loosening one of the stakes on the tent. Marc stepped outside to fix it. He slipped and fell to his death. He was twenty-six years old. His death put a deep crack in the shield of invincibility that most of his fellow pilots wore. The other climbers were deeply affected, grieved, and distraught. One of those men was Danny Sullivan.

Seven weeks later, on June 24, Danny was on routine F-15 alert maneuvers out of King Salmon Air Base when he noticed a warning light on his instrument panel alerting him to a problem in his aircraft's ventilation system. He decided to land at Galena Air Base, the closest base, to have it checked. The ground crew found no problems. Danny climbed back into his fully armed and fueled aircraft and took off, initiating a maximum performance climb at the end of the short runway. Within moments, one of the wings appeared to separate from the fuselage and the plane exploded. Danny was 24 years old. There was another funeral, another honor guard, another missing man formation, and another reminder that the number of our days is in the hands of God. Flying operations were suspended for several weeks.

A Fond Farewell

In the years following his T-38 IP assignment, Bob Fleer flew F-4s and then was the logistics officer for USAF Thunderbirds. In 1984, the friends were united when Bob was assigned to the 43rd Tactical Fighter Squadron at Elmendorf AFB. When they first met, they both had the dream to become fighter pilots. For both of them to realize that dream and to be able to share the experience together was an amazing gift from God. When it came time for Charlie to leave Alaska, of course Bob was the appropriate person to give the "farewell roasting."

Charlie was a funny guy, but he was also tenacious when defending standards. In the F-15, he was a stickler about shot discipline, sound training, and sound tactics. Occasionally, his passion ruffled the feathers of superior officers, who might have wanted to maintain the status quo. So, right before his going away party in Alaska, he spread the rumor that his farewell speech "might make some people uncomfortable." He told others that people might not like what they were going to hear. To others, he admitted that what he was about to do might be considered tasteless. Well, the air became filled with intrigue as the lieutenants and captains looked forward to Major Yates' going away party. The colonels, on the other hand, were feeling a little uncomfortable as the rumors drifted their way. Bob, was called into the wing commander's office, and the commander asked him if he knew what Charlie was going to say. He didn't. Charlie had not said a word to Bob, and Bob had not asked. Bob was asked by the wing commander if he could tamp Charlie down a bit. Bob said that he doubted it. Charlie was his own man. Bob was not concerned anyway, but he didn't tell the wing commander that. Bob knew Charlie, and he knew Charlie would never hammer anyone on his way out the door to his next assignment. Besides, Bob recognized the set up from a mile away.

The party was held in an Italian restaurant at Charlie's request, and Bob was tapped to "reminisce" about Charlie. His sole goal was to make Charlie laugh. He wanted to see those eyes well up with tears and get bloodshot, the way they did when he laughed really hard. So Bob, dressed in a "coat and tie pilot uniform" t-shirt, came to the podium with a large paper bag. He set the bag on the floor and began telling stories. He presented Charlie with the red plastic smoking fish that had been Charlie's hood ornament in high school. As he talked, he adorned himself with items from the bag that had in some point in time been associated with Charlie. There was a ball cap with a bear face, a pair of big plastic ears, a pair of oversized yellow work gloves, a pair of bloodshot eyeballs, and a pair of "nose-n-glasses." Bob succeeded. He looked ridiculous. Not only was Charlie in a fit of laughter, but the whole place was in stitches.

Then Charlie got up. He composed himself, wiped away the tears and looked steely-eyed at the audience. There was a hush in the room. He said, "Some people are not going to like this, but I just have to do it." The colonels traded uneasy glances. Then, Charlie reached under the podium, pulled out a violin and a bow and announced, "I have always wanted to play a violin in an Italian restaurant." Bob knew that Charlie had never played a violin in his life, and he doubted that Charlie had ever held one. Charlie announced that his "first number" would be "The Carnival of Venice!" Then he proceeded to assault his audience with the most horrible screeching ever heard. Those in the room helped him along by humming the tune, and he brought the house down. Everyone was laughing. Bob could hardly contain himself, but those colonels laughed the loudest.

Valley of the Sun

1986-1989

Charlie delayed his departure from Alaska as long as he could. We were able to take advantage of the best of Alaska in a little over four years, including five summers. We sold our beloved Cessna 170. That little blue and white plane with the oversized tundra tires took us on many memorable adventures. We sold our worn out Toyota station wagon, and to our relief, we sold our house on the creek. At that point in time, it was not easy to sell an older house in Alaska. Interest rates were greater than 12% and there were many vacant newer homes on the market. However, we had a great advantage – our neighbors, Al and Judy Jonsen. Al is the kind of neighbor that helped with projects. Such as the time he and Charlie put on the "nose-n-glasses" and supervised the tree service company that cut down a dead towering birch tree that threatened to damage both of our houses. Al and Charlie fished together many times including several excursions in Charlie's plane. Since the Jonsen twin boys and our son, Andy were about the same age, the Jonsens and the Yates attended birthday parties and school events together The Jonsens' were part of the Yates' property package deal.

We nailed a "For Sale by Owner" sign to a big tree near the entrance to our driveway. Within a few days, a man knocked on our door. He introduced himself as the pilot who was to be Charlie's replacement at the squadron. It was a beautiful late summer day, so they sat on the porch steps and talked a little shop. Al saw them and came over to chat. They talked fishing and wandered back to the creek to see if they could spot a trout. After they finished telling their best fishing stories they came back out to the driveway. The "new guy" said, "Aren't you going to show me your house?" We did, and he bought it a few days later.

Lt. Col. Charlie Yates' new assignment was in the "Valley of the Sun," at Luke AFB, Arizona, just west of Phoenix. It would take us a while to adjust to the new climate. We bought a newly constructed house in Glendale. It was early fall, and the first thing we did was landscape the yard and put in a pool. At Luke, Charlie still flew F-15s, but the mission was different. He was assigned to the 550th Tactical Fighter Training Squadron. There were three training squadrons at Luke, the 461st Deadly Jesters, the 550th Silver Eagles, and the 555th Triple Nickel. They were responsible for training new pilots from the Air Training Command and veteran fighter pilots transitioning from other fighters. The basic course was five months long. The instructors built the air-to-air foundation for 12 operational squadrons around the world. They could boast that the F-15 achieved the highest kill ratio of any fighter, 144:0.

Just as Charlie was beginning to experience the 115 degree plus temperatures on the flight line in early summer of 1987, with subsequent cooling dips in the pool at home, the fishermen of Alaska were trekking to the wilderness to fish. Al Jonsen's new neighbor invited Al and two others to join him on a float plane trip to a new fishing spot. They planned their trip to cut through a mountain pass. Bob Fleer called Charlie to let him know that the four men perished when their plane hit the side of a mountain, another tragedy that not only affected us personally, but also another loss for the squadron in Alaska. Once again, I had to deliberately dismiss from my mind the fears that Charlie, too, could die in a plane crash.

On June 12, 1989, after three years of training other pilots how to fly the F-15, Charlie's Air Force flying days ended. Charlie knew that he was an extremely fortunate man to have been able to fly the Eagle for eleven years. That acknowledgement, however, did not make it easy for the knight to take the "fini flight," his last ride, in that powerful steed. When his plane landed for the last time, Andy, Angela, and I rode out to meet him in the flight line van. He was wearing the "nose-n-glasses" as he climbed out of the plane. Andy had the honor of dousing him with the fire hose, a tradition well received in the Arizona desert. I could hardly speak, afraid that

I would cry. I knew how much he loved flying that plane. He had mentally prepared himself to keep his composure at this moment. He didn't need his wife to sabotage his efforts.

Stress Training

1989-1991

Charlie's last tour of duty was with the Office of the Inspector General (IG) based at Norton Air Force Base in San Bernardino, California. During his two years as an IG Team member he traveled all over the world inspecting flight operations. His destinations included Germany, England, Korea, Ecuador, and bases in the continental US. Twice a year all of the inspection teams were at the home base for several weeks. This time was spent in briefings, training, and planning for future inspections.

At one meeting, Lt. Col. Yates sat at a conference table with members from Teams A and B and the colonel who was the commander of those teams. The colonel explained that they would be attending a briefing on "stress" that afternoon. Something in Charlie's head just snapped. He stood up, slammed his notebook on the table and hollered, "Doggonnit, Sir. We don't need no stinking meeting on stress!" There was no sound for a few moments until everyone realized it was a joke. Then they all burst out laughing.

A little later that afternoon as the teams gathered outside the auditorium for the "stress briefing," Charlie was standing in a group that included one of the IG commanders, a general. They were chatting and the general said something about the briefing. In a fateful instant, Charlie thought, "It got laughs the first time." He addressed the general, stomped his foot and forcefully blurted, "Doggonnit, Sir. We don't need no stinking meeting on stress!" The general, who towered over Charlie, picked him up off the ground by the lapels of his blue suit, shook him, and retorted, "We do too need a meeting on stress!" The general then set Charlie back on the ground and patted Charlie's jacket back into place. This was one joke that went awry.

Charlie's 20-year Air Force career ended in April, 1991. His worldwide travels continued as he began a fourteen-year-career flying for Delta Airlines.

Charlie Yates, Delta Airlines (2003)

CHAPTER 9

Family Stories and Lessons

1979-2007

"How blessed is the man who does not walk in the counsel of the wicked, nor stand in the path of sinners, nor sit in the seat of scoffers! But his delight is in the law of the LORD, and in His law he meditates day and night. He will be like a tree firmly planted by streams of water, which yields it fruit in its season and its leaf does not wither; and in whatever he does, he prospers." – Psalm 1:1-3

Father's Rools

When I was growing up, I remember the expression, "I'm going to lay down the law!" Sometimes, this meant that it was time for a paddling, and other times it meant that it was time for some new rules of behavior. When Charlie and I became parents, we instituted the "Rules." A carefully-crafted Father's Day card was evidence that the rules were firmly imprinted into the mind of our son. Andy made the card in Sunday school when he was seven years old. The teacher asked the children to spell the word "father" lengthwise down the side of the paper. They were then asked to write a word that described their fathers for each letter in the word "father." Andy wrote "F-15" because that was the airplane his dad flew. "Astroids" was the video game they played. "Teaser" was an appropriate description, as were "Handsom," and "Educated." "Rools" referred not only to his authority in the household but to the family rules which had been instituted to keep peace and harmony in the family and to teach obedience and self-control. The rules were instituted as the need was demonstrated. The first three rules were: no whining, no crying, and no fooling around. An example of fooling around is when you tell your son to go put on his pajamas and brush his teeth, and instead he takes off his play clothes and proceeds to drive hot wheels around the track he just built. Rule #4 was no coloring on the walls; #5 - no talking while others are talking; #6 - keep the gum in the mouth, and #7 – flush the toilet. There may have been a few others that I can't remember. The really expeditious thing about the rules is that they became such a family institution that it was not necessary to say the rule; we only had to hold up a hand signal – one finger for rule #1, 2 fingers for #2, etc. This was especially helpful with rule #5 – no talking while others are talking. The hand signal worked because it was a distraction that caused an interruption in the behavior. The child had to think and then decide to obey or disobey. Obedience pleased the father. Disobedience, of course, had consequences. A good father who loves his children will lay down the law for his children for their own well-being. God showed us the way.

Tough Love

There comes a day of reckoning in every child's life. "I reckon I will do as my parents say," or "I reckon I won't." Angela had her "day" on the evening we celebrated her third birthday. We had tickets to the Anchorage Symphony. Andy, who was then eight years old, was dressed in his best (and only) suit, and Angela wore her birthday outfit, a purple velvet vest with matching Capri pants, white blouse, and stockings. She looked adorable. This was the deal: "If you behave at the symphony, we will go to Baskin-Robbins for ice cream after the concert." It was a very cold Alaska January night so we donned our heavy coats and drove the ten miles to town. The concert hall was a new experience for the kids, and it probably wasn't the best choice of a birthday outing for a three-year-old. As we settled in our seats, there was the problem of what to do with the coats. We decided to sit on ours, but the best place for Angela's small coat was her lap. Charlie gave instruction about whispering when we talked. The birthday girl had some trouble understanding this concept. With the mouth "zipped," the body began to fidget. She was also having trouble with the concept of "being still." Angela began to whine about the coat in her lap. Then, she held the coat up over her head, blocking the view of those behind us. Her dad told her to stop messing with her coat. Just about that time a hush settled over the hall in anticipation of the orchestra tuning up. As she opened her mouth to begin a loud protest, Charlie put his hand over her mouth and whisked her out of her seat and up the aisle. He commenced with a lesson in obedience outside the auditorium while the conductor raised his baton inside.

After the concert, we were hungry. We had anticipated the ice cream as much as the concert. But, there was a problem. Someone in our party had not behaved. We ordered three ice cream cones and sat at one of the parlor tables. Bubble gum, praline and chocolate chip ice cream was eaten, but not enjoyed, because a three-year-old little girl in a purple pant suit with a tear slowly rolling down her check was watching every lick. The lesson was not forgotten. She did not truly appreciate this story until she had a three-year-old of her own.

> "Train up a child in the way he should go; even when he is old he will not depart from it." – Proverbs 22:6

The Blue Fox

Most of Alaska is wilderness and the best fishing spots were inaccessible by car or truck. A pilot's solution to this problem is an airplane on floats or a plane with oversized (tundra) tires. Charlie found an airplane for sale, and he found a partner who would share the expenses. We were so excited about the adventures to come. We went to the airfield and did some maintenance and cleaning in anticipation of our first outing. Before we could go, however, the partner took our plane on a fishing trip and crashed it. What a disappointment! The partner promised to pay back the money we invested, and he did, but it took some time. The wilderness was still calling. Charlie located another plane, even nicer than the first one. This time the partner was not another pilot; it was his wife. If she wrecked the plane it would be a family matter. The bird was a sharp looking, blue and white Cessna 170. We called her the "Blue Fox." One winter, Charlie was out of town for several weeks. A volcano in the Cook Inlet erupted and spewed ash throughout the region for days. The "Fox" was parked out on the ramp at Birchwood Airport and she was covered with several inches of snow topped with a layer of acidic ash. I enlisted the help of my neighbor, Al Jonsen, and together we swept the toxic mixture from the much loved "wings to the wilderness."

Charlie appreciated my dutiful care of the family toy, and he hatched a plan to show his appreciation. The squadron went to Nellis AFB, Las Vegas, Nevada, to participate in a Red Flag exercise (practice for war). While in Vegas, he shopped the furriers until he found the perfect blue fox jacket. It was to be a Christmas/anniversary gift. Since it was early November he gave the jacket to his commander to bring back to Alaska in his F-15 and then keep it for him until December. While Charlie was gone, I cut out and began to sew a formal gown for the Officers Club Christmas Ball which was the first week in December. When I showed Charlie the metallic gold fabric, he made a face and said he didn't like it. He said, "Why don't I buy a formal dress for you this time, and I'll go shopping with you!" This was an unusual offer; I should have known something was up, especially since he picked a very expensive, silvery gray dress with a jeweled neckline. Charlie was so proud of the extravagant gift that he was to bestow on his wife. All the guys at the squadron knew he planned to give it to me on Saturday, the day of the Ball. He was going to wait until I went into the bathroom to shower and get ready and then when I came out, he would have that soft, white fur with the silver tips to wrap around me. How many times did he go over in his mind what he was planning to do. Friday when he left work, he picked up the box from his commander and drove the ten miles home to Eagle River. He left the box in the back of the Toyota station wagon in the garage. Saturday was spent playing with the kids and doing chores until "it was time." I went into the bathroom to do my ritual.

Charlie ran downstairs to the garage to get the box. He opened it and then closed it quickly. He opened it again in horror. The blue fox was gone. In its place was a child's faux fur jacket. This was not a good joke. There was no time to drive back to the commander's house. Charlie's best friend, Bob, lived a mile away. Could he be in on it? Charlie frantically dialed his number. "Where is it?" are the only words he tersely barked. Bob answered in kind, "It's here." There was a fumble at the scrimmage but Charlie was determined to complete the play. Just as I emerged from the bathroom he walked in the bedroom door with the gift. The guys pulled a good one and no doubt it was Charlie's turn to get "the business." However, on the night of the Christmas Ball, Charlie was my hero. I stayed close to my prince all night.

The Bear Story

Mark and Ann, friends from California, were coming to visit, and we wanted to give them a real Alaskan adventure. We had heard that the silver salmon were running at Silver Salmon Creek.

The creek was southwest of Anchorage across the Cook Inlet from the Kenai Peninsula. It was accessible only by air and when you flew in you had to land on the hard-packed sand of the beach when the tide was out. We decided to check it out one Saturday before our guests arrived. We packed our fishing equipment, the survival gear, and our kids in the "Blue Fox" and took off from the Birchwood airport. About an hour and a half later we landed on the beach. The creek ran parallel to the shore. It was forty feet wide in places and the water flowed so slowly that it mirrored the backdrop of spruce forest and blue-green mountains highlighted with patches of snow. Other than our voices, the only sound was that of waterfalls. As we explored the area, we found many, many tracks – bear tracks! This would be a good place to sing the song that the bears hate, the theme song to "Gilligan's Island." As vacation scouts, it was necessary that we test the fishing. We weren't the only ones fishing. As Andy pulled his line through the water a grizzly stepped into the creek on the other side about thirty feet away. We froze in our places, Charlie with a camera in one hand and the other hand on the gun at his hip. Andy said "Pop, he's getting too close!" His dad replied, "Just let me get this one picture." The bear waded into the water, took a drink, and then went back into the woods.

Charlie decided I needed to learn how to use the short muzzle shotgun. As soon as we landed back at Birchwood, he gave me lessons. I needed to be able to shoot a bear in the face because my dear husband was going to leave me and the kids alone at Silver Salmon Creek. The plan was for us to fly down with the camping and fishing equipment. The kids and I would set up camp while Charlie flew to the Kenai Peninsula to pick up Mark and Ann. The trip was to take about an hour. However, if there was a delay and Charlie missed the low tide landing opportunity, his family would be alone overnight. It would be an understatement to say that I was relieved when that Blue Bird landed on hard packed sand. We stowed our food in the trees far away from our campsite and the plane. We also decided not to fish until the next day, the day of our departure, so that we would not have fish smell on us or our belongings. It was late summer so it was about 11 p.m. when it began to get dark. Barely visible in the gloom, several bears began to fight in the creek. We huddled in our tents and listened to the roaring, growling, and splashing of the feared grizzlies. After a while, Charlie and the kids dozed off. I didn't. That's why I heard the snorting outside the blue nylon wall. I could feel the thud of his feet as the beast closed in on our tent. I screamed, "Charlie, there's a bear outside!" The transition from sleep to "wide awake" was instantaneous. Charlie grabbed his gun, barking "Get down! Get down! Get Down!" He didn't want to blow the heads off his wife and children. He was ready for bear! And so we spent the rest of the night, Charlie crouched with the gun, slowly turning as the bear circled the tent. Andy and Angela went back to sleep, confident their parents would take care of things, and I prayed that the bear would find something else to eat.

Sometime before morning the bear wandered off. "Mark, Ann, are you okay?" From the other tent they replied, "We're here." Charlie slowly unzipped the tent and rain fly. He jumped out with gun ready for action. Bear prints were everywhere. We walked down to the beach to check on the plane. If the bears wanted something in the plane, they could rip the aluminum to shreds with their massive claws. The plane was untouched, but several half gallon water bottles left on a log where we cooked the night before were punctured and flattened. We walked up a hundred yards along the creek and found another campsite. These guys had fished the day before. Their coolers were demolished and the fish consumed – better the fish than us. The mission was "fishing" so we fished, keeping in mind that Charlie had to take Mark and Ann across the inlet and then come back for his family while the tide was out and before the bears came out to eat.

Sand Trap
(Story written by Andy Yates at 14 years old)

Dad and I drove out to Birchwood Airport on the morning of June 8, 1985. Our blue and white Cessna 170B sat to the south of the runway, eager to carry us to a favorite fishing spot as it had faithfully done so many times before. The Alaskan sun already shone high above the horizon and reflected brightly off the snow of Mt. McKinley's glorious face. I quietly fulfilled my duties as first mate, removing the tie-downs and the chocks, checking the tires and the surfaces of the airplane, and loading up the gear. "Clear Prop!" Dad's voice broke the morning stillness with the compulsory warning. The cockpit shuddered as the newly awakened engine roared and all the previous morning grogginess left me. We rolled slowly forward. Dad masterfully played with all the switches and knobs, testing the flight controls and doing all of those mechanical things that pilots do. I knew that nothing could go wrong because my dad was in control. Whenever we took the Cessna out, Dad always let me fly some and that trip was no exception. He taught me the controls and the instrumentation and let me go at it. I would do my best to keep the aircraft right on course but was not always successful. He'd tell me quietly which way to go and redirect my path. Dad was in control the entire time, never allowing me to put us in a dangerous situation. I had to rely on him completely. Even when I thought that I was in control of the aircraft, it was actually Dad who was constantly directing me and making sure the situation was under his authority.

Virtually, the only way to get to Alexander Creek is by light aircraft, and the only place to land is a narrow sand bar in the middle of the river. As we approached and circled the island, we saw several other airplanes lined up on it and mused that it resembled a miniature aircraft carrier. Dad wondered aloud if it was long enough for landing. The sand looked hard packed, and the others who had parked were already fishing so he figured it would be all right. We circled around it once more and entered a flight path for final approach. Dad lowered the flaps; his eased manner comforted me and I did not fear. Confidently, I watched our shadow get bigger on the water and then on the sand until we touched down. We slowed and stopped quickly, quite short of the end of the island. Yes! We made it! That was easy. Plenty of room left, I thought. "Oh great! We're going to have a hard time getting out of here" Dad murmured. I had forgotten about getting out. Dad explained that the sand was deceiving. Though it had looked inviting as firm-packed sand from above; it was actually very soft because it hadn't rained in some time. Soft sand was great for slowing us down on landing but would make takeoff extremely difficult. Since we had already gotten ourselves into this morass, we decided to go ahead and attempt some fishing before worrying again about getting out. We cast for about an hour, trying different lures and different spots, but we never hooked into anything. A number of anglers had brought with them inflatable rafts to take them to the opposite bank, but we didn't have one. That was the trick. People on the opposite shore were catching good-sized king salmon, but no one on our side caught anything. We risked our lives to be there and didn't catch any fish.

We gave up on the fishing and decided to try to get out. Dad and I pushed the airplane through the soft, shifting sand to the downwind edge of the island. Dad yelled his compulsory warning and started the engine. After testing the flight controls, he opened the throttle full out. The plane did not move. He cut the power, and we pushed the little plane through the deep sand to an area that was slightly firmer, thus shortening our runway and narrowing the window for success. Once more, at full throttle, the plane would not move through the sand, and we pushed on. At this point our window for likely success was virtually nonexistent, though I never would have known by my father's cool demeanor. On the third attempt, the plane slowly began to edge its way down the short island. I know that Dad prayed, and I began to murmur a prayer, too. As we gradually picked up speed against the sand that wished to keep us, I looked out the window at the rapidly approaching river. I prayed again to God that He would keep us from that icy end. Then the river was there. It rushed not two inches below the tires of the plane as we broke from the grasp of that island. We made it. WE MADE IT! WE DID IT! If it had not been for our flying expertise, we'd be dead in the water. Yes, WE did it! Dad rejoiced because he had flown the plane so coolly. I rejoiced because I did not panic; I kept my cool. We knew we could do it. We had gotten ourselves into it, and we knew that we could get out of it. I prided myself in having held on in that tight situation.

Not until every last bit of our pride left us did we realize God's faithfulness to us in our virtual faithlessness. We knew then that it was God who was our pilot who lifted us from the sand trap and protected us even in our fit of foolish pride. If it is possible to have faith smaller than a mustard seed, I had it. But God answered that small prayer and protected us to show us once again His great faithfulness. I see now that our attitude about the sand bar was about the same attitude I take when I sin. Something looks inviting, and I see others taking part in it and even being successful at it. So, I go ahead and jump in. God convicts me then and causes me to realize my situation, but sometimes I resolve to go ahead and sin more since I've already messed up. It gets worse and I pray. Then, for some reason that I don't comprehend, God gets me out of the situation. But instead of worshipping God, I praise my own efforts and my ability to "hang in there" during the tough times. Only later do I realize that it is God who lifted me from the sand bars of Alexander Creek. When will I learn that God is always faithful? When will I give Him the glory?

White Water

We carried the canoe to the water and there was a sign posted for all to see. WARNING. The authorities (the park service) had posted a warning. (1) The conditions on the Eagle River vary with the season and amount of glacial melt. Conditions may be hazardous. (2) Do not take a canoe on the river unless you are an experienced canoeist. (3) The river has class III and IV rapids. All canoeists must exit the river prior to the class III rapids. A sign is posted for last take out. (4) There are bears in the area; take the appropriate precautions. DECISION TIME: Do we go or not? The considerations were: we've come this far; it's a beautiful day; the river is pretty; look how gentle and slow it is; we have a gun; we have a babysitter; and there's nothing to worry about; we won't capsize; Charlie is experienced.

For hours, the trip was spectacular, incomparable scenery with a leisurely picnic on a sandbar (so we wouldn't be ambushed by a bear). As the slope of the valley became steeper, the river straightened and we no longer needed to paddle for the river carried us speedily onward. Anticipation set in as the river became noisy. It was gushing and splashing and then we could see the rocks jutting out of the river like an obstacle course scattered across the width of the river. The river here was flanked by steep banks so there was no way to get out. We had to go through them. At this point Vicki (Charlie's sister) and I were frightened. This wasn't quite what we expected. I was sitting in the front of the canoe. Over the noise of the river, Charlie hollered at me to pay attention, warn him of the rocks and to do what he told me to do.

Water was splashing into the canoe from all directions as we maneuvered through the rocks, with Charlie steering from the rear and I sometimes pushing off the rocks from the front with my oar. Vicki and I were in survival mode. Charlie knew he had control of the situation and was laughing and enjoying the sport of it. I wondered how long we could keep this up and then we saw the "last chance" sign next to a flat place on the river- bank. We aimed for the spot and paddled diagonally across the current with all our might to the place of safety. It was a good thing we thought ahead and brought extra clothes because we were soaked. We changed and as we hiked through the woods, carrying the canoe on our shoulders, I told Vicki, "We don't do drugs, we do rivers." The point of course is that they are both risky behaviors.

About fifteen years later, after hearing a story told by our son and daughter, Charlie and I were wondering why our children did such risky, adventurous things. We looked at each other and simultaneously said, "We taught them everything we knew."

Like Father Like Son

Charlie was in the sixth grade in 1961. The teacher rolled the book cart into the room. The assignment was to select one of the books on the cart, read it, and write a book report. Charlie listened as Miss Jones read the titles: "Treasure Island – He had read that one before. "Robin Hood," "King Arthur" – he had read those. "Heidi," "Little Women" – he was not reading those. The teacher read the titles of several girly horse books. The girls snatched those up. She continued through the titles. None of them interested Charlie. There was only one book left and he didn't have one, so it was his. "Strawberry Girl!" "I don't want to read 'Strawberry Girl'!" So he didn't read it until the night before the report was due. He pulled his first all-nighter reading and then writing a book report on that "stupid" book.

Twenty-six years later his son Andy, later to be known as Smedly, was in the seventh grade. Mrs. Phillips rolled the book cart into the room. Alphabetically, she called up the students to select a book. Andy Yates picked the last book, "Strawberry Girl." There was no reason to hurry up and read that book. The night before it was due, he went into his room to read the book and write the report. His dad wandered in and said, "What 'cha doing Sonny-boy?" "Oh, I've got to read this "Strawberry Girl" book and write a report on it by tomorrow." "Strawberry Girl!" Charlie yelled. "You're not reading that book!" After he recovered from the agitation of that painful memory, he called Andy's teacher, told her the story, and made arrangements for a substitute book.

There are many ways in which Smedly is like his father. They both were gifted with musical abilities. Smedly could carry a tune when he was a toddler. They sang and harmonized together and when Smedly became a man, their voices were hardly distinguishable from one another. Smedly played the trumpet in band as his father had done. They were athletic and especially enjoyed snow and waterskiing. They were sharp-minded and quick-witted. Their greatest shared loves were love of God and love of flying. Smedly realized he could study theology and earn his flight ratings by pursuing a degree in Missionary Aviation at Moody Bible Institute. One of his dad's proudest moments was the day he received this e-mail.

From: Andrew E. Yates
To: Charles D. Yates
Date: 9/16/96, 1:03 PM
RE: Smed's Solo

"Oh, I have slipped the surly bonds of earth......" Today at school, my instructor and I flew around the pattern at Elizabethton Municipal Airport four times; and then my instructor slipped out of the aircraft, gave me a thumbs-up, and said, "You've got the airplane." He walked away. From that point on, freedom held new meaning. "No longer was I an earthbound misfit, tongue-tied and twisted, staring at the circling sky. Rather, across the clouds I could see my shadow fly, out the corner of my watering eye."

The fact that I am sending this e-mail is proof that my landings were acceptable (any landing you can walk away from.....). This is something I have dreamt of for years. To have finally realized this goal is a bit overwhelming. To know that the Lord may someday choose to use me to fly for the furtherance of His Kingdom is much more so.

Seek Him and have a good day! Smed

The Toyota

When Charlie came back from the war in 1973, we needed a second car. I was driving the green Cutlass to work, and we just purchased a house, so Charlie bought a new low budget car, a baby blue Dodge Dart. That car was a lemon in the days before "Lemon Laws." Almost every week when he drove that thing, there was another quirky anomaly. Sometimes the wipers didn't work; the speedometer was faulty and he got a ticket; the door locks were finicky. The most annoying thing was that the trunk lid would pop open for no reason while he was driving. He had to backtrack and retrieve belongings from the road several times. On the last occasion, it was raining and everything in the trunk got soaked. Within six months of purchase, he traded the Dart in on a navy blue Toyota station wagon. The Toyota was our transport to the wildernesses areas of New Mexico. Our backpacking gear and two small children filled the little wagon. During the winter, our snow skis replaced the camping equipment. We had several close calls in that car: a spin-out on a snowy mountain pass in Colorado, and a slide off an icy road in Cloudcroft where we ended up at the bottom of an embankment wedged against a tree. I was eight months pregnant with Angela.

The day we almost died was due to "road rage." Charlie's dad gave him a "message paddle" for a Christmas gift. The yellow plastic paddle was about the size of a ping pong paddle. There were two rings at the top of the paddle and a number of message signs were attached, similar to a notebook, where you could flip the pages back and forth. The "messages" on the pages were: "Idiot," "Nice Move," "Slowpoke," "Speed up," "Stupid," "Slow down," "Nice car," etc. Instead of the driver complaining to the passengers in his vehicle about other drivers on the road, he could tell the other drivers himself with the message paddle. One day, Charlie decided to tell the driver of a big rig what he thought about a bad move he made. When we were stopped side by side at a light, Charlie paddled him a message. The truck driver gestured his appreciation. Of course, we pulled ahead when the light turned green. Soon the 18-wheeler caught up with us and ran us off the road. I threw the paddle in the dumpster at the next gas stop.

We took the Toyota with us to Alaska. It was not suitable for our Alaskan adventures but rather than replace it, we decided to buy a plane. At that time, the cost of the plane was $13,000, which was about the same as a truck with a camper top. Charlie continued to drive the aging wagon with the unfixable oil leak to work until 1986. When we were getting ready to leave Alaska, Charlie posted a "For Sale" sign in the window of the car. One day, he went to the base hospital for a physical and left the car in the parking lot. Several hours later when he returned to where he parked it, the car was gone. After a thorough search he called the military police and filed a stolen vehicle report. I picked him up, and we figured we might have to make do with one car for the next several weeks until we moved. Three days later, the police called and told us our car had been returned. A car detailing service had taken our station wagon by mistake. They were supposed to pick up a different navy blue Toyota wagon. It was coincidence that the key they had also worked on our Toyota. It had been ten years since our car looked that good. We sold it within a week.

The Yates family (1988)

Going This Way

We left our beloved plane in Alaska and decided that our next assignment in Arizona was the place to introduce the children to boating adventures. We purchased the 1967 Speedliner from Charlie's parents for $3000. The boat was twenty one years old and showing its age but we reupholstered it, had some engine work done and taught our kids to ski. We taught them the 1966 boat rules with some adaptations to fit the family of four and their friends.

When we moved to Texas in 1991, we began teaching the rules and the art of skiing to many kids, young and old. We taught the friends of our children and then we began having ski days for junior high, high school, and college-age kids from our church. In 1996, we found it necessary to buy a newer, larger boat to better serve our "ministry." It was during the steamy Texas summers when we taught so many to ski that Charlie coined the phrase, "I'm going this way; I suggest you do the same." It was inevitable that a new skier would get tangled in the rope, struggle with putting on the skis and would wind up facing the opposite direction than the boat was headed. Soon, everyone in the boat knew what to say to the confused novice in the water. "I'm going this way; I suggest you do the same." Charlie would always give an instructional briefing before the skiing began.

The lessons on skiing inevitably led to a presentation of the gospel. Charlie compared the skier to the child of God. The skier could not ski under his own power. It was the power of the boat that brought him up out of the water. So it is with man; he is unable to save himself; it is only by the power of God through faith in Jesus Christ that man is saved. It was up to the skier to stand firm (on the skis) and to keep his eyes on the pole in the center of the boat. The child of God is to stand firm in his faith, keeping his eyes on the cross. Many beginning skiers did not pay heed to the admonitions. They tried to pull themselves up on the skis and they looked down, resulting in a fall. Of course, the falls provided a reason to reiterate the key components not only of getting up and staying up on water skis, but also the basic tenets of the faith. The analogy proved a great way to teach, as Charlie would say, "young skulls full of mush."

Boat Rules

Rule # 1—Follow all rules

Rule #2—No coloring on the walls

Rule #3—No shoes in the boat

Rule #4 – When a man is washed overboard, throw him a lifesaver immediately! At a critical time like this, any flavor will do.

Rule #5 – There is a right way and a wrong way to approach a dock. Wrong way: Never approach from the land side as this is not only hard on the boat, but is rather rough on the grass. Right way: Always approach the dock from the water side.

Rule #6 – Be careful in fog! The biggest trouble is that fog never occurs on a clear day.

Terminology: To fully appreciate the nautical life, it is important to have a thorough understanding of the terminology. Such technical terms as *boat* and *water* will be unavoidable. There are four sides to a boat—front, back, left, and right. The front of the boat is called the *bow*. The back of the boat is called the *stern*. The two sides are called *port* and *starboard*. These are often confused. A reliable way to recall which is which is to remember that *port* has four letters and *left* has four letters. We have thus far discussed three sides of the boat, *bow*, *stern*, and *port*. It should be obvious to the casual observer that there is only one other side left and that is *starboard*. Therefore, *starboard* is left. (If you are puzzled by this, read it again, it is a joke.)

Almost every boating outing required that we purchase ice and gas. There is an old gas station at the corner of Kimball Avenue and Dove Road in Grapevine, the crossroads on the way to the nearest boat ramp. The building is a white wooden bungalow with a large hand painted sign over the front door. The faded red letters on the sign read "Yates Corner Grocery." The store also sells minnows, beer, cigarettes, snacks, and lottery tickets. There was another sign posted by the tattered screen door which said, "There are no public restrooms on the premises." Every time Charlie stopped at the corner store, he would ask two questions of the attendant: "Do you have a public restroom here?" and "May I have the Yates discount?" The attendant always answered "no" and "no." When the attendants became familiar with Charlie's routine, they would add, "maybe next time on the discount."

A lot of people thought that we owned the store since our name was "Yates." One summer day a family was coming to our house to join us on a ski outing. We asked them if they would stop by Yates Corner Grocery and pick up some ice. We told them that they wouldn't have to pay but just to ask for the Yates discount. Charlie drove up to the store earlier in the day and prepaid for the ice and asked the attendants to humor him in his prank. Sure enough, they walked into our store and walked out with the ice, no charge. They were quite impressed.

Journey in Grace

There was once a spunky, stubborn, delightfully funny little girl in our house. At the age of fourteen the spunky, stubborn parts weren't so funny anymore. Sometimes, her father and I wanted to "pinch her little head off," in love, of course. We had what we called a "straightening out" program in our home, which was often put into effect when there was talking back, pouting, or a bad attitude. "Straightening out" included restrictions of various types: from the phone, television, spending the night with friends, and such. Even very minor infractions were not tolerated during "straightening out" programs. Angela got tired of these programs. One day, she came to her father and me with "a deal." She proposed that if she did not "talk back" for one year that we would then buy a telephone for her with her own number. "Everyone else (meaning her friends) has their own phone. This was in the days before there were cell phones. Since I pay the bills in the family, I quickly blurted out, "Not your own number." I was thinking how the monthly expense would add up. But, my wise husband said, "Let's talk about this." He said, "Okay, Angela, but this is the deal. If you can go a whole year without talking back, we'll get you a phone, the one you pick, with your own number, but if you talk back, you have to start over from that point working toward your year. And, talking back includes slamming doors, rolling your eyes, stomping your feet, huffing, heavy breathing, and any other body language that communicates defiance."

The deal was made. She did well for about a week, and it was a wonderful, peaceful week. We liked the deal. She failed and had to start over. I think she even made it for a month one time. I can still hear her dad saying these words, "Angela, it is November 23, 1995. It will be at least November 23, 1996, before you have your own phone." After nearly a year of trying to keep "the law," Angela came to us and in great frustration said, "I'll never get a phone." Her daddy said, "I know. In fact, I knew it when you made the deal that you couldn't do it. But, I have another deal for you. This one is based on grace, and it is God's idea. God gave the Ten Commandments knowing we couldn't keep them. Later, He gave a "new deal," the new covenant of grace. We want you to try as best you can to have the right attitude and not talk back to us, but if you do, you must recognize that you have done wrong, and you must apologize, and then earnestly try to do better. I know a hollow apology when I hear it. We will know if your heart is right and your repentance is genuine, and we will forgive you. With true repentance, the clock does not start over and one year from now you will have your phone."

During that year with this application of the concept of grace, we had opportunities to share with Angela what it meant to live a life of obedience, why God calls us to be obedient, what Christ did for us, and how through the help of the Holy Spirit we have a new nature, a new attitude. She had heard all of these things since she was a toddler, but now she was learning what these things meant with regard to living the Christian life. At the end of the year, she had her phone and by the grace of God we had a daughter with a new heart. As it turns out, she didn't like to talk on the phone much and rarely used it.

Phone Etiquette

The day Angela entered high school the phone calls began. "H'lo. Is Angela there?" Her dad answered, "May I ask who is speaking?" "Scott," the young man responded. Charlie proceeded to instruct Scott in proper phone etiquette. "Well Scott, when you call I expect you to say, 'Hello, Mr. Yates. My name is Scott and I am a friend of Angela's from school. May I speak with her please?' Why don't you call back and try it that way." Click. Scott didn't call back. Charlie called Angela from her room and told her what had just transpired. He told her to brief any other boys who wanted to call her with regard to the proper procedure. He also informed his precious daughter that her parents were there to protect her and if she did not want to talk to someone on the phone to let us know and we would cover for her. A few weeks later, another boy called. "Is Angela there?" Charlie answered, "What's your name, son?" "Trey." Charlie told Trey the same thing he told Scott. Trey responded, "Oh, yes sir. I will sir." Click. Trey called right back, respectfully following instructions. Charlie then bantered a bit on the phone with him. Angela is standing behind her dad trying to get his attention, mouthing "I don't want to talk to him." When he realizes what she wants he hands her the phone anyway. At that moment, he felt more obligated to Trey than to his daughter.

The Prom Dress

In the spring of Angela's senior year in high school, we went shopping for a prom dress. After browsing through several local stores, we found one that was a "maybe," but it was $125 and we weren't sold on it. That evening, she asked her dad if he would take her shopping for the dress. He was flattered and said, "Absolutely!" He was surprised to find out that there were stores that specialized in prom dresses. They went through the racks in a few stores in Ft. Worth and then moved to Dallas. At the prom dress "megastore" Angela selected a handful of dresses and headed for the dressing room. Charlie settled into a chair to watch the drama that was unfolding on a stage near the dressing rooms. The stage was backed by large angled mirrors so the gowns could be viewed front, sides, and back. A young lady stepped up on the stage, looked at her image and wasn't convinced it was "her." The mother and a companion "oohed" and "aahed" and told her how beautiful it was. The dress was blue and short with a long dress on top of it that was made out of a lighter blue, see-through material. Charlie thought it was atrocious. He caught the eye of the girl with a "psssst" and gave her the "thumbs down." She seemed relieved that he verified her skepticism. She exited to try on another dress.

Angela paraded before her dad in a succession of dresses, and they rated each one. They liked a white one the best so they held that one back and headed for the racks to pick out a few more. After watching her do this several times now, Charlie thought he could help. He picked a black one. Once again, Angela modeled the dresses for her Pop. He liked the black one the best. Angela said, "We can't get this one." "Why not?" he asked? "It's $400." She replied. "$400!!!!" he thought, without letting it show. "Why don't you try the white one on again?" was all he could say. The white dress was lovely and several girls were waiting around, hoping she would put it back out so they could try it on. After a few minutes of viewing before the mirror, Charlie said, "Go try the black one on again." It was an elegant gown, black jersey trimmed in rhinestones, with straps that crossed her back. He decided, "That's it! That's the one we're buying."

They weren't anxious to hurry home and show Mom. They decided to have a late lunch and plan a strategy. "The dress is like a classic tuxedo. It won't go out of style. You can wear it over and over again." I greeted them when they came in. "Did you find one? Great! How much did it cost?" Charlie said, "Just wait 'til you see it. Angela, go try it on." While Angela changed, he continued to dodge the cost question. Angela was stunning. It was a quality dress and I knew it so I asked again, "How much did THAT dress cost?" Under his breath, Charlie said, "$400....but it's a tuxedo....she'll wear it a lot..." It was Angela's lucky day; she took her Pop shopping. The next morning was Sunday. On the front page of the newspaper was *that* dress, worn by the winner of the Miss USA pageant, crowned the night before. A mom can't argue with good taste.

The Interrogation

One of the hardest things Charlie had to do in his life was to give permission for his precious daughter to marry. The young man who asked the question had been a frequent visitor to our home since he was Smedly's best friend. He had known Angela since she was eleven years old, and he teased and annoyed her as if she was his little sister. Five years her senior, Ryan Guthrie came home from college on Christmas break a few weeks short of Angela's eighteenth birthday. The little sister had become a young woman. Ryan asked Charlie for permission to date Angela and a year later showed up at the front door to ask the harder question. Charlie told the story often......

"When a young man who has an interest in your favorite daughter leaves a flight school and drives sixteen hours straight to ask you a question, you know it's not going to be about instrument approach procedures or techniques for cross-wind landings. It was certainly not a conversation I was looking forward to until I thought, "Wait a minute! I'm not in the hot seat; he is! I'm going to milk this for all it's worth." He drives up to the curb, there's a knock on the door, and he is escorted into the interrogation room – I mean formal living room. The doors are closed and instructions are given, "No, you can't listen in." I begin, "My daughter lives under my umbrella. I provide her a nice home, fine clothes, health care, a car, and an education. You don't even own an umbrella. How do you plan on taking care of my favorite daughter?" Ryan responded, "Sir, she's your only daughter." "That's beside the point – a mere technicality," I said. What follows is a two-hour-discussion of theology, economics, the world geopolitical arena and an in-depth oral exam on flight instrument procedures. After all, I am an instructor pilot. By the slimmest of margins, Ryan barely completes the interrogation; after all, she is my favorite daughter. Who could possibly pass such a test with flying colors? Now, my dreadful day is approaching. I have to answer the question, "Who gives this bride?" There is no way I'll make it down the aisle without tears streaming down my cheeks. I can't even tell Angela how beautiful she looks without losing it. A young associate pastor we befriended will be at the end of the aisle to receive us and ask "the question." I handed him a packaged brownie and said, "You know what to do." "I know what to do," he replied with a grin. The music swells. There's our cue. The people stand and turn to see the second most beautiful bride in the world come down the aisle with her proud dad. Only two people can see my young friend at the front of the church with a big brownie-coated smile on his face. All is well. The question is answered with a solid, "Her mother and I do."

The Other Bear Story

Smedly Yates and Janet Anderson were wed on May 20, 2000 in a mountain meadow in view of Pike's Peak on the outskirts of Colorado Springs, Colorado. The wedding party arrived at the Black Forest Bed and Breakfast on Thursday. The wedding was to be outside and would be set up on Friday in preparation for the wedding on Saturday. It snowed Thursday night but by Saturday the skies were blue with puffy white clouds. By the time the guests arrived, it was warm with gentle spring breezes – a perfect day. Janet looked like an angel as she walked down the aisle with her veil softly blown about her. They spoke their vows. The pastor prayed a long prayer and then asked for the token, the ring. There was some fumbling among the groomsmen. No one seemed to have it. The pastor asked, 'Where is the ring bearer?" And then over a slight rise in the meadow came "the ring bear." Of course, he would have the ring! Everyone, especially Charlie, laughed to see such sport, and the "dish" ran away with the groom.

The ring bear was none other than Janet's brother, Jonathan, one of the groomsmen. During the long prayer, he slipped into the woods and donned the bear suit. His childhood disappointment had been rectified. When he was a young boy, he was a ring bearer. He heard ring "bear" and assumed that he would be wearing a bear suit. When the wedding day came and his suit was a miniature tux there was a lot of explaining that had to be done. And so was true this day, there was a lot of explaining to be done.

Couples left to right – Charlie and Diane, Smedly
and Janet, Ryan and Angela (2002)

It is Well with My Soul

My mother, Jean Coggins, died on February 7, 2003, and her memorial service was held at the First Baptist Church in Rocky Mount, North Carolina. Mom had requested that Smedly, her oldest grandchild, play one of her favorite hymns at the service. When it came time for him to play, he exited the family pew at the front of the church, made his way up the middle aisle, around the back of the sanctuary and down the far side to the beautiful grand piano on the right side of the stage. As he walked the length of the sanctuary toward the piano there was a strange rhythmic "ker plop" with every other step. The sound was magnified by the wooden floors and it echoed through the lofty angles of the room. The "ker plopping" stopped when Smedly sat down and began to play "It is Well with My Soul." The tears began to flow. There will be a reunion one day. Smed stood up and returned to his place on the family pew. "Ker plop, ker plop, ker plop, ker plop......." All was well with Mom. However, all was not well with Smedly's sole. From behind, one could see the shaking shoulders in the family pew. There was plenty of emotion – laughter not tears. Mom would have loved it. She once told Charlie she could see better out of her glass eye that she could the other one. On this day, we all knew she could see perfectly.

Order of the Arrow

My dad loved Charlie and Charlie grew to love my dad. Joe devoted his career to ministering to soldiers, particularly those who served in the United States Air Force. He saw in his son-in-law the talent, drive, and courage it would take to do the mission that would be required of him. He had the wisdom to know when to encourage and when to stand aside and let God do His work in Charlie's life. As Charlie grew in spiritual understanding, he and my dad shared more than the brotherhood of military service; they shared in the mission of Christ's great commission to share the Gospel. Joe lived eighty years and died on January 5, 2007. At the funeral, one son gave a soldier's tribute. Not only did the father faithfully serve his country, but more importantly he faithfully served his God. The evidence was a cornucopia of fruit, the fruit born of the Spirit – love, joy, peace, patience, kindness, goodness, faithfulness, gentleness, self-control. The inheritance of value that he left his children was not the few dollars in his wallet, the gold pocket watch given to him by his dearly departed wife, the gray felt dress hat with the red feather and black grosgrain ribbon, the military medals or the scout leader's uniform, but rather the inheritance of value was the good name and the spiritual blessings that only a godly father can give. Another son recounted the sixty plus years the father lived out the law of the Boy Scouts. A scout shall be trustworthy, loyal, helpful, friendly, courteous, kind, obedient, cheerful, thrifty, brave, clean, and reverent. He was bestowed the honor of chaplain emeritus for life and was tapped into the esteemed Order of the Arrow.

Joseph Harold Coggins had more than one arrow. The soldier and scout had a quiver full. *"Like the arrows in the hand of a warrior, so are the children of one's youth. How blessed is the man whose quiver is full of them..."* – Psalm 127:4-5. The soldier who fought the good fight and finished the race released his arrows. He had gone home where his heavenly Father welcomed him with open arms saying, "Well done, good and faithful servant." Fly high, straight, and true ARROWS blessed with his good name. Hit the mark that has been set before you. Bring glory to God as did your earthly father. Remember Dad in his chair, Bible open, reading, meditating and praying. This was the source that fueled his life of loving service to our Lord and Savior Jesus Christ and to everyone else who crossed his life path.

"Redeemed, redeemed, redeemed by the Blood of the Lamb. Redeemed how I love to proclaim it, His child and forever I am." (hymn lyrics– Fanny Crosby)

CHAPTER 10

Travels with Charlie

1990-2011

*"We have relationship. You need to come back sooner." –
Restaurant owner*

Out to Lunch

Not everyone understood Charlie. Is he serious? Is he for real? Is he
joking? One Sunday after church, we went to lunch with Michael
and Elaine Flory and their four-year-old granddaughter, Michaela.
At the restaurant, Charlie told a story about the blind man who
went into an ice cream store with his seeing-eye dog. The man
picked up the dog and swung him around in circles. The store clerk
said, "Hey you, what are you doing?" The blind man said, "Oh, I'm
just taking a look around." Well, Michaela didn't quite follow the
story and didn't know it was a joke. She told her mother that she
had lunch with a man who abuses animals.

Medical Evacuation

Ordinarily Charlie would have been traveling with an Air
Force inspection team, but the team was at home base preparing

for the next trip, and he was at his desk talking on the phone. The phone was cradled between his ear and his shoulder. As he was talking, he was multitasking- scraping the label off an empty Dr. Pepper bottle with an X-Acto knife. The knife slipped and cut his left hand across his palm between his index finger and his thumb. I received a call from his boss. The colonel told me not to be alarmed. Charlie had an accident and was at the base clinic with a hand injury. He asked me to pack some civilian clothes and take Charlie to the hospital at the Naval Air Station in San Diego. Charlie had cut a tendon in his hand and was no longer able to bend his index finger. His left hand was in a permanent Texas Tech University "guns up" position.

The hospital in San Diego had a special medical unit that treated hand injuries. As I drove him to the hospital, I asked him to tell me again exactly how he had managed to cut himself with the X-Acto. When we got to the hospital, a treatment room was ready. The nurse did some preliminary work, and then the doctor came in the room with an intern. He asked Charlie a few questions, and then Charlie had one for him. He asked, "Doc, will I be able to play the piano after you fix this?" The doctor replied, "Yes, you will be able to play the piano just fine." Charlie retorted, "That's great! I couldn't play the piano before the accident." The doctor should have known what was coming next. He asked the intern to observe the position of the fingers of the injured hand. He then asked him to look at the normal relaxed position of the fingers in Charlie's right hand, the uninjured one. Well, by golly! The right hand looked just like the injured one, another "guns up." It wasn't an ordinary day in the operating room.

Relationships on the Fly

Travel with Charlie was interesting. Even "lunch" could be memorable. He would strike up a conversation with just about anyone. If a restaurant was one he frequented, the conversations developed into relationships. At many of his favorite places, he only had to say "the usual" and the counter clerk or the waiter would know what he meant. The wait staff also knew not to refill his tea after it had been "sugared" up. Because of his relationships, beverage or dessert was often on the house. For a while, he flew frequent Delta trips to Orange County, California. A Chinese restaurant was near his hotel, and he befriended the owner. His schedule changed, and he didn't make that trip for about a year. When he did return to the restaurant, the owner asked him, "Why you not come to see me in long time? We have relationship. You need to come back sooner." That Chinese woman knew how to run a business. She knew the value of relationship.

Groaners

Opportunities to build relationships with fellow employees at Delta Airlines varied. He flew with some crew members on multiple occasions and with others sometimes only once or twice. On occasion, Charlie set the ground rules for "conversation." During down time with the crew, invariably someone would ask, "Do you know any jokes?" Charlie knew the tendency for the jokes to become off-color, so he would volunteer to "set the standard" with the first joke. More often than not, it was the one about the burly, dusty cowpoke who approached the door of the local watering hole. The bouncer said to the cowboy, "You can't come in here without a tie." The cowboy went back to his pickup and scrounged around for some kind of tie. The only thing he found was a set of jumper cables, so he tied those around his neck and returned to the bar. The bouncer eyed the even rougher looking customer and said, "I guess you can come in, but don't start anything."

Charlie loved "gotcha stories." One of his favorites was easy to work into normal conversation so he told it repeatedly. On morning Delta trips, if there was leftover fruit from first class breakfast, the flight attendants would offer the pilots some cantaloupe. That was the cue line. Charlie would respond, "Oh,

I'm sorry but I don't eat melons." The flight attendant would ask, "Why is that?" "It is because of a sad childhood memory. When I was a boy we had a little dog. He loved melons, especially cantaloupe, and he would beg and do tricks for a bite of melon. Dad would always tell us not to feed melon to the dog, that it would make him sick. One time when Dad went on one of his long B-52 missions, we had cantaloupe for supper. Our little dog begged and begged so we gave him a bowl full of melon. He ate it and then curled up in his bed. He looked puny. When we woke up the next morning we found him dead. Mom took him to the vet and asked what possibly could have happened. 'Did the cantaloupe kill him?' The vet said, 'No. He died of a broken heart.' You see, the dog was a little 'melon collie.'" (That is melancholy for those who are a little slow on the uptake.)

There was an addendum to this joke that was funnier to the family than the original story. Charlie told the joke to the family and relayed how the story got a lot of groans and laughs on his trips. Charlie's dad, Charles, especially liked the joke because Charlie added the details about the B-52 missions. Charles decided to tell the story to a group of his friends, expecting the same response. He began, "When I was a boy, we had a little cat." His wife, Dottie, interrupted and said, "No dear, I believe it was a little dog." Charles told her not to interrupt him, that he was telling the story. He continued on. "The cat loved melon and would beg for it." Dottie once again tried to tell him it was a "dog." He silenced her with "the look," and said, "No, Dot. I'm certain that it was a cat." He continued with the story and finished with the punch line, "You see, he was a little 'melon cat'." It was obvious that Charles did not know what the word "melancholy" meant, and the joke fell flatter than a pancake. Dottie made the pancake delectable when she poured on the syrup, "Dear, I told you it was a little dog. He was a 'melon collie'." Fortunately, or not, his friends knew the meaning of "melancholy."

Encounters with the Famous

Charlie was standing in the lobby in a hotel in New Orleans with some of the Delta flight crew. One of the flight attendants was engaged in a conversation with a tall thin man sporting a distinctive hairstyle. Charlie thought that he was the boyfriend or at least an acquaintance with the flight attendant. After a few minutes, Charlie and the rest of the crew walked over to her, as they were ready to go find a place to eat dinner. She told the crew, "This is Lyle Lovett." Charlie then asked Lyle, "What do you do for a living? What brings you here to New Orleans?" The flight attendant indignantly slapped Charlie across the arm and said, "This is Lyle Lovett. He's doing a gig here at the hotel." Then Charlie retorted, "Do you sing country and western or something? You know I always turn off the radio in my car when that stuff comes on because I think the motor is slowing down." It was a joke of course. Charlie didn't know who Lyle Lovett was because Charlie's musical diet usually included genres with brass, especially the trumpet, the instrument that he played. The flight attendant hit him again. It was retribution for "foot in mouth" disease.

I was traveling with Charlie on one of his trips. It was getting late in the evening so we were trying to find something to eat at an airport in between legs. He walked faster than I do, so he told me to go on to the gate and he would get some food. I asked him to buy a bagel for me. First, he stopped at Au Bon Pain to purchase his favorite sandwich, cracked pepper chicken on whole wheat with honey mustard. As he was standing in line, a tall young woman pushed past him and stood in front of him. She turned around, looked down at him and said, "I'm sorry, I didn't see you there." Of course, he was in his pilot uniform, part of the Delta customer relations team, and he said, "No problem. Where are you headed?" She responded, "I'm going home to Indiana." Charlie asked her where she had been. She said that she had traveled to Russia and France in the last 48 hours. Charlie asked her, "What were you doing there?" She was dressed in sweats with her hair in a ponytail and a ball cap pulled down low on her forehead. She said, "I'm a model." Charlie questioned, "No kidding?" She said, "Really." She leaned over and whispered in Charlie's ear, "I'm Angela Mellencamp. You know. My husband is Steve Mellencamp, the singer." Charlie didn't let on, but at the moment he didn't know who Steve Mellencamp was, though he realized later that he was familiar with some of his music. Meanwhile, their sandwiches were ready. After straightening out a mix-up with the sandwiches, he had hers, and she had his, she told him that she was on the cover of Glamour Magazine this month. She asked if he would like to have one. He said, "Yes, of course," and she beckoned to a porter who was carrying a large portfolio. She pulled a magazine out of the bag and handed it to Charlie. He looked at it and then looked at her again, and then back at the magazine and said, "Wow! I mean you look really different!" (foot in mouth again). She signed the cover and sauntered off toward her gate. Charlie had to book it to his own gate as it was nearly time for departure. I was waiting by the desk at our gate. He was grinning from ear to ear. I was starving. "Where's my bagel?" Unfortunately for me, I didn't care for cracked pepper chicken on whole wheat with honey mustard.

Another one of Charlie's conversation starting techniques was to ask, "Could I have the rest of your sandwich?" or "Could I have the rest of your french fries?" He was joking, but it was surprising how many kind people said, "yes." On one of his strolls from one airplane gate to the next, he stopped at a Pizza Hut kiosk. An attractive woman was sitting alone at a table and had just opened her pizza box. Charlie stepped over to her table and asked, "Could I have a piece of your pizza?" He was not a poor beggar. He was a nicely groomed middle-aged man in a black suit with brass buttons, a necktie, and pilot wings on his chest. She looked up at him and said, "Here, take the whole pizza." Trying to get out of the awkward situation he had just created, he changed the subject. "Where are you headed? Oh, I just brought that plane in from Dallas at Gate 12.

The weather is good. It should be a nice trip. Do you have family in New Orleans?" The woman responded, "I'm headed to a television convention. I'm trying to get a television show syndicated." "Which one?" Charlie asked. "Touched by an Angel." Charlie asked if she was one of the writers. "No, I'm one of the angels. I'm Roma Downey. The show is on Sunday nights." The feet were finding their way to one of their usual places. "I'm not usually home on Sunday nights. I'm also a little leery about shows that depict angels because they aren't portrayed as the Bible describes them." She replied, "But it's a very wholesome, uplifting show that the whole family can watch." Mr. Customer Relations needed to find a way to gracefully excuse himself to buy his own pizza. "You better go ahead and eat. Your plane will be leaving soon. It was nice to meet you. Have a successful trip."

A Day at the Museum

There was enough time on one of his Delta trips to Washington, D.C. for Charlie to visit a museum. He and the captain decided to go to the National Museum of History. One of the exhibits was a display of ancient columns. The columns were in pieces and in disarray as if they had toppled over in an earthquake. After viewing the artful display, Charlie sauntered back to the information desk near the entrance to the museum. There was a young woman at the desk. He said, "Ma'am, I want you to know that you don't have to worry about that exhibit with the columns. Someone knocked them over, but I put them back together for you." She paused, mentally processing what the man in front of her just told her. Then she said, "I'm sorry. You did what?" Charlie continued his little game and repeated what he told her. The young woman then said, "Please wait right here. I want you to tell that to my supervisor." A few moments later an older woman came up and said, "Now tell me what you did." Charlie told his story again. The supervisor said, "O my! You didn't! Those columns are supposed to be like that. You see it depicts the fall of the Roman Empire. Oh dear. I need to call someone and get those put back the way they belong." Charlie tried to tell her that he was just kidding, but she hurried off to take care of setting things right. Maybe she took the rest of the day off.

Nine-Eleven

Charlie's good friend, Tim McManus, made an offer we couldn't refuse. He invited us to go on a safari to South Africa, and he would take care of our accommodations if Charlie would take pictures and video of the hunt. Tim arranged safaris for other hunters but on this particular trip, he was on a quest to add to his own personal trophy collection and make a publicity video. On Tuesday, the 11th of September 2001, we were on our fourth day of safari, isolated on a game ranch near the northern border of South Africa. Tim and his guide were tracking a large kudu. The animal proved to be quite elusive, so they struck out alone while Charlie and I spent the morning in a blind on a game ranch. The ranch belonged to a Swiss man who had immigrated to South Africa four decades ago. The blind was disguised as a rock outcropping, nestled in some bushes and a cluster of trees. Our hiding place was not fifteen feet from a watering hole. Through slits in the "rock" we watched a parade of animals take their turn at the water. Charlie took pictures as I hurriedly thumbed through the African bird watchers' book trying to identify the amazing avian display before us. Throughout the morning, the four-legged animals made their appearance. Warthogs and a variety of deer-like animals wandered into the small clearing surrounding the water. At one point, we were startled by a loud barking noise. The bark belonged to an enormous kudu, crowned with two majestic spiral horns. Several mature female and young kudu cautiously approached the water. When they finished, the buck took his turn in front of our cameras.

After several hours in the blind, the rancher invited us to his home for lunch. We sat a picnic table under a tree on the lawn of his Eden. The air was filled with the songs of a myriad of birds, and sunlight filtered through the filigreed canopy of trees, fashioning patterns on the grass. Other than the wilderness of Alaska, we couldn't remember having been in a more peaceful, beautiful place. For a while, it felt like time stood still. The rancher's wife brought us a tray with bowls of chicken soup, fresh baked bread, and iced tea. We savored every moment of that morning and early afternoon, not knowing that it was the calm before the storm.

At dusk we were back at our base camp. Tim and his guide drove up, all smiles with the elusive kudu in the bed of the truck. We gathered around to hear the story of the hunt when the guide received a cell phone call from his wife. She urgently gave him some sketchy news from the United States, something about an airplane crash. Within an hour she brought the evening meal to our camp and told us all she knew. Several planes, the exact number unknown, had been hijacked and crashed into the World Trade Center and the Pentagon. Up to 80,000 people had been killed. All flights had been ordered to land, and the borders to the United States were closed with no air, land, or sea travel in or out. That was it! That was all the news. Our immediate thought was that this is war! We have been attacked, and we will have to fight back. Just the past week in Durban, South Africa, an international conference on racism had condemned the United States for its association with Israel. Osama bin Laden was a prominent participant. We had some immediate concerns about when we would be able to get out of the country, especially since we traveled on stand-by tickets. To add to the surreal nature of the evening, lightning started brush fires on a nearby ranch. There was a red glow on the horizon; the night air was clouded by smoke and filled with the smell. The wind was blowing the fire away from our camp so we were not concerned for our safety, but the effect of it was to add to the gravity of the events half a world away.

We spent the sleepless night just thinking, wondering, and praying. The next morning, we left this camp to travel to another game ranch in the southeastern coastal area of the country in Kwazulu-Natal. We were able to catch a few minutes of CNN news at the hunting guide's home before we left. We saw the segment of video that showed the plane flying into the World Trade Center. It was reported that the fatalities were in the thousands, the prime suspect was Osama bin Laden, and air travel was suspended indefinitely. We purchased a newspaper several hours later and found that the government of South Africa expressed outrage over the atrocity and conveyed condolences to the American people. Since we could not leave the country, we pressed on to our planned destination. Sometime during the next week, we were able to get another newspaper and follow developments. We had no news or information on our government's response, President Bush's address to the nation, or of the memorial services. We wanted to be home in the USA. We wanted to reassure our grown children.

We were able to leave on Sunday the 16th as we had originally planned, but we had to fly from Johannesburg to New York instead of to Atlanta. There were more seats available on the New York flight since travelers were avoiding going to New York if at all possible. Upon landing in New York, the passengers on the plane whistled, clapped, and hoorayed. Some were crying. When we left New York for Dallas, we flew just north of Manhattan Island and were able to view the devastation. Since we had not seen any television, we had not expected to see smoke still billowing from the site, filling the streets, and trailing off toward the Statue of Liberty. The intense security, the long waits at the airports, and the repeated document checks gave us the sense that all was not right with our world, and the reality of the smoky ruins below us confirmed it.

The tragedy gave us opportunities to share our faith in God, in His absolute sovereignty, in the power of His love, in His provision for our salvation through Jesus Christ, and in God's victory over evil. However, it was hard to reconcile the beauty and serenity of the isolated camps where we stayed with the turmoil across the Atlantic. As we thought about these things on the long flight home, we decided that the first thing we would do was to put our flag on the brick pillar by the front door. It wasn't necessary. The stars and stripes, already posted by our daughter, welcomed us home. As a result of our nation's response to the attack, over the next thirteen years, four of our immediate family members would serve multiple tours in Iraq and Afghanistan.

Address in Athens

While Charlie was studying the book of Acts in preparation to teach the college group at our church, an idea took root. One of Charlie's regular Delta trips in the 767 was to Athens, Greece. He had done some sightseeing in Athens and some of the coastal islands. He wanted to take me to see the magnificent temple ruins, and he also needed me to help him with a project. On his next Athens trip, I flew on standby status and accompanied him. We flew all night, took a short nap, and then began our walk through the city to the Acropolis. We hiked up the citadel and toured the temples built for the worship of the ancient Greek gods. Then we climbed the Areopagus (Mars Hill), the marble hill across from the entrance to the Acropolis. It was here that I became Charlie's project assistant, his videographer. Charlie wanted to give the college kids an idea of the setting of one of Paul's missionary journeys.

Paul was waiting in Athens for Timothy and Silas to join him. Acts 17:16-17 records, *"...his spirit was being provoked within him as he was observing the city full of idols. So he was reasoning in the synagogue with the Jews and the God-fearing Gentiles and in the market place every day with those who happened to be present."* Some of the Epicurean and Stoic philosophers took Paul to the Areopagus, which was a public forum where the locals and visitors gathered for the telling or hearing of something new. As Paul stood before the crowd in the natural amphitheater that is Mars Hill, the Acropolis, crowned with the temples to these false gods, was his backdrop. Charlie set up the tripod, camera and microphone, carefully positioning the temple ruins in the frame. He stood before the camera and gave me the sign to start recording. He earnestly and energetically recited the sermon that Paul had given.

"Men of Athens, I observe that you are very religious in all respects. For while I was passing through and examining the objects of your worship, I also found an altar with the inscription, 'TO AN UNKNOWN GOD.' Therefore what you worship in ignorance, this I proclaim to you. The God who made the world and all things in it, since He is Lord of heaven and earth does not dwell in temples made with hands; nor is He served by human hands, as though He needed anything, since He Himself gives to all people life and breath and all things; and He made from one man every nation of mankind to live on the face of the earth, having determined their appointed times and the boundaries of their habitation, that they would seek God, if perhaps they might grope for Him and find Him, though He is not far from each one of us; for in Him we live and move and exist, as even some of your own poets have said, 'For we also are His children.' Being then the children of God, we ought not to think that the Divine Nature is like gold or silver or stone, an image formed by the art and thought of man. Therefore having overlooked the times of ignorance, God is now declaring to men that all people everywhere should repent, because He has fixed a day in which He will judge the world in righteousness through a Man whom He has appointed, having furnished proof to all men by raising Him from the dead."

A few bystanders clapped. Charlie reviewed the video and said "Take two." Several tourists had walked behind him as he recited the sermon. I didn't mind a repeat performance. The words that rang powerful and true 2000 years ago were just as powerful on this day to an audience of a few.

The Russians Are Coming

Charlie received a call from someone he knew who was working at the Pentagon. At first he thought the call was a joke or a set up. "No, no. You won't be shadowed by the FBI or the CIA. This is the real deal. Two Russian film makers want to meet with you and talk about your experiences flying F-15 intercepts of Russian bombers during the Cold War." Charlie responded, "You mean I'm allowed to talk about what we did and how we did it?" "Yes, all of that information has been declassified. They have seen your videos and your interviews with reporters and they want to videotape an interview with you. They will be getting in touch with you, and I am just letting you know that the interview has been approved." When Charlie got off the phone, he said to me, "Remember when I told you that I could not tell you what I was doing at work or I would have to kill you. Well, I've just been given permission to tell the enemy."

The Russians called and set up the rendezvous. Charlie was flying trips for Delta Airlines that month in and out of California. They met him at his hotel near Los Angeles, set up a green screen in the room, positioned the camera on Charlie in front of the screen, and began to ask questions. Charlie was still a little skeptical of this project even though it had been almost 16 years since he flew top cover for America. The Cold War was over and the United States of America had prevailed, but Charlie was not so sure he could trust the Russians. What were they going to put on that green screen when they edited the videotape? He also wondered about those pictures of himself with the "nose-n-glasses" taken by the photographer in the Russian bomber so many years ago. Charlie enjoyed his encounter with the Russians but he still kept some of the secrets under wraps.

An Evening at the Theater

Though he was a world traveler, Charlie sometimes took in the local culture. On several occasions we attended amateur musicals and plays at the Artisan Center Theater in Hurst, Texas. It was not unusual that some of our young friends from choir were cast members, so it was our custom to go with a group of choir members and others from the church. One lucky night, Charlie sat next to

Alyssa Kern, the teen-aged daughter of Randy and Eileen Kern, fellow choir members and boating buddies. We have known the Kerns about twenty years, and Charlie taught Alyssa jingles and songs, and how to make funny faces ever since she was a toddler. They had a special handshake. (Partly, because of their special handshake, Charlie had to come up with dozens and dozens more for the other youngsters who also wanted a special handshake.) Every show night at the theater there would be a drawing at intermission. Each attendee was to write their name and contact information on the small form that was provided. These were collected by staff and put in a rotating drum. A volunteer was selected from the audience to spin the drum draw out the name of the winner. This night, Charlie and Alyssa conspired together, and Charlie wrote a mystery name on his piece of paper. A young girl pulled a paper from the drum, but she could not read the name. The owner of the theater, who was standing beside her, gave it a try. "Mel Puhuu." Alyssa started giggling. Charlie began to turn red. The owner tried again, "Mel Nerput." Alyssa pointed at Charlie and he started laughing. One of the fellow choir members said, "No, you didn't." Others were beginning to catch on that something was up and they began laughing. The flustered owner thought that the audience was laughing at his mispronunciation of the name. He apologized and tried again, "Mel Perputs." Charlie stood up and said, "That is P(i) nerputz, and that would be me." (There was no 'i' in the spelling.) The little theater only seats about 150. There were probably 50 people there that night who knew that "Mel Pnerputz" was not Charlie's real name, and they were laughing themselves silly. Lucky Charlie won two tickets to the next play. He told a lot of people he was lucky, which was why he did not play the lottery. If he played, he would win and it would ruin his life. Someone who attended that night told the story to one of their friends. That friend enjoyed the tale so much that he had a name plate made for Charlie's office desk. It was an impressive clear acrylic block emblazoned with a small airplane and the name, "Mel Pnerputz."

Charlie, the funny man (2009)

In the Neighborhood

Traveling to a nearby suburb could often provide as much entertainment as more distant destinations. On one occasion we were invited to a party at the home of our dear friends, Larry and Priscilla Snyder. Larry was adopted when he was a baby and had never known who his birth mother was until he became a grandfather. She made a search for him and found him. The reason for the party was to introduce Larry's mother to some of his closest friends. As people arrived at the party they were introduced to her and then the guests were all were visiting and snacking. The house was full of people when Charlie met Helen Jean. After he was introduced he knelt in front of her and said very seriously "Lady, I don't know how to tell you this but none of us know this man. We met him on the street and he guaranteed us $5 and free food if we would come in here and pretend to be his friends." She fell for it hook, line, and sinker. Her look of horror even caught Charlie off guard. It took several seconds of laughter from everyone within earshot and a great deal of explanation from Larry and Priscilla to convince her that he was indeed a dear friend, and that Charlie's story was a joke.

The Paris Honey Shop

On every trip to Paris, Charlie bought honey. He had discovered a honey store on his first trip to the city and thereafter, he made a beeline to the shop every trip so he could replenish his honey supply. The first time he walked into the store, the owner said to him "Bon jour." Charlie replied in the French that he had learned 30 years ago in high school, "Bon jour." The man then began to speak to Charlie in the "king's" English. Charlie asked him, "How did you know I wasn't French?" The store owner replied, "By your accent." Charlie replied, "I'll have you know that I learned from the master?" The Frenchman asked, "And who would that be?" "Inspector Clouseau. You know. He's the detective in the Pink Panther movies in the 1970's." Charlie recited several lines in Peters Sellers' slaughtered French from the "Does your dog bite?" routine. The store owner didn't miss a beat and finished the bit where Charlie left off. The shared appreciation of the humor of those old movies was the start of another relationship. Charlie learned about honey from that Frenchman, and every trip he brought home a variety of small jars, some that were his favorites and some new ones to try.

Masks in Mumbai

Many of Charlie's Paris trips were followed by a leg to Mumbai, India. His last trip as a 767 pilot with Delta Airlines was the New

York-Paris-Mumbai-Paris-New York trip. Since it was his final flight before retirement, I was given a ticket so that I could accompany him. The flight crews stayed at the historic and beautiful Taj Mahal Hotel. We arrived late and spent the night in that gorgeous hotel. It was filled with antiques and ancient art works from all over the world, yet the rooms were appointed with all the modern amenities. (A few years after our stay, the hotel was attacked by terrorists and set on fire. What a senseless act of violence that resulted in death and destruction.) The next morning, we woke early and hired a cab driver to take us around the city. The cab driver asked us, "Do you know what the unemployment rate in India is?" After seeing the great numbers of people who lived in the streets, some with pieces of cardboard and fabric as shelters, and many with no shelter at all, Charlie guessed that it might be 30 percent. The driver replied, "No, we have 100 per cent employment in India. In India, if you are a beggar, that is your job. If you camp in the park and clean the ears of those who pass by, that is your job. If you gather grass and tie it into little bundles to sell to people to feed the 'holy' cows that are in the streets, that is your job. When you go to the store to buy groceries, someone helps you find what you need, someone checks you out, someone bags your groceries, and someone delivers them to your house. Each one of those tasks is someone's livelihood. If you carried your own groceries you would be depriving someone of a job."

As we toured the city, the driver stopped at a Hindu temple and told us that we could go in and look around if we liked. We were curious so we followed him inside. The walls were lined with chest high platforms and pedestals. Carved and ceramic images of their gods were on every surface. A number of worshippers were scattered throughout the temple. Many sat on mats around a chair height platform in the middle of the room. They appeared to be in prayer with their eyes closed. It was a good thing their eyes were closed so they could not see the mice that darted from dish to dish of grain offerings that were placed before the idols on that platform. Many of the people wore hospital-style face masks across their noses and mouths. Our driver took us to a narrow back room where he told us that the gods on the platform lining the back wall were some of the more important and powerful ones. Those carved idols also wore the face masks. We quietly asked the man why the idols and the people were wearing the masks. He told us it was so that the idols would not catch a cold. We both asked, "Are you kidding? Who are these people here who believe that?" The driver told us that we were in an affluent section of the city, and this is where the professional people came to worship during their lunch breaks. They were doctors, lawyers, accountants, college professors, and politicians. We asked the nature of their prayers. He responded, "They pray that nothing bad will happen, and that the next life will be better. Most people pray to Lakshmi, the goddess of wealth and prosperity." Charlie asked him, "How do you think that has been working out for most Indians?"

The unspoken prayer of our hearts was "Open their eyes that they may see." The words of Isaiah from this time forward would be colored by our experience in India.

"Gather yourselves and come. Draw near together you fugitives of the nations. They have no knowledge who carry about their wooden idol and pray to a god who cannot save. Declare and set forth your case. Indeed, let them consult together. Who has announced this from of old? Who has long since declared it? Is it not I, the LORD? And there is no other God besides Me, a righteous God and a Savior. There is none except Me. Turn to Me and be saved, all the ends of the earth; for I am God, and there is no other." (Isaiah 45:20-22)

Mission in Kenya

Many times when Charlie would get into spiritual conversations, someone would ask, "But what about those people in Africa who haven't heard about Jesus, would your God condemn them?" Then Charlie would ask, "If you care so much about those people in Africa, why don't you go there and tell them about Jesus? I've been there and told them the good news, and they embraced it. Now, what will you do with it?" Charlie made four mission trips to Kenya from the years 2003 to 2011. On two trips, I was with him. On the other two, he went unsupervised. The mission trips were arranged by Dallas Turner of Onboard Ministries. His ministry in Kenya was to train pastors. At least once a year, he put together a team to go to Kenya and hold training conferences in several locations. The men on the team taught the pastors during the week, and on Sunday they taught at several of the local churches. The women and young people on the team taught classes to the wives and children of the pastors. Most team members also taught at the schools in the communities we visited.

The trips were full of challenges, surprises, and immeasurable rewards. Security was a concern in the aftermath of "nine-eleven" and the shoot-down of an Israeli airliner near the airport in Mombassa, Kenya. So the mission teams stayed at a guarded German resort hotel that overlooked the Indian Ocean in the suburbs of Mombassa. During the days, we traveled by minivan over potholed dirt roads into the rural hillsides north of the city. Our meetings were sometimes in small buildings made of bricks of crushed coral, with dirt floors and tin roofs. Other times, we sat on crude benches or plastic chairs under the palm trees. It was sticky hot, and sometimes it was hotter. We always brought gifts for the attendees - Kenyan translations of the Bible, rice, and beans. Several of the Kenyan women would cook the rice and beans over wood fires for five or six hours while the teaching was going on. Then everyone would be fed before they trekked home to their villages. Many had walked five to ten miles to attend the conference. The mission team as a rule, for health reasons, refrained from eating anything but that which was served at the hotel. However, on occasion it was necessary, out of respect, for us to eat a roasted goat or a "coocoo" (chicken) that had been prepared as a gift for us. The term "tough old bird" had new meaning for veterans of these mission trips.

213

Charlie entertained the children with his harmonica and a slight-of-hand "magic trick." He had a small silk hankie that he would stuff into his balled fist where it disappeared. He could also make it reappear. At first the children were aghast and moved away from him in fear. They thought that he had connections to the evil spirit world. Stateside, Charlie used this trick as an object lesson to teach about deception but soon realized the translation into this culture did not work, and he had to reveal the secret of the trick to the Kenyan children. The trick was that he stuffed the hankie into a hollow, rubber fake thumb that he slipped on his own thumb. Several of the young Kenyan boys then wanted to try the "trick." Somehow it was hard for the boys with their "black thumbs" to pull off the trick with a "white" rubber thumb.

Charlie's second exposure to the spiritual darkness in Kenya occurred as he and two other men on the team went into a village with the intention of sharing the gospel with any who would engage in conversation. A crowd gathered around them, and a deranged man grabbed Charlie by the hand and started dancing with him. The deranged man was laughing and carrying on. Several men in the crowd grabbed him and tried to drag him off. He grabbed a stick, wiggled free from his captors and started chasing kids. There was mayhem. The crowd hollered at him. The crazy man screamed back at the crowd. Charlie asked some of the men what was going on. They responded that the man was demon- possessed. Dancing with demons, that was a scary thought. Charlie asked, "Well, what was he saying?" They said it was something like the demoniac who confronted Jesus. "I know why you are here. You are here to preach Jesus Christ." The man was harassing Charlie to disrupt his efforts to share the gospel.

On one trip to Kenya, the suitcases were delayed. John Melton and Charlie made a special trip back to the airport to go through customs and pick up the bags. The customs official asked John, "What do you have in your suitcase?' Any Kenyan in an official uniform is a person of importance. A stern deportment is part of that uniform. John respectfully replied, "I have some clothes and some snacks. The Kenyan looked him in the eye and said, "We Kenyans are not afraid of snacks." (He thought John meant "snakes".) John opened his suitcase and showed the peanut butter and cheese crackers, beef jerky, and M&M's. The official laughed loud and long and let Charlie and John go on their way with no more questions.

Charlie's last trip to Kenya in 2011 was memorable for several reasons. He traveled with his dear friend and fellow elder, Daryl Bennett, and he played the role of surrogate father to two young women who were a part of the team. Beth was a senior in high school, and Rebecca was a junior in college. The hotel sat on a cliff overlooking the Indian Ocean. There were stairs that led down to the beach. At high tide there was no beach; the ocean waves crashed against the cliffs. At low tide the beach was lined with vendors selling African carvings, t-shirts, scarves, and jewelry. It was impossible to take a quiet stroll along the water. The only way to avoid getting entangled in prolonged wrangling over the tourist trinkets was to completely avoid eye contact and any conversation with the vendors. Charlie wanted to take the girls down to explore the waterfront. He briefed them on how to handle the onslaught of the merchants. He told them that when they approached to talk to them, to let him do all of the talking. The first man asked Charlie, "You speak English? German?" Charlie acted like he didn't understand. The man asked again, "Do you speak English? Where are you from? Would you like to buy my carvings?" Charlie again feigned no understanding. Then he began to speak in a made up language similar to "pig Latin." The merchant now looked puzzled and confused. He walked away from Charlie and the girls. Daryl joined them, but he was unaware of the plan. The vendor approached the new victim and asked, "Where are you from?" Daryl, with no hesitation, drawled, "Texas." The ruse was foiled. The beachfront sales force converged like ants on a discarded popsicle stick.

During the course of his prior trips to Kenya, Charlie had developed deep and abiding relationships with many of the Kenyan pastors whom he taught. The pastors were greatly encouraged by Charlie's teaching of the Word of God and by Charlie's desire to equip them to do the same. Charlie loved them, and they reciprocated. Being able to share this teaching experience with Daryl was a special blessing. The opportunity to encourage the young women as they taught the youth and children was the cherry on the sundae. The icing on the cake was the Sunday morning when Charlie and Beth sang a duet of "Amazing Grace" in the church service.

God has called people to Himself from every race and every nation. One day they will all join voices and worship Him before His heavenly throne.

Opportunistic Evangelist

Charlie was passionate about his faith, and he was faithful to obey the "Great Commission" of Matthew 28. He was a naturally friendly guy, but as he matured spiritually, his friendliness and desire to cultivate relationships was purposeful. He wanted to share Christ's message of salvation and hope with anyone who would listen. It is God's kindness that draws us to Him. Charlie was an ambassador for God. He worked in a world where thousands of people passed each other by as they moved toward their destinations. He offered a smile, a conversation, a humorous story, an interest in the person traversing an oblivion of strangers. He considered every trip a mission trip, including a trip to the hardware store. He was an opportunistic evangelist. He prayed for those he would encounter, especially the flight crews and his flight students, because he knew he would have time for prolonged conversations. He planted the seeds that beget new life. God took care of the follow-on assignments of watering and reaping. And God in His kindness, sometimes allowed Charlie to witness the fruit of the planting.

CHAPTER 11

You Ain't Heavy; You're My Brother

Newton

Charlie called his brother Bill, "Newton P. Duty," Newton or Newt for short. There was no rhyme or reason for that name. Charlie bestowed special names on those he loved. There were times when "love" was not demonstrated. Charlie was four years older than Bill, and often the relationship was characterized by Charlie as the bossy big brother and Bill as the aggravating younger sibling. In the early years, they shared a bunk bed. Of course, Charlie was on the top and Bill was on the bottom. When lights were out, Bill would kick the underside of the top bunk when Charlie was trying to go to sleep. Charlie would "pound him to a pulp" to make him stop. The brothers told that story often, but it wasn't the whole story. They watched scary movies together, played games, waterskied, and were best buddies on family camping trips. Charlie left home to go to college when Bill was a freshman in high school. He was not around when Bill began making poor choices that would have an impact on the rest of his life.

A Reunion

Charlie had not seen Bill in a few years, and a lot of water had passed under the bridge. Charlie had spent a year in Southeast Asia and was now a T-38 instructor at Reese AFB in Texas. In the meantime, Bill attended Texas Tech for a year and then enlisted in the Air Force. He was a military policeman stationed at McChord AFB, Washington. Charlie had the opportunity to take a T-38 to McChord. He called Bill to let him know, and Bill arranged a deep sea fishing trip. Bill and five of his buddies picked up Charlie at the Visiting Officers' Quarters near midnight. They were to be at the chartered fishing boat by five in the morning. Before they headed for the coast, they stopped for gas and purchased several cases of beer. Then, they stopped at a pancake house and finished the fueling for the trip. The men, other than Charlie and Bill, consumed beer during the rest of the journey. When they arrived at the boat, it was misty with light rain. The captain warned them, that the seas might be a little rough. All the young airmen were quite jolly by this time and told the captain, "No problem." Not long after the boat exited the harbor and began traversing the swells, there were five problems. Those young men who ate pancakes at midnight and drank beer until morning were green. They were either groaning as they lay on the deck of the ship or tossing their 'cakes' into the ocean. Charlie and Bill fished, reminisced, and caught up on each other's lives. The trip gave Charlie some insight into the vast difference in their stations - two brothers, same surname, same employer, vastly different worlds.

Two Brothers Yates

When Charlie was flying for Delta Airlines, he often flew to Salt Lake City, Utah. At that time, Bill lived in a neighboring town. On one occasion Charlie had a layover and was staying at a hotel in downtown Salt Lake City. Bill came to visit him and they had some time on their hands, so they toured the Mormon Tabernacle. They walked through the main visitor center and were especially impressed with the beautiful murals, models, and other artwork that depicted well-known Bible stories.

Charlie was familiar with the history and beliefs of Mormonism. In the mid-1980s when we lived in Alaska, two Mormon missionaries knocked on our door. Charlie had a good friend who was Mormon, but Charlie and I knew little about the religion at the time, so we invited them in to talk. We asked a lot of questions, they gave us some materials to read, and said they would return in a week. We read their materials, and we purchased some of their other books such as the "Book of Mormon" and read those, too. When the missionaries returned, Charlie was ready with another set of questions, and then he proceeded to try to persuade the young men that they had been deceived. Though they claimed to believe the Bible, the doctrines of their faith were contrary to Biblical truths.

Since Charlie knew there was more to the Mormon story than what was depicted in the visitor center, he asked one of the tour guides, "Where is the Mormon stuff?" She asked, "Have you been to the South Building?" Charlie and Bill proceeded to the South Building. Several topical presentations were staged there at different times of the day. The only one that fit their time schedule was one entitled, "How You Can Know That in Eternity You Will Be Reunited with Your Family." The brothers were ushered into a large foyer with a number of other tourists. As they were standing there, a woman introduced herself to them. She said, "Hi. I'm Sister Boardman. What should I call you?" Without hesitation, Charlie responded, "I'm Brother Yates." Sister Boardman, replied "No, no. I mean, what is your real name?" Charlie repeated, "I'm Brother Yates." At that point, she turned to Bill and said, "Well, sir, what is your name?" Again, without hesitation, Bill responded, "I'm the other Brother Yates." Sister Boardman moved on.

Sister Boardman garnered the attention of the group and told them they would be seeing a video. Also, "according to teachings of

Jesus Christ," they would learn about life in eternity. They walked through a door and lined up two deep along a narrow hallway. There was a diorama along one side, fronted by stanchions and a rope. There was a variety of animals, the work of a taxidermist – a black bear, squirrels, a raccoon, a bird, and various others. The animals were perched and nestled in a forest-like setting, and an exquisitely painted mural was the backdrop. Sister Boardman pushed a button on the wall. The diorama came alive with tactically-placed lights, and the sounds of the forest and soothing background music filled the hall. After a few minutes, all the lights went out, and then there was a flash of light in the dark room and a peal of thunder. The lights came back on and the sound of soft rain filled the room. Then Sister Boardman said, "Wasn't that just great? Does anyone have anything he wants to say?" Before Charlie's hand could go up, Bill grabbed his arm.

They went into a big auditorium with plush theater seats. Sister Boardman introduced the movie, again reiterating that what they would see was "according to the teachings of Jesus Christ." In the opening scene, a family is sitting at the kitchen table. The husband sits quietly throughout the 15 minute film, and the wife does all the talking. The couple had two daughters. One daughter, tragically, was struck by a Mac truck as she was riding a bicycle, and she is no longer with us. There was a reenactment of the truck accident. The wife said, "I was so angry with God. I was so angry with God until I remembered the teachings of Jesus Christ that we will be all be reunited as a family in heaven. We will be husband and wife in heaven, and we will all be together. Isn't that a great thought?" When the movie ended, Sister continued with some other descriptions of family life in heaven. When she finished, she asked if anyone had any questions.

Before Bill could grab Charlie's arm, he raised it, and Sister Boardman called on him. Charlie said, "I'm a little fuzzy on some things here. I'm just a little bit fuzzy. Now you're saying that when you get married, you are going to be with your wife in heaven again?" Sister responded, "Oh yes, isn't that wonderful?" Charlie then said, "Well, according to the teachings of Jesus Christ" in Matthew 22, Jesus is responding to the Sadducees with regard to a woman who had been widowed and married to seven brothers successively. *"In heaven, whose wife of the seven would she be?"* Jesus said, *"For in the resurrection, they neither marry nor are given in marriage, but are like angels in heaven."* So, Christ said that in heaven, there would be no marriage. I'm a little fuzzy here. What's going on?"

Sister Boardman said, "Oh my! Is there anybody here who can help us out?" Charlie knew that of course, there was. There was another plant in the audience. A large, older woman stood up and said, "Listen, you. You were invited to come here and hear what we have to say. We don't want to hear your opinions. You can join the tour outside the facilities." Then Bill said to Charlie, "Well, now you've done it!" Charlie responded, "Yep, I sure have."

Letter to Bill

Charlie knew that Bill was in deep trouble, and he longed for the opportunity to share his concerns with him. That opportunity came when Bill called to talk to him about problems he was having with his teenage son, Chris. Bill was worried that Chris had joined a group called the Vegans, had become a vegetarian, and meal times had become a source of conflict in the home. Charlie had a long talk with Chris on the phone, and he wrote Chris a letter. Then, Charlie wrote a long letter to Bill and zeroed in on the heart of the matter. He told Bill that as the father, he needed to be exerting some spiritual leadership and influence in his home. He also told him that he had heard that their cousin, Marc, had overcome his dependence on alcohol through his faith in Jesus. The letter continued....

Bill, you too can have this same peace and joy and be free from this vice that has you under its control. I know you really want to do something about it because you keep telling me you are ready to make some changes, get the family back to church, and so on. I know it's tough to get it started. If you are really ready to listen to what I have to offer as you said you were, then now is the time! I have two things to offer. First, "you ain't heavy, you're my brother," and I love you. Second, I offer you God's Word, the Scriptures, because here is where you are going to find the answers. I did. Vicki did. Marc did. You can.

"All Scripture is inspired by God and profitable for teaching, for reproof, for correction, for training in righteousness; so that the man of God may be adequate, equipped for every good work." (2 Timothy 3:16-17)

God's Word will instruct you and, as it has done for me over the years since I became a Christian, and it can correct any misconceptions you may have about faith in Christ and what it means to be saved. By your own efforts, you are powerless and ineffective to make the necessary changes in your life. It is God, through the Holy Spirit who gives you the faith and ability to act on the problem.

"I can do all things through Him who strengthens me." (Philippians 4:13)

"I am the vine, you are the branches; he who abides in Me and I in him, he bears much fruit, for apart from Me you can do nothing. "If anyone does not abide in Me, he is thrown away as a branch and dries up; and they gather them, and cast them into the fire and they are burned. "If you abide in Me, and My words abide in you, ask whatever you wish, and it will be done for you." (John 15:5)

"As He spoke these things, many came to believe in Him. So Jesus was saying to those Jews who had believed Him, "If you continue in My word, then you are truly disciples of Mine; and you will know the truth, and the truth will make you free." They answered Him, "We are Abraham's descendants and have never yet been enslaved to anyone; how is it that You say, 'You will become free'?" (John 8:30-34)

This is pretty good news. When Jesus was talking to the Jews, they really didn't understand this freedom He was talking about. They had their freedom; they were slaves of no one—just like you and me. We live in the "land of the free and home of the brave," yet until we are saved we are "slaves" not in control of ourselves. Read this passage from Luke 4:17-18:

"And He [Jesus] opened the book and found the place where it was written, "the spirit of the Lord is upon me, because He anointed me to preach the gospel to the poor. He has sent me to proclaim release to the captives, and recovery of sight to the blind, to set free those who are oppressed..."

This passage has nothing to do with poor people, blind people, or slaves. It has everything to do with the spiritual state of mankind—depraved! Read Chris' letter and discussion from Roman's chapter 1. The "poor" are poor in spirit, the "blind" are blind to the truth of God (that man is a sinner, separated from God and in need of a Savior), and the "oppressed and captives" are controlled by their sin. Satan wants to deceive you into thinking there is no problem and keep you right where you are. He is the slave master.

"Jesus answered them, "Truly, truly, I say to you, everyone who commits sin is *the slave of sin.* "The slave does not remain in the house forever; the son does remain forever. "So if the Son makes you free, you will be free indeed." (John 8:34-36)

*If you are truly interested in changing, you need to start now. Don't wait; do it now. The Bible offers a warning not to put the decision off because God, although full of patience, love, and compassion, will not always answer when **you** think you are finally ready.*

"And just as He called and they would not listen, so they called and I would not listen," says the LORD of hosts; (Zechariah 7:13)

"Then the LORD said, "My Spirit shall not strive with man forever," (Genesis 6:3)

"Seek the LORD while He may be found; Call upon Him while He is near. Let the wicked forsake his way and the unrighteous man his thoughts; and let him return to the LORD, and He will have compassion on him, And to our God, For He will abundantly pardon." (Isaiah 55:6,7)

"He who conceals his transgressions will not prosper, but he who confesses and forsakes them will find compassion." (Proverbs 28:13)

If the Bible simply said "Thou shall not drink", I'd say, "Bill, the Bible says, 'Thou shall not drink' and that would be the end of that. But it doesn't. Here's what it does say:

"Wine is a mocker, strong drink a brawler, and whoever is intoxicated by it is not wise. (Proverbs 20:1)

'Therefore be careful how you walk, not as unwise men but as wise, making the most of your time, because the days are evil. So then do not be foolish, but understand what the will of the Lord is. And do not get drunk with wine, for that is dissipation, but be filled with the Spirit ...' (Ephesians 5:15-18)

"Do you not know that the unrighteous will not inherit the kingdom of God? Do not be deceived; neither fornicators, nor idolaters, nor adulterers, nor effeminate, nor homosexuals, nor thieves, nor the covetous, nor *drunkards*, nor revilers, nor swindlers, will inherit the kingdom of God." (1 Corinthians 6:9-10)

This puts those who abuse alcohol—get drunk—in some very bad company! It's pretty clear—they will not go to heaven! But there is good news, of course, or a lot of us would be in trouble. Read on.

"Such *were* some of you; but you were washed, but you were sanctified, but you were justified in the name of the Lord Jesus Christ and in the Spirit of our God." (1 Corinthians 6:11)

Notice that it says, "were some of you" not "are some of you." Paul is speaking to believers, not unbelievers. He continues, "but you were washed... sanctified... justified in the name of the Lord Jesus Christ and in the Spirit of our God." They were saved! No, the Bible does not come out and directly say not to drink. It does say not to get drunk.

"And do not get drunk with wine, for that is dissipation, but be filled with the Spirit." (Ephesians 5:18**)**

There are numerous Biblical references to the legality of wine. Jesus first miracle was turning water into wine. Paul tells Timothy to drink a little wine for his stomach. While a Christian is free to drink, is it necessarily the best option? Consider this:

"All things are lawful for me, but not all things are profitable. All things are lawful for me, but I will not be mastered by anything." (1 Corinthians 6:12)

All things are lawful for me, but not all things are profitable. All things are lawful for me, but I will not be mastered by anything. Drinking is a master over your life. You may *think* that you are the one in control because you ultimately decide when and where to drink and you think you can stop anytime you want. This is part of the deception.

"If we say that we have no sin, we are deceiving ourselves and the truth is not in us. If we confess our sins, He is faithful and righteous to forgive us our sins and to cleanse us from all unrighteousness. If we say that we have not sinned, we make Him a liar and His word is not in us." (1 John 1:8-10)

Bill, it is because you are my brother and I love you that I'm giving you this information. It is my intent to do this Biblically so that you may experience the joy and freedom that God wants you to have.

"If your brother sins go and show him his fault in private; if he listens to you, you have won your brother. "But if he does not listen to you, take one or two more with you, so that by the mouth of two or three witnesses every fact may be confirmed. "If he refuses to listen to them, tell it to the church; and if he refuses to listen even to the church, let him be to you as a Gentile and a tax collector." (Matthew 18:15-17)

So what do you need to do now?

1. **ADMIT your spiritual need**—*you are a sinner in need of a Savior.*
2. **REPENT**—*that means that you agree with God and you are willing to turn from your sin. It also means you need to stop drinking immediately and toss out every bottle of beer and all your beer-making "stuff."*

3. **BELIEVE** that Jesus Christ died for you on the cross to pay the penalty (wages) of your sins.

4. **RECEIVE,** through prayer, Jesus Christ into your heart and life.

"Whoever will call on the name of the Lord will be saved." (Romans 10:13)

"For this reason also, since the day we heard of it, we have not ceased to pray for you and to ask that you may be filled with the knowledge of His will in all spiritual wisdom and understanding, so *that you will walk in a manner worthy of the Lord, to please Him in all respects, bearing fruit in every good work and <u>increasing in the knowledge of God</u>;*" (Colossians 1:9,10)

How can you "increase in the knowledge of God" unless you go where His word is preached? How can your children avoid the pitfalls of youth and false philosophy unless you teach them or take them where they can learn God's will and purpose? Bill, it is imperative for you to get good instruction and support. You will get that from a good Bible-teaching local church, and I guarantee that you will get it from your family—all of us!

I pray for you every day because I love you. Charlie

Estrangement

Bill didn't think that he needed, nor did he want, any advice from his big brother, Charlie. Over the next decade, Bill would call Charlie on occasion. Sometimes, he would ask for advice. Charlie would counsel him, and Bill would seem to listen. But, he wasn't listening. Rather, he would call his parents and sister and complain that Charlie was "browbeating" him with the Bible. Charlie's dad told Charlie to lay off Bill with the Bible stuff. Meanwhile, Bill's life continued to unravel. There were still problems with Chris. And Cori, his daughter and oldest child, had her own set of troubles. Soon after a family reunion to celebrate the 50th wedding anniversary of his parents, Charles and Dottie, Bill left his wife and kids and moved in with a woman he met on the internet. Bill now had even more reason not to talk to his brother. There was nothing that Charlie could have to say that Bill would want to hear.

Building a Bridge

There had been a total washout in communication between the two brothers. What would it take to bridge the gap? God works in mysterious ways. In this case, God used two sisters and a kidney. Our first date had been a double date with brother Bill, and my sister, Janet.

When Janet was 28 years old, she was diagnosed with lupus. Over the next twenty-five years, she battled with both that disease and the diabetes she had since she was 12. In 2003 she was in the final stage of kidney failure. I knew better than to ask the questions: "Why has Janet suffered so much?" and "Why have I experienced such good health?" These things are in the hands of God for His purposes. My brother Mike was eager to donate a kidney. Since he was an Air Force chaplain, he began the process in a military hospital before the procedure had been approved by the insurance company. Brother David began some preliminary testing on his own and discovered he was the wrong blood type. Just about every time I talked to my Dad or visited him he would ask me, "Are you going to give your sister a kidney?" I would respond, "I'm on the list Dad." The doctors were trying to get the transplant arranged for the May to June time frame which was when Mike would have leave from his assignment in the Azores. It didn't happen. The insurance company had not come through with the approval and there was a complication. Essentially, the chemistry set in Janet's body was broken. She had strict limitations on what she could eat and drink, and this complicated the diabetes management. A drop in blood sugar with no warning caused her to pass out, fall down, and break her leg. Surgery and a metal plate were required to put her back together, and of course, there were more complications. The first week in July, Mike did come to North Carolina. He and I took Janet to the beach to see David and his family. As we made the drive, I was concerned about her and asked her several times if she needed to eat something. The kidney dysfunction greatly affected the management of her diabetes. At one point, she became belligerent which is not like her, and she seemed to be on the verge of passing out. I told Mike to pull off the highway immediately. Janet by now was not responding to instructions. I'm not a nurse, but I had to play like one: be calm, rip open that glucose gel packet, squeeze it into her mouth, and make sure she swallows it. I thought, "This is not fun; that was too close; we have to get her a kidney."

However, it still was not time. The leg had not healed, and another surgery was required. It was September when the insurance company granted approval for the transplant. Mike was in the Air Force and serving overseas, so my sister, Kathy, began testing to be a donor. The doctors told Janet that her kidney function was minimal and that if she didn't have a transplant by November she would have to begin dialysis. Janet knew what that meant. She had watched our dear Uncle Clay's struggle while he was dialyzed the last few years of his life. The last weekend in September, I retrieved a call from my answering machine. It was Kathy, who anxiously asked, "Are you still on the donor list?" I sat down. I knew it. It's me. I'm supposed to be the donor. When I called her back she told me she had been disqualified because of unexplained high blood pressure. She didn't want to tell Janet unless she knew there was still a possibility of a transplant. It was Sunday night, and she told me to call the transplant coordinator on Monday. A week later all the tests were scheduled, and I was in North Carolina. Three weeks later the surgery was scheduled for mid-November.

When Bill heard of the pending surgery, he was very concerned about Janet and me. He called Charlie to talk. The talks continued in the days leading up to the transplant surgery and in the weeks after. Bill's life was a shipwreck, and he came to the point where he said, "Charlie, I need you to be my big brother and help me." Bill and his new wife both pleaded with Charlie to come to Iowa and give them the "big picture" about God and His plan of salvation. Charlie took a leave from his job and flew to Iowa the next day. He taught them and prayed with them and helped them find a church. He bought a study Bible for Bill and gave him a list of Scriptures to look up and study. He directed him to some good Bible teachers on the radio. Then, Bill's big brother came back home to take care of me.

Truth and Consequences

Bill repented of his sin and disobedience. He asked for forgiveness, not only from God, but from his first wife, Betty, and from his children. God forgave Bill and gave him new life. Bill called Charlie often to talk about Scripture and ask questions. On one occasion, both of them were in tears as they asked for each other's forgiveness for the unsaved years when they had mistreated one another. Bill came to visit Charlie for a week, and they spent that time combing through the Scriptures. Bill asked Charlie, "How are we going to get through to Dad. I don't think Dad gets it." Bill knew his dad regularly attended church services, but he also knew he didn't hear well and even admitted to sleeping through the sermons. His dad also attended a Sunday school class where he often arranged social functions. For a time he served as class president with the duties of making announcements and introductions. With these things in mind, Bill wrote his dad a letter, took it over to his house, and read it to him.

"Dear Daddy, I want to tell you how much I love you and respect you as my father. First of all, I am so proud of your military service and the fact that you don't brag or gloat about the things you have seen and done. We are proud people of the United States of America, and we will keep our freedom because of you and the dedication of all military members of all branches of the military. Dad, when I am doing my job, whether it's copper or fiber optics, I always make sure that I am doing a good job because in the back of my mind I feel that you are watching me, and I think to myself, is this the way my dad would do it. Your perfection motivates me. You are my dad. I want you to be proud of me, of the work I do. You have created a great family. Dad, I know you do a lot of public speaking, and you are good at it. You speak at the podium at your Sunday school to members of your church. Dad, teach Scripture. It is very important. You need that knowledge. I am giving you this little book, "What the Bible Teaches." It will help you in your understanding and tell you where to go in the Bible to answer questions that people may have. This is what Caryn and I have been studying because we want to be sure we are ready to be baptized together. Dad, I am "born again." I want to follow God's Word through Jesus Christ, Who is in fact my Lord and Savior. Dad, I have made bad choices in my life. This is the only way of salvation. This is not a soap box; it is a fact. Dad, do this for me. I want to see and be with you in heaven! After all, you are my dad and I love you dearly.

Your loving son, Billy

P.S. There were a lot of tears writing this letter. I love you! Thanks for being my dad.

Charles listened but had little to say. Bill poured out his heart hoping that his dad would understand. His mom put the letter and the little booklet in Charles' Bible on the table next to his recliner.

She hoped he would read it again. She gave him the study Bible. She hoped he would read that, too. If he did, it was never in her presence. He never talked about it.

Though Bill had a spiritual birth, there were consequences from his life of sin. His body was a wreck. The years of alcohol abuse had nearly destroyed his liver, and he was on medications to prevent seizures. He lost his job, and his second wife packed up her things and left the state. Then Bill deliberately "fell off the wagon." He bought a trunk load of beer, locked himself in his half-empty house, and began to drink.

Charlie told me that he had been trying to get in touch with Bill. After several days with no answers from his phone calls, Charlie contacted his dad. The elder Charles tried calling Bill and his wife. After a day of no return calls, Charles called the police station. A squad car was dispatched to check out Bill's house but they found no lights on, and they got no response when they knocked. Another day passed and the father called the police again and asked that they do a forced entry if necessary.

I was reading in the next room when I heard a wail come from Charlie's study. His dad had called to tell him that Bill had been found dead in his house. I rushed in to find Charlie weeping. He kept saying, "Bill is dead. Bill is dead." Their relationship had grown stronger than that of blood brothers. They had become brothers in Christ, and Charlie was not ready for the earthly part of that relationship to end.

Getting Through to Dad

Charlie and his dad flew to Iowa to take care of legal matters and arrangements for the funeral. Bill was to be buried at the National Cemetery in Grand Prairie, Texas. The funeral service was to be at our church because Bill had expressed a strong desire to move to Texas and worship with us. Charlie and Charles gathered up some of Bill's personal things, those things they thought his children would like to have. They packed them in Bill's beat up pickup truck and drove from Davenport, Iowa to Fort Worth, Texas. That was a long, sorrowful trip. The radio did not work well, but the tape player did. Charlie found some sermon tapes in the glove compartment, tapes that Charlie sent to Bill. Would his dad listen? Something was wrong with the sound system. The tape played, but the volume could not be adjusted; it was stuck at full blast. Charles was hard of hearing, but he heard those sermons. However, hearing is not the same as listening.

Charlie spoke for the family at the funeral. He was also speaking to the family – to Bill's children and wives, to cousins, and nieces and nephews, and to his mom and dad, especially his dad. Bill's story was tragic, but at the end, there was victory. Compared to eternity, life on earth is just a vapor that is here for a little time and then vanishes away. God is eternal, and He is in the business of rescue. He rescued Bill. *"According to the teachings of Jesus Christ,"* there is no marriage in heaven, but our loved ones who have died, and who have trusted in Him for salvation, will welcome us into the heavenly kingdom. Jesus said, *"I am the way, the truth, and the life; no one comes to the Father but through Me."* Listen.

Not So Heavy Brother

Charlie kept a few of Bill's things for himself, a sweatshirt, some red pepper seasoning that Bill used to make his award-winning chili (without beans), and a postcard that Charlie had recently sent to Bill. The postcard was mailed from Brussels, Belgium when Charlie was there on a Delta Airlines layover. At this time, he was flying the Boeing 767 on international flights based out of New York. The picture on the postcard was of the Atomium, a place where Charlie and Bill had been together when they were young boys. Charlie wrote:

Newton P. Duty — not heavy, my Brother! They've got it all right here — Belgian waffles, mussels in Brussels, and Brussels sprouts, and the Atomium — and you were here! I once was lost but now I'm found, blind but now I see!
Love,
Your not so heavy brother

Charlie and Bill (2005)

He Ain't Heavy; He's My Brother

The road is long with many a winding turn
That leads to who knows where
But I'm strong enough to carry him
He ain't heavy; he's my brother

(ballad by Bobby Scott and Bob Russell)

CHAPTER 12

He Chose the Nails

"What God did to win your heart" – Max Lucado

What I Learned from Harry

A testimony of Charlie Yates in 2012

I taught chapter one in the book of James thirteen years ago (1999) at an evening home Bible Study. God afforded me a practice run that same morning in Harry Sands' hospital room. Harry and I were Air Force pilots. We both flew OV-10s in Southeast Asia (SEA) in the early 1970s. I didn't know him then because I was leaving SEA just as he was arriving, but I knew of him. We were stationed together in New Mexico in sister F-15 squadrons in the early 1980s. We did not fly together but we had a casual acquaintance and the common bond of being NAILS (part of the OV-10 squadron). In the 1990s, we were hired by Delta Airlines and occasionally crossed paths in our travels.

Harry had two boys who played football in high school. He loved those boys and spent a lot of time supporting their love of football. On those occasions when I talked to Harry, he talked about his boys, football, and golf. I knew that Harry and his wife had visited my church once, but on those times we spent some time together, I could not get into a spiritual conversation with Harry. He always steered the conversation to his boys and sports. Several years passed and I had not seen him. A mutual friend told me that he had terminal cancer and was in Baylor Hospital in Dallas. I had an overwhelming desire to go see him. I typed the words to the hymn "It is Well with My Soul" so that I could leave those with him if we did not have an opportunity to talk.

When I walked into the hospital room, I could tell by Harry's physical appearance that he was very ill. I gave him the paper with the hymn words. Harry read it and asked me to put it on his bulletin board. My lesson for that night was on my mind, *"Consider it all joy, my brethren, when you encounter various trials, knowing that the testing of your faith produces endurance. And let endurance have its perfect result, so that you may be perfect and complete, lacking in nothing."* (James 1:2-4) I thought, "How will Harry react when I tell him to count it all joy." I asked, "Harry, do you realize that God's Word says that you should respond with joy to this trial?" I told him a little about the lesson I had prepared. Harry asked, "Can you give me the whole lesson?" So, I did. When I finished, Harry responded, "Would you do me a favor and come back and teach me the Bible? It has to be Bible 101 because I know nothing."

For the next month I went to the hospital whenever I could. Sometimes, Harry was in "la la land." If Harry was asleep, I would give the Bible lesson to his wife and sons and to anyone else who was in the room. One day after the lesson, I prayed for Harry, his family, and the professional staff who cared for him. I also prayed that God's purposes would be fulfilled in this trial. Then, Harry prayed. After he finished, he looked up said, "I am healed." I didn't know what he meant because as I looked around the room, I noticed there were books on healing. I was familiar with the author of some of those books, and I knew that the teaching was not based on God's Word. As I looked at Harry, ravaged by the stomach cancer that had spread throughout his body, I doubted that physical healing was part of God's plan for him. Then Harry said, "By His stripes."

That's all he said. So I knew that Harry was saved, and I knew that Harry knew how he was saved. In just that little time we had spent together, Harry knew that God sent His Son, Jesus, to suffer and die as a ransom for his sins. Harry was washed clean of the guilt of his sins through the precious blood of Jesus. Harry knew the "way, the truth and the life," and of equal importance to Harry was that his boys also knew it. Both of them came to know the Lord. I talked to them about their salvation. Harry said this, "If I had known the effects of my cancer on me and my boys, I would have volunteered for this (cancer) twenty years ago." No one makes a statement like that unless he understands the advantage, unless he has an eternal perspective on life, unless he is looking forward to the "crown." Harry was looking forward to the crown of life, an eternity in God's presence, and he knew hardly anything about what lay before him. He didn't know much about theology, but he knew the gospel, and he was seeking wisdom, as much as I could give him in the four weeks that he was still alive.

There is one thing Harry asked me to do. Near the end, he said, "All I want to do is be a good witness to the world." I thought, "What is he going to do. All he *can* do is lay in bed and have his family and a few friends visit him." I told Harry, "You do have a lot of friends out there who need to hear." He said, "Tell them." On my last visit with him, he told me, "I'm going home next week." I said "Really?" I knew he was going home for hospice care sometime soon. Harry then said, "Yep, going home. But, then, somebody's got to do it." I thought, "That doesn't make sense." At the hospital a few days later, he told our mutual friend, Howie Pierson, "I'm going home tomorrow." Harry did. He went to his eternal home. His wife, Nancy, asked if I would speak at his funeral. My answer was, "Yes, absolutely!"

The day of the funeral Nancy asked me, "Are you going to give the gospel?" I said, "That's why I'm here." I looked out into the audience and saw the Sands family and their friends. Many were mutual friends of mine from the Air Force and Delta Airlines. I was able to do what Harry asked – to be his witness.

Several months later, I was at Delta Airlines recurrent training in Atlanta, and I went with five or six guys over to a local restaurant for Mexican food. As we were eating, one of them asked, "Hey, did you hear about Harry?" I said, "Yes, I have. Let me tell you about Harry."

I studied the book of James, but much of what I came to learn about joy in the midst of trial I learned from Harry.

Several years prior to Harry's death, I was flying for Delta on a long leg across the country. The captain and I engaged in a spiritual conversation. At one point, the captain became very angry and he said, "A loving God wouldn't allow such things. If this is the way God is, killing women and children, then I would just as soon go to hell." (He was referring to the Israelite conquest of the Promised Land after their forty years of wandering in the wilderness.) I responded, "Wait, wait, wait. You mean to tell me that when you get up to heaven and are at the pearly gates, and St. Peter greets you, which by the way is fictional, and you say, 'I know about this God up here, and I want nothing to do with Him, send me to hell,' that is exactly what God is going to do. He is going to send you to hell. Do you know what hell is?" Then I described hell to him. The captain said, "That's it. This conversation is over and we are no longer talking about this!" He is the captain. I am the co-pilot. I said, "OK." I'm thinking that this is going to be a long four-day trip. So, I sat quietly in my seat and the only thing heard occasionally over the radio was, "Delta 437, contact Albuquerque Center on 23.7." And, I would say, "Roger." The plane is on autopilot and the captain is just sitting there, stewing. Finally, he said, "Just one more question...." I said, "You know what we need to do? We need to start at the beginning." On a napkin, I sketched out Genesis to Revelation, and all the major events that happened in between, how God has dealt with people, why He passes judgment, and why these things happen. He said, "Man, I never heard it presented that way before. I've never heard this before. That's incredible!" At the end of the four-day trip, he said, "That's one of the best trips I've ever been on and the best Bible lesson I ever had."

By the way, he was one of Harry's friends, and he was at Harry's funeral. He is an Aggie and a marine. I know that explains some things. As I stood up before the packed congregation at Harry's service, I planned to read from Scripture, so I asked the guests to take out a Bible from the rack on the back of the seat in front of them. "There are two red books there, one is a Bible and one is a hymnal, and for you Aggies and marines out there, the Bible is the one without the musical notation. The captain came up to me after the funeral and said, "You were talking to me, weren't you?"

The Next Assignment

Harry died in December of 1999. Several months later, Howie Pierson, Charlie's dear friend and former squadron commander (1973), gave him book called "He Chose the Nails" by Max Lucado. The book had special meaning for Howie because his squadron of forward air controllers, the 23rd TASS, was called the NAILS. The dedication the author wrote at the beginning of the book was, "To Jesus Christ, because you chose the nails." In the book Howie gave to Charlie, he added the following words to those of Max Lucado, "For all the Buds! How could Lucado know of our unique call sign and symbolic message? Stay in position – on His wing – forever. Your Bud, Howie." Howie also referenced Matthew 6:33, *"But seek first His kingdom and His righteousness, and all these things will be added to you."*

Ever since Howie Pierson became a follower of Christ in 1991, he made it his mission to keep tabs of those who had served under him, especially those who had served in combat in Southeast Asia. His desire was to encourage them to join him and become fellow soldiers for Christ. When one of Howie's former NAIL lieutenants, Harry Sands, became gravely ill, Howie called Charlie. In the front of Charlie's book, Howie also wrote, "NAILS – anointed, saved, holy. To Charlie – obedient servant! God – 01." The cryptic inscription meant, "I know that God is your commander-in-chief and that you are His obedient servant, therefore, take the gospel to the NAILS."

Howie had plans for Charlie. A forward air controller (FAC) reunion was scheduled to be held at Ft. Walton Beach, Florida on September 22-23, 2000. The reunion was called, "FAC Homecoming 2000." Howie was the master of ceremonies for the event. He asked Charlie if he would give the benediction on the evening of the banquet. Charlie told Howie that he would think about it. The FAC reunions were held every two years, and Charlie had attended a number of them, but he was so busy with his job at Delta, a home movie business, and his responsibilities at church, that he was reluctant to commit to going to the reunion. Besides, he had recently seen many of his "Buds" at Harry's funeral. Howie continued to press him on the issue. He wanted Charlie to talk about Harry and share the gospel with the FAC community. Charlie talked to two of his friends and fellow church members, who had also been Air Force combat pilots. They advised him not to go, because "Those guys would not be interested in what you have to say. Why waste your time throwing pearls to swine?" Then, Charlie consulted his pastor who told him, "If you get to share the gospel, you should go." Charlie called Howie and told him that he would do it. "How much time do I have?" Howie gave him five or six minutes.

As the weekend of the reunion drew near, Charlie had misgivings about his assignment. At previous reunions, many of the attendees spent time on the golf course and in gatherings where they swapped stories and consumed great quantities of "adult beverages." On the banquet night, the culmination of a weekend of parties, there was a moment of remembrance of those who had died in the war, and there was a guest speaker, often a high ranking officer, who gave them an update on the current state of the armed services. Charlie's ·benediction was the last thing on the evening's docket.

The day before, we were to catch a plane to Florida, a hurricane that had been slowly churning in the Gulf of Mexico made a right hand turn and started moving in a northeasterly direction. Ft. Walton Beach was in its path. Charlie thought, "Perhaps the reunion will be cancelled, and I won't have to speak." He called our hotel in Florida on the morning of our flight. The hotel employee said that they had only a little rain. There would be no cancellation.

The die had been cast. Our course was set. We landed in Pensacola, rented a car, and visited the Naval Air Museum. From there, we drove to our hotel and spent a beautiful afternoon on the beach. That evening, we met up with several of Charlie's FAC buddies and their wives and had a wonderful time catching up with regard to jobs and family life. On the morning of the 23rd, a memorial to the FACs was dedicated at nearby Hurlburt Field. A former FAC, who was at this time a pastor, gave an inspiring and comforting message at the dedication service. Charlie was beginning to feel more comfortable about his role at the banquet that night.

FAC Memorial Inscription

The Forward Air Controller

This memorial is dedicated to honor those special aviators who lost their lives during the Southeast Asia war while serving as forward air controllers (FACs) in the O-1, O-2, OV-10, U-10, U-17, PC-6, and T-28 aircraft. From 1962 through the end of formal hostilities in 1975, thousands of USAF officers trained at Hurlburt Field in these aircraft. Flyers of all ranks and backgrounds learned the basics of aerial reconnaissance, air power employment, command and control, damage assessment, and search and rescue operations. Once deployed, they were assigned to air commando detachments, the 504th Tactical Support Group, and the 19th, 20th, 21st, 22nd, and 23rd Tactical Air Support Squadrons.

The banquet hall was filled to capacity. In fact, there were two banquet halls because attendance at this reunion was so large. In the second banquet hall, a large video-projection screen had been set up so that the guests in that room could view the live program in the other room. Charlie's confidence that had built during the morning program began to dissipate when the guest speaker took the stage. The speaker's jokes and stories catered to the bawdier side of military life. The tenor of the room ratcheted up into rowdiness. When the speaker finished, Howie made several awards and appreciation presentations, and then he announced that NAIL FAC, Charlie Yates, would give the benediction. Charlie confided in me that he had been nervous until it came time for him to walk from our table at the back of the room to the stage. Then he said that he had a peace that could only come from God.

Howie shook Charlie's hand and gave him the microphone. Charlie began, "God chose the NAILS." He told the story of Harry Sands and of the joy Harry found in his trial. Many of those men in the room either knew Harry or had heard of him. Charlie told them that Harry was at peace with God, and he appealed to those who were at war with God to be reconciled through faith in Jesus Christ. Some of the FACs stood up and started yelling at Charlie. He was told to "Shut up and sit down. We didn't come here to hear this!" There was profanity. Others stood up and left the room. Charlie continued to finish his planned six minutes. "God loves the NAILS and every other FAC squadron represented in this room." When he finished, he walked over to Howie and returned the microphone. Howie saluted him. Charlie walked back to his seat and Howie dismissed the crowd. There was an awkward silence. There were those who resented the message and a few who were embarrassed by the public rejection of it.

Our table was next to the exit. I whispered to Charlie that perhaps we should quickly leave and go to our room. Before we could leave, however, several men surrounded Charlie, desiring to talk to him. Harry told Charlie to "tell them," and Charlie did.

During the next few weeks following the reunion, the e-mail traffic concerning Charlie's benediction was brutal. Charlie did not see it personally, but others told him. One FAC sent the following e-mail:

> I wanted to write to you – especially after all the bantering on the FACNet after the reunion about the benediction. Matthew 5:11 says, "Blessed are you when people insult you, persecute you, and falsely say all kinds of evil against you because of me." We all needed to hear what you said, and to leave the Lord out of that reunion would have been a tragedy and disgraceful, especially since we were there to also pay tribute to those who were not able to join us. So, I say thank you from my wife and me for your from-the-heart words. Also, the reunion reminded me of all those times you made the war not so miserable – with your energy, fun, movies, harmonica, and speeches. You gave us all those gifts of yours – especially in a place that took so much from us.   Respectfully, T.S.

The Next Storm

Charlie was "done" with FAC reunions. The brouhaha in Florida was merely a Category 1 hurricane. The next storm we would have to face was a Category 5. As a follower of Christ, one expects to encounter opposition from the world. We were not prepared for opposition from within our church. Charlie was serving as a deacon in the church, and an incident occurred in which a teacher was placed on church discipline for unspecified charges. Charlie was uncomfortable with the situation because it had not been handled according to Biblical principles or the church's by-laws. He encouraged the church leaders to repent and to publicly apologize to the teacher. When they refused to do so, Charlie stepped down from his position as deacon. We had been members of the church for eleven years. Charlie was well-known and respected. When he and another man resigned, other members began to ask a lot of questions. Two of the church elders confronted Charlie and told him that he was not to discuss the issue with anyone, or Charlie himself would be dismissed from the church.

Charlie loved God, his church, and his church family. He did not want to cause division within the body. He did not want to become the problem. He just wanted, for the sake of Christ's church, for the integrity issues to be resolved. That could be simple. Confession, repentance, and forgiveness would set everything right again. It was an agonizing decision, but for the sake of the unity of the church, Charlie and I discreetly left the church. We privately grieved deeply over the loss of fellowship with our dear brothers and sisters in Christ. We remembered the lesson we witnessed in Harry – count it all joy when you encounter various trials.

We knew that God could take care of any problems within His church. We just needed to get out of the way and wait for Him to set things right. During the next year, God, the Great Healer, did the surgery that was required to bring health back to His ailing church. There was calm after the storm. Charlie and I returned to the church and began to serve as we had done before. A year later, Charlie was asked to serve as an elder in the church that he so deeply loved.

God Does Not Grow Tired or Weary

People grow tired and weary. Time passes; life happens. The great enemy, death, is menacingly close. Perspectives change as a result of experience and through the grace of God. In 2010, the FAC reunion was held in Ft. Worth, Texas. Howie Pierson was to be honored at the event. His health had been deteriorating for a number of years, and most of his friends believed that this would be the last reunion he would be able to attend. Charlie was not "done" with FAC reunions after all. Howie had moved to California and Charlie had not seen him in a few years. Charlie wanted to see Howie and the rest of his "Buds." The coordinator of the reunion was Jim Hodgson, a former marine FAC, an airline pilot, the executive director of the Fort Worth Aviation Museum, and our neighbor. He called and asked Charlie if he would speak at the memorial service. Charlie asked, "How much time do I have?" The answer was, "As long as it takes."

Charlie knew what he would say, and it would begin with "One nation under God" and end with a plea to every person to become reconciled to God through Jesus Christ. His target audience was not just the FAC community, but it was his dad, Charles. He knew that his eighty-seven- year-old father would come to a military memorial service. Maybe the father would listen to the son in this venue.

In 1999, after the intense spiritual conversation with the Aggie-marine-Delta Airlines captain, when Charlie sketched the events of the Bible from Genesis to Revelation on a napkin, he had an idea. He had tried for years to have a meaningful spiritual conversation with his dad. Often those conversations would become trivial arguments over meaningless rabbit trails. Charlie thought that if an Aggie-marine could understand a "Big Picture" timeline, perhaps his dad, also, would understand. Charlie spent weeks on the computer perfecting his timeline of events that explained God's eternal plan and purpose for mankind. He also typed up a manuscript of explanations and Scripture references to go with it. He took his "refined napkin" over to his parents' home and spent a day going through it with his dad. At the end of the day, Charlie left the timeline and manuscript, encased in a nice binder, with the father he so dearly loved. The elder Charles never read it. Arguments over the mindless rabbit trails continued on over the next decade. People grow weary; God does not become weary or tired.

Charlie knew that Howie was ready to meet God face-to-face. Time was running out for Charles, and Charlie could not say with confidence that his dad was ready. Charlie poured himself into the memorial message. His desire was to appeal to the hearts of the old soldiers. There would be many old soldiers there besides his dad. They were proud, patriotic men. They had sacrificed for others. Charlie had to make sure they understood that though they may have done good, honorable, and sacrificial things in their lifetimes, those things did not earn them a place in heaven. To God, all of their 'good' works are as filthy rags. But God in His mercy provided the free gift of salvation through faith in Jesus Christ. The service was held in the beautiful Water Gardens in downtown Ft. Worth. David Nall sang the national anthem as a missing man formation of FAC planes flew overhead. Charlie spoke. Don Harris, in plaid Scottish regalia, played "Amazing Grace" on the bagpipes. The bell tolled for those who had died in service to their country. How many who were still living heard the message and took it to heart? Charlie could not know. He only delivered the message; it was up to God to do the rest.

Epilogue

Charlie's father, Charles E. Yates, Jr., died November 14, 2011, a little over a year after the FAC memorial service. His wife Dottie, his daughter Vicki, and Charlie hovered over his hospital bed as he took his dying breaths. He had a breathing tube and was unable to talk to them. They held his hands and pleaded with him to squeeze theirs as they asked him if he knew Jesus Christ as his Savior. He squeezed. His family said goodbye with hope. Maybe he truly understood and believed the gospel but never told them.

Charlie died less than a year later on September 22, 2012. Those who knew him are confident he is now in the presence of his beloved Savior. Howie Pierson was heartbroken that he was too ill to attend the funeral of his fellow soldier in the faith. He died less than six months later on March 10, 2013. Howie's funeral service was in California in March. On April 7, a memorial service was held for him at the Lonesome Dove Ranch in Southlake, Texas. Howie's friend, Ron Knott, recounted their meeting and told of Howie's conversion and baptism. Family members and friends took turns telling stories about Howie. Two of those who spoke were Mike and Steve Sands, the sons of Harry. I had not seen them since their dad's funeral in 1999. When the service was over, I reintroduced myself to Steve and Ray Sands, Harry's brother. (Mike left with his young family before I could talk to him.) I told Steve and Ray that Charlie had been faithful to tell Harry's story again and again. In his death, Harry wanted to be a witness. I knew that there was an audio recording of Charlie telling Harry's story in a Sunday school class. I asked them if they would like for me to send them the link to the recording. Of course, they wanted it. I sent it to Steve, Mike, and Ray the next day and promptly received the following e-mail message from Mike.

Diane,

You are so thoughtful and wonderful to send this sermon from your sweet late husband. I just sent an e-mail with your link to our entire family. This sermon was amazing and it brought tears to my eyes, hearing Charlie talk. Your husband was such a kind and gentle soul and everyone loved him so much. You two are the salt of the earth, and we can never repay Charlie for helping our father see the light of salvation and the Glory of God.

I knew that Charlie had been the one teaching the Bible to our dad, and Howie came in towards the end when our dad was already on his new path. That is true friendship in its purest form, and I hope I can impact other people the way you and your husband have done in your lives. Isn't it amazing how Charlie would witness to anyone and everyone, and he didn't care if he was going to ruffle their feathers because to him it was worth it if he could get through to them in the slightest way.

What a treasure he was, and I know you miss him dearly. I'm so terribly sorry that he's not with us anymore, but it's so comforting to know where he and my dad are right now. That takes away a lot of the worldly pain when you really think about it. You will see Charlie again one day as our lives on this earth are so brief. God bless you and thank you for reaching out to us. I'm so sorry I didn't get to see you yesterday. Let's get together soon when my mom comes in from Florida.

Much love, Mike Sands

God is Not Finished

Charlie loved people enough to tell them about his God. God decided that it was time for the seeds that had been planted over four decades to be harvested. In John 13, beginning in verse 24, Jesus said, *"Truly, truly, I say to you, unless a grain of wheat falls to the earth and dies, it remains alone; but it if dies, it bears much fruit. He who loves his life loses it, and he who hates his life in this world will keep it to life eternal. If anyone serves Me, he must follow Me; and where I am, there My servant will be also; if anyone serves Me, the Father will honor him."*

Some sow, some water, some harvest. Harry wanted to be a witness of God's saving grace, and he still is through the retelling of the story. Charlie, one of the storytellers, has entered into his reward, and now his story of God's transforming grace is also being told. God is in the business of rescuing the lost. He will raise up His standard bearers until all of His sheep are brought into the fold.

CHAPTER 13

The Debriefing

"For I am not ashamed of the gospel of Christ, for it is the power of God to salvation for everyone who believes, for the Jew first, and also for the Greek." - Romans 1:16

2012

Before the mission began, the pilots would go to the briefing room to discuss the goal and the means by which the goal would be attained. The details included the type of aircraft, the armaments, fuel needs, enemy offense and defense, weather, and tactics. The meeting before the mission was called the "briefing," and the meeting following the mission was the "debriefing." In the debriefing, all who had been involved would discuss what happened on the mission: Was the goal achieved? Was there any loss of aircraft or personnel? Did anything unusual or unexpected occur? Was some tactic particularly effective? What could be learned and applied from what transpired?

Our purpose or mission in life on this earth is to glorify God. When life is over, the only question that matters is: "Did I glorify God?" Charlie believed that he was saved by grace through the blood of Jesus Christ, God's perfect Son. That glorified God. Charlie loved God. He loved his family. He loved his brothers and sisters in Christ. He loved his neighbors and his enemies. He shared the gospel. All those things glorified God. When his life on this earth came to an end, he went home to heaven to glorify God in His presence forever. The "debriefing" of his life is for those who are still mortal, and the purpose of the debriefing is to glorify God. Only God can cause a sinful man to be "born again" and be transformed into a vessel serviceable to the King. What can be learned about God from the life of a faithful servant? The words of those who knew him bear witness.

There were two memorial services in the week following Charlie's death. The first one was at Northwest Regional Airport. Marc Barth, Charlie's employer and the owner of Marcair, sent out the following invitation:

We invite all aviators who have been touched by Charlie's life in any way to come to a short memorial in his honor. There will be an opportunity to remember him, to give a short testimony, and to pray for his family. We will meet on Tuesday, September 25, at 10:00 A.M. in the Marcair hangar.

The hangar was full of people who were still in shock over the death of their coworker, friend, teacher, mentor, and fellow aviator. A long line formed and each took his turn, sharing a little about Charlie's impact on his life. Many penned their thoughts and messages.

Tributes from His Cohorts

Remembering Charlie –

Charlie and I spent many hours in the air together, and many hours on the ground, just talking, enjoying each other's company. We also shared a great passion for waterskiing. He often talked about dragging Diane out of bed so she could drive for him in the early morning hours when the water was like glass on Lake

Grapevine. We talked about many things. His stories were such an education in history, and he was always willing to share. His videos were amazing, especially the movie about the F-15 where he played a role in military history by intercepting and doing recon for the first time ever, on a Russian Bear bomber. I was a National Champion barefoot water skier and he picked my brain on many occasions about my success on the water. We often talked about our mutual envy of each other's backgrounds. He always wished he could have been me on the water, and I always wished I could have been him in that F-15. His sense of humor knew no limits. In a video that I still have on my YouTube site, Charlie and I were flying the Decathlon, just for a brush up on landings for me. I had my GoPro video camera with me, and asked Charlie to video a bit for me, so I could make a fun video of my crappy wheel landings. At one point in the pattern, Charlie had the camera in hand, in the back seat, and asked me something. In a completely serious voice, he said, "Have you ever done a four point roll in this airplane, in the pattern?" Rolling the plane out in the practice area was one thing, but in the pattern? No way. I laughed. He remained silent. Then he asked again. "Well, have you?" I said "Of course not, Charlie." The only thing I heard from after that was a Charlie giggle over the headset. I had no clue. It was just crazy Charlie. Not until I got home and uploaded the video, did I finally see what all the fun was about. He simply did a four point roll with the camera, while we stayed upright the entire time. I had to laugh out loud. Charlie was being Charlie. Every flight, every encounter, I always left with a reason to smile. – *Doug Dunbar*

Thanks for everything you taught me about flying and about God. – *Brian Jones*

I am grateful for the short time I was able to spend with you. Selfishly, I wish it could have been longer. I was looking forward to grabbing lunch at the Blue Hangar again. Thank you for the unashamed example of a godly man, father, and leader you were to me. – *Jon Warren*

We are praising our Father that you are in His presence today and for the rest of eternity. We are so thankful that our lives were touched by you and your family. Thank you for standing for truth and for doing it full of joy. We are looking forward to worshiping with you in heaven. – *Tracey Carter and Family*

I am a better man today for having known you. I'll miss you deeply. – *Scott Christ*

Thanks for everything you have passed on to all of us. You are one quality person. – *Ken Volk*

You were such an inspiration to me on and off the tarmac. You made me realize that there is so much that I could do for others. You also taught me the importance of living the best I can, living for Christ. I hope to fly with you again my friend. - *Chuck Lansford*

You had such joy in everything you did. It really displayed your love for Christ. He was, and is, and always will be your first love. I am more than thankful for the impact you had on my life. – *Reilly Carter*

Thanks for being such a great role model and voice for our Lord and Savior. I will miss our lunch time conversations. – *Brian Kelly*

It was a pleasure and an honor to have you as my Chief Flight Instructor. I am a better Christian because of you. Thank you for the encouragement as you pushed me to follow my dream as an Air Force pilot. I will always remember you, Charlie. You are now good like God. – *Andy Hart*

Thank you for everything. You may not have realized just how much of an impact you had on my life, but I am thankful to God for being able to call you "friend." – *Ken Ihrig*

Words cannot express the love and admiration I had for you. It was an utmost honor to have met you and to have been able to work alongside you and absorb your knowledge of life, flying, and most of all, God. Thank you for your wonderful humor and sense of life. Our lunch meetings will be so greatly missed. We thank God for lending you to us, to experience your life. I will always carry you with me. – *Henry*

You have changed the lives of so many people. I am blessed to have met you, and I am only sad that I could not spend more time with you, especially learning more about God. Flying was our passion. The Lord is our purpose, the end of all our journeys, and the beginning of our walk with Him. Enjoy your walks with Him. I will be thinking of you every time that I fly. - *Rick Sage*

You made the biggest impression in the shortest amount of time than anyone else I've met in my 47 years of flying. You will be missed. – *Ray W*

We flew fighters for the same Air Force and worked in the cockpit together at Delta Air Lines. Charlie was as good at stick and rudder flying as any man in aviation. He will be missed. - *Scott S*

I cannot begin to express my great shock and sadness at learning of the passing of Charlie. Over my years at MyFBO.com, I had the pleasure to work quite a bit with Charlie, not only in troubleshooting but in developing enhancements. I deal with a lot of people day in and day out, and in this fast-paced business, Charlie was always a joy to work with and has always been one of my most favorite customers. In a day where kindness is often forgotten, Charlie was always a kind spirit. The Marcair staff, his family, and friends were truly blessed to have him in their lives, and I know without a doubt that he will be greatly missed by all. – *Annemarie Jasko*

My guess is that Charlie sized up all his students early in the training process to see if they were believers. On my first Saturday morning of aerobatic flight instruction, I got two lessons. The first lesson was Charlie's Sunday school lesson for the next day. It started out with a question that Charlie was prepared to answer, and he did in short order. Obviously, I got the abbreviated version as Charlie had about 10 minutes from takeoff to the practice area to rehearse his lesson plan. About once a month the Bible lessons continued over lunch at the Blue Hangar Cafe. Charlie and I argued occasionally about theology, but in most cases he prevailed. He knew his Scripture. These are very special memories for me and in hindsight I realize that Charlie was mentoring me. – *Chuck Grice*

Charlie, you were my spiritual mentor. I love you. – *Thomas R. Meyer, "Son of Toot"*

All of your friends at the Blue Hangar will miss you terribly. All of our lives are better for knowing you! We look forward to seeing you again. - *Love, Tavia Ovens and Family*

Eulogy

On Monday morning, only the second day after the accident and before any plans had been made, one of the pastors from First Baptist Church in Grapevine, Texas, called me and asked if I would like to use their facility for the services. Charlie had been a guest speaker at a Sunday school class at the church. Our home church, Countryside Bible Church in Southlake, Texas, did not have the seating capacity that was needed for the service, so the gracious offer was an answer to a prayer that had not yet been made. It was evidence of God's care and provision for His children. Jacob Williamson, Charlie's nephew, and Kevin Wills, one of Charlie's students from the church college group, spent much of Thursday and the early morning hours of Friday at the funeral home, transforming Charlie's plain gray coffin into a masterful piece of artwork. The result was reminiscent of the decorated war planes of WWII and the Vietnam conflict. Love and respect motivated the two young men to spend those long hours with a spray of roses, a bucket of chicken, and Uncle Charlie as they painted glorious clouds, shark teeth, the Air Force insignia, and rusted bullet holes. Charlie would have been proud. The second memorial service was held on Friday, September 28, 2012.

The Countryside Ensemble turned the hearts of the assembly toward God with a song.

Bow the Knee
Bow the knee; Trust the heart of your Father
When you know the answer goes beyond what you can see.
Bow the knee; Lift your eyes to heaven
And believe the One Who holds eternity.
(Words and music: Chris Machen and Mike Harland)

The Words of a Lifelong Friend

Ecclesiastes 3:4 tells us that there is "a time to weep," and there is "a time to laugh." I suggest that in the case of Charlie Yates, both of those times have come together today because I believe nothing characterizes Charlie more than the gift of laughter. But before we move on, I want to pause for just a moment at the "weep" part of that Scripture and state what we all know: Charlie Yates had his spiritual bags packed for this journey for a very long time. I met Charlie 47 years ago, late summer of 1965. He had just turned 16 years old. We had been auditioning for trumpet chair positions with the Pascal High School Band. We were both new to the area, and neither of us had made many friends yet. He gave me a lift home. By the time he had dropped me off in my driveway, we had only known each other about 35 minutes but realizing we had an enormous amount in common, we had already enthusiastically made plans to meet the next day. As I got out of the car, I turned, leaned into the window and said, "Thanks a lot, Charlie! I'll see you later!" And he said ... "Gee, I hope not, but thanks for the warning!" Then he put the car in reverse and sped out the driveway, leaving me in a fit of laughter and the knowledge that I had just met my friend for life.

The car he drove was an English Ford, a 1959 Anglia. It was a nondescript little car only about so long (2 arm lengths). There were not many foreign cars on the road back then, a few Beetles maybe but mostly cars from Detroit. So this was an odd little car. It looked like a cartoon car. From the side you could not tell if it was going to the right or the left. We fixed that. We attached a great big hood ornament - a big red fish with large glassy eyeballs. And, of course, we filled the glove compartment with packs of cigarettes. Oh no; I know what you are thinking. No, Charlie didn't smoke. And, I didn't smoke. The fish smoked like a chimney... Marlboros... filter tips. We would light one up and stick it in a little hole between its great big lips. It smoked two or three cigarettes on the way to school and two or three on the way back home. On the weekends when we were cruising around, it could go through two or three packs. It got about two and a half miles per cigarette. It cost us more to keep that fish in cigarettes than it did to put gas in the car! Charlie was good. He would lollygag going up to the next light to ensure that we were the first car up to the cross walk in downtown Ft Worth. People would walk by, and there would be that fish: big green eyes and tendrils of smoke curling up over those big grouper lips. That car had a phone. This was before cell phones, and I doubt that there were more than a handful of limousines in Ft Worth with car phones. Few cars on the road even had air conditioning back then, so most people drove with the windows down on a pleasant evening. But, we had a phone. It was a big black old time receiver that fit perfectly, vertically on the dashboard. It looked like it was made to go there. We tied the cord under the dash. We also had an old, loud alarm clock from which my sister had twisted off the arms. I would pull the alarm button, "B' RING!" "B'RING!" Charlie would wait until he was certain he had the attention of the car next door; then he would pick up the receiver and answer the phone, "Hello! Just a minute." Then he would hand it out the window to the next car, "It's for you!"

We attended high school together, went to Texas Tech together, learned to fly and each gave the thumbs up on each other's choice of spouses. We were participants in one another's weddings. We joined the Air Force and shared a couple of assignments together. If you want to know the Genesis of our playing trumpets in church, photography, making movies, waterskiing antics (We used to ski around in long night gowns with big puppy dogs sewn on the front and wore seven foot long night caps.), and the nose and glasses among many others, you need look no further than our early friendship.

Once when we were stationed together in the F-15, Charlie intercepted a pair of Soviet Bear H bombers. The Bear was an old design, but this particular variant was new off the assembly line and various intelligence agencies wanted some air to air pictures of the planes. So Charlie's job was not only to shadow and monitor the Bears, but also to get some good pictures. When we intercepted Soviet bombers, they frequently had their cameras out, too, to take pictures of us. The Soviet crewmen would pull out large format, mapping cameras. Well, you know what happened if somebody pulled out a large camera in front of Charlie. Immediately, he pulled from the wing position and moved right up close beside the rear blister window of the Bear, raised his helmet visor, pulled off his oxygen mask and you guessed it. He donned the nose and glasses.

Charlie flew as an OV-10 forward air controller in Southeast Asia. He was "Covey 25" and then "Nail 50." The OV-10 was a little twin turbo prop airplane used by the forward air controllers to vector fighters in support of ground troops. Being a FAC in that plane was a very hazardous job, requiring exposure to small arms fire, anti-aircraft fire and shoulder launched SA-7 surface to air missiles. Yet Charlie, while jinking around these threats, still took time to recite John Wayne's "Republic" speech to the Cambodian ground commanders. He also took song requests to play on his harmonica while waiting for the fighters to arrive. When the fighters checked in, they often asked for a "hold down" on the microphone switch. The hold down might normally include the count, "1,2, 3, 4, 5, 5, 4, 3, 2, 1." The ADF needle in the fighters would turn toward the transmission and the fighters would follow that course to the FAC's position. However, in Charlie's case, he would offer a "normal" or the "special" hold down. The "special" was "Turkey in the Straw" on the harmonica. Charlie gained a certain amount of fame with that. If you read the Time magazine account of the very last minutes and seconds of the war, you will read about the combat frequencies slowly going quiet, except for some one playing "Turkey in the Straw" on the harmonica.

Charlie was funny, but he was also tenacious when defending standards. In the F-15, he was a stickler about shot discipline, sound training, and sound tactics. Occasionally his passion ruffled the feathers of superior officers, who might have wanted to maintain the status quo. So, right before his going away party in Alaska, he spread the rumor that his farewell speech "might make some people uncomfortable." He told others that people might not like what they were going to hear. To others, he admitted that what he was about to do might be considered tasteless. Well, the air became filled with intrigue as the lieutenants and captains looked forward to Major Yates' going away party. The colonels, on the other hand, were feeling a little uncomfortable as the rumors drifted their way. I was called into the wing commander's office and asked if I knew what Charlie was going to say. I didn't. Charlie had not said a word to me, and I had not asked. I was asked by the wing commander if I could tamp Charlie down a bit. I said that I doubted it. Charlie was his own man. Well, I was not concerned anyway, but I didn't tell the wing commander that. I knew Charlie. He would never hammer anyone on his way out the door to his next assignment. Plus, I recognized the set up from a mile away.

The party was held in an Italian restaurant, at Charlie's request. I gave the farewell speech about Charlie. My sole goal was to make Charlie laugh. I just wanted to see those eyes well up with tears and get bloodshot the way they did when he got to laughing really hard. I succeeded. Then Charlie got up. He composed himself, wiped away the tears and looked steely-eyed at the audience. He said, "Some people are not going to like this, but I just have to do it." The colonels looked uncomfortably at one another. Then, Charlie reached under the podium, pulled out a violin and a bow and announced, "I have always wanted to play a violin in an Italian restaurant." I knew Charlie had never played a violin in his life, and I doubted he had ever held one. He announced that his "first number" would be "The Carnival of Venice!" Then he proceeded to assault us with the most horrible screeching you have ever heard. The entire audience helped him along by humming the tune, and he brought the house down. I have never laughed harder, but you know what? Those colonels laughed the loudest.

I don't know what to expect, exactly, when my time comes and I step on the other side. It is a mystery. I mean, is Charlie going to meet me with a palm buzzer or his normal trick handshake? I don't know if Charlie's spirit can hear us today. I do know that, for now, I am not permitted to hear him. So, I will take this opportunity to say one last time, without the possibility of a retort: Thanks a lot Charlie! I'll see you later. – *Bob Fleer*

The Words of a Young Friend

All of you here know Charlie Yates, his passion for life, his seemingly boundless energy, his penchant for humor no matter how corny, his love of a good practical joke, his joy in catching someone unawares with his special mustard and his "melon collie" story, most importantly though, his love of Jesus and the gospel. Today, I hope to shed some light into the memory of how he ministered to young men and women of the college group at Countryside Bible Church and many other places through a few precious memories of my own with him. Look at Facebook today and you will see many examples and stories of how he ministered and taught others of the college /career bound, not to mention everyone else.

Think back to the first time you met Charlie, when you were first confronted by his larger than life personality. You know that moment. Now imagine yourself as a 16-year-old young man at your front door announcing that you are there to take his favorite daughter to school. The first words you hear from him are, "Son, what exactly are your intentions with my daughter?" This was definitely not what I expected, and I most certainly was not prepared to answer anything else other than a stuttered, "Uh, take her to school?" This is how I first met Charlie Yates, and it was the beginning of a wonderful friendship that we called, "pal-dom." Charlie and I were pals. From that point on Charlie became a mentor, friend, and spiritual father to me. I wasn't a believer in Jesus Christ then, but Charlie would become a great teacher to me once I became a Christian.

Let me take you to another moment in history about three years later. I was 19 and a new believer in Christ, home from college. Charlie and Diane had invited me to dinner on the lake at a restaurant called Sneaky Pete's. I remember we hadn't been seated long when somehow I uttered a phrase that received one of the first of many lessons on the Bible. I said something about how the earth was millions and millions of years old. I hadn't ever thought about it. I didn't know what was coming, but boy was it fascinating. Charlie launched into one of his great topics of passion, God's creation! This is when God first taught me the truth of His word on the topic of creation. I had read and heard it many times before, but now I had been redeemed by the blood of Christ and had repented of my sins. Now I was a Christian and could understand. And God used Charlie to teach me.

It didn't matter whether you were out on the boat skiing, playing ultimate Frisbee, learning the finer techniques of crud, or simply enjoying a meal, Charlie always loved you enough to minister to you. Sometimes, you didn't like it. Most times you did. Everyone to whom Charlie has ministered over the years knows this. He cared about me enough to share the gospel with me, to teach me how to teach a small group Bible lesson, to give advice biblically and not with a worldly perspective, to show me the best way to choose a 'plant' for a Sunday school answer. He taught me what to say if asked, "What is at the end of the universe?" (Cinder block is the ridiculous answer that makes the point that the Creator of the universe is there.) He taught me to give an answer not only with right information, but also in the right way. Yes, he also taught me how to go about wooing a lady. I remember many a lesson after Frisbee, or on the boat, or at his house about how to woo a lady. He was always careful to make sure we had our next few moves planned out. You can ask some of the other young men around the church. They know.

Charlie's life was about ministering. He was constantly working interactions toward the gospel and the glory of God. His life is still ministering today and even this morning. He was a friend, mentor, small group leader, exhorter, and pal to many people. He will be missed. – *Drew Michael*

The Words of a Partner in Ministry

I am one among a vast multitude of men privileged to know Charlie as a friend and mentor. I met Charlie after starting to attend Countryside Bible Church about five years ago. Charlie extended himself to me with such a welcoming spirit, packaged with his typical humor and energy. Little did I know then of the coming impact this man would have on me and my family. Charlie was a magnet; I was drawn to him. I came to see and experience an incredibly genuine and godly man who modeled Christ. **Charlie loved the Bible.** I discovered a man who loved the truth, - God's truth. He had a drive for studying and deeply understanding Scripture. He passionately and tirelessly taught it to others. Charlie encouraged and invited me to teach with him in his adult Sunday school class. For my first teaching assignment, he gave me 1 Corinthians 14-16, which included some difficult text and material. I was terrified. Every time I reminded him of that unfair initiation, he would just pat me on the shoulder, smile, and beam with pride. **Charlie loved Christ.** We taught together recently through the book of Hebrews where the superiority of Christ above all things is made clear. There, and throughout all of Scripture, Charlie would revel in the perfections and glories of his precious Savior and in the power that Christ offers to forgive sin and transform the heart through repentance and faith. Charlie shared the gospel everywhere. He told me that it had been his routine during preflight inspections to pray for his assigned copilot and for an opportunity to minister and advance the kingdom. He shared the gospel where he worked, where he ate, at nursing homes, at funerals, and at all kinds of events. Sharing Christ with others was the norm for him in the course of daily living. It was not the exception. **Charlie loved people.** He loved what Christ loves - the church, made of people. He poured his life into young and old alike. Charlie used all kinds of tools to make connections, things like humor, handshakes, games, lunch, flying, boating. Charlie was a wonderful and patient shepherd who counseled and strengthened myriads of people with biblical wisdom. He attended my Home Fellowship Bible study twice a month, not because he had spare time, but for personal support and encouragement. Charlie was tender. Big tears could be seen in his eyes as he recounted guiding a rebel heart over time to repentance, or as he listened when my wife told him of her dad's cancer. **Charlie loved life.** Among many things, Charlie loved to waterski. He was accomplished at it, just as he was in practically everything else in life that he pursued. He was my ski buddy this summer on many early morning runs. He would call me just after 6 a.m. and say "all systems are go." That meant the wind direction and speed were within acceptable parameters and it was time to hit the water. Precision and procedures describe Charlie. There are certain procedures for configuring the rope, sequencing ski gloves, entering the water, and specific things you are supposed to say when a fish jumps out of the water, or you put on a wet life vest. Over time, I joked about naming them rule 23a or 37c, which he thought was pretty funny. The first time I drove the boat, he was standing in his ski on the back platform ready to gently step and sink into the water. I accidentally gave the boat a sudden burst of power, and in a panic I looked back. The expression on his face in midair confirmed that I had just broken rule 16b. He later told my wife, Denise, that "It was pure buffoonery" on my part. Charlie trained you to drive the boat a certain way when he was skiing. He would give a directional signal with his hand. He was pointing you at precisely the right direction to turn and drive. Don't waste skiing time with a gradual turn; turn the boat on a dime. And once you do, don't zigzag, but drive in a straight line to a fixed point ahead. Maintain steady and appropriate speed. What a beautiful picture of the spiritual lessons he taught. Quickly get on the right course; don't deviate from your heading; maintain your speed; don't slow down.

Charlie was an exceptional church elder, a leader, and a man's man. Using the imagery and exhortations from 2 Timothy, Charlie was a good soldier of Christ, undistracted and undeterred in carrying out the ministry instructions of his Commander. He was the disciplined and prize-winning athlete who competed with endurance according to heavenly rules. He was the hard-working farmer who labored to plant spiritual seed, and who nurtured people to maturity and fruitfulness. The two greatest commandments are to love God with all your heart, and to love others as yourself. Do all these things not describe our Charlie? I was not done with Charlie Yates. There was so much more I wanted to learn and enjoy with him. Yet, what I was privileged to learn and observe in a few short years provides a lifelong challenge and example to follow in pursuing ministry and Christlikeness. I will forever love Charlie Yates. – *Terry Tyler*

The Words of His Son

My Dad is my hero: defender of country, husband, my "Pop," my friend. And he was a hero to many. When I was a little kid, my Dad called me on the phone. And at the end of the conversation, for some reason, when it was time to say "Goodbye," I said, "Bye, BOI-ING!" My Dad liked that so much that every time thereafter when we talked on the phone, I had to say, "Bye, BOI-ING!" It became one of the "procedures." It was on the checklist. I never did not say that, whether I was on a date, or I was with my buddies in high school. I would whisper, "Bye, BOI-ING!" I did it through college and until a week ago today. We talked about heaven in our last conversation on the phone. He had just taught Revelation 4 and 5, and he was preparing to teach Revelation 6-8. He had planned to teach on heaven at a retirement home this last Sunday. That is what he was thinking about.

I love my Dad. And I know that you love my Dad. He had many loves. He had many friends, I didn't know until this week how much I shared my Dad. He was a dad to many young men and many older men. I never felt like I shared him. Many of you have expressed how you did not feel like you shared him either. He gave. And he gave. And he gave. God's outlandish love was manifest in him, and you felt it. I felt it. His greatest love, of course, was Jesus Christ. He loved Jesus! The power of God made my Dad who he is. There is no explanation other than that God invaded his life through the gospel. The death, burial, and resurrection of Jesus Christ transformed him. He was born again. I had the privilege of living with my Dad, watching my Dad, and watching my Dad be transformed. God's coming was evident in him. I have no doubts what he would say if he could be here. He preached others' funerals. I heard what he said. The words from Paul to Timothy have been in my heart and my mind this week. I direct your attention to the four things that Paul said to Timothy in some of the last words that he gave to his young protégé in 2 Timothy, Chapter 2. Paul tells Timothy first of all, "Be strong in the grace which is in Christ Jesus." My Dad would echo those words. He called himself the chief of sinners. He was not a good man, and he would tell you that. If you had the audacity to answer his question, "Hey, how are you?" with, "Oh, I'm good," then he would say, "There is no one good, not even one!" And, he would rehearse to you the rest of Romans 3 and give you the gospel presentation. That was his entrance into talking about eternal things from "How are you?" He probably had faster ways than that! My Dad is a good guy. But he had imputed to him the righteousness of Jesus Christ, which made him acceptable to God, and there is no other way. All of his earthly achievements, which are many, are not worth a thing in eternity. The only things that have lasted are the things that God, Himself, did through my Dad, letting him live for Him. My Dad did many good things, but the good things that he did, the good things that last, are the things that God produced in him. He lived for God's glory. He would say to us, "Be strong in the grace of Jesus Christ." If you don't know Jesus personally, you do not know what made Dad who he is. He would want you, more than anything else, to know Christ.

Paul gives another command to his protégé in verse two. He says, "The things which you have heard, pass these on." Paul told Timothy to pass the baton. My Dad invested in so many people. There is a baton too big for any one of us to carry. There is an unfillable hole where my Dad stood, where my Dad served, where he spoke, where he loved. It is going to take an army of people to carry the baton. Third, Paul told Timothy to suffer hardship as a good soldier of Jesus Christ; to be bold, to be willing to endure scorn. My Dad endured scorn for the gospel, a lot of it from me. We would walk into a gas station, or a grocery store, or step onto an elevator, and he's thinking, "How can I get to the gospel? I know- a really bad joke." I would roll my eyes. Dad was not afraid! He was not ashamed to be thought of as silly, corny, cheesy, or foolish. My Dad wasn't embarrassed by anything, except if one piled on the compliments. He would run from this. But he was not embarrassed to tell anyone about what changed his life, about Who changed his life, and how others can know Jesus.

There is a fourth command here that has been on my mind recently. That command is "Stay on *target*." Paul tells Timothy, *"No soldier in active service entangles himself in the affairs of everyday life, so that he may please the one who enlisted him as a soldier."* But I know my Dad's motto: "No slack!" The definition of "slack" at our household was half a pair of pants....... You're still thinking about that! He got you again! There were no empty spaces in my Dad's life. He filled every nook and cranny with something! He would get up early in the morning and weep over his Bible and pray for his family and friends. He would go to work where he was the chief pilot at the flight school. My Mom said that he spent his entire paycheck in the Blue Hangar Café buying lunch for his friends where he would talk to them about the gospel and any other topic in the Bible that was appropriate for that day. He would come home, open his Bible again, and study for hours to prepare to teach God's Word. His foot was on the gas full time. We talked about each other's funerals after my grandfather died. We agreed that if I preached his, or if he preached mine, we would say this, "He got what he wanted." My Dad is doing better than all of us. He had been studying the book of Revelation, meditating on the throne room, the concentric circles of worship surrounding the glorified Christ; he had been meditating on singing with the multitudes. I read his notes this morning, the message that he did not give here on Sunday, Revelation 6 through 8. And it was filled with awe and wonder, with the glory and the beauty, and the magnificence of what it would be like to be in Christ's presence. I can't wait to tell him of the serving illustration his life has been. My Pop ran hard. He passed the baton to many of us. And we must run hard for the glory of God, for the gospel. I love you, Pop. Bye, BOI-ING! – *Smedly Yates*

The Words of His Pastor

The memorial service has been a wonderful celebration of Charlie's life. It has also been a powerful reminder of the deep imprint his life has left on each one of us. All of us are forever rich for knowing him. There were qualities about Charlie that stood out. You didn't have to be around him any time at all to see them. Charlie loved people, and he had a unique gift of making everyone feel like they were his best friend, whether they were eight years old or eighty. He was quick to laugh. In fact, he was one of the funniest people I have ever known. But he also knew how to be serious about those things that are important. He loved his wife, Diane; he loved his family; he loved life; and he loved God and God's Word. There are countless other qualities we all loved about Charlie. Let me challenge you, especially you young men into whom he poured his life, to step up and to begin to follow his example and to imitate those qualities. If Charlie were here today, he would be very uncomfortable with all the praise that he has received. He would want everyone to know that he owed whatever he became and whatever he accomplished to Jesus Christ.

In fact, I think I know exactly what Charlie would say and what he would want me to say to you. Diane reminded me this week that there was one verse from the Bible that he quoted most because it best captured the most important realities in his life. These are the words of the apostle Paul in his first letter to Timothy: *"This is a trustworthy statement, deserving full acceptance, that Christ Jesus came into the world to save sinners, among whom I am foremost the chief of all."* Jesus came to save us. Unfortunately, the word "save" has become so familiar that I think it sometimes gets in the way. The Greek word simply means "to rescue." Jesus came into the world to rescue sinners. Jesus of Nazareth, the Messiah whom the Jewish Scriptures had promised, came into the world for one great reason: "To save (or rescue) sinners." He came to rescue them from what? Jesus came to rescue sinners from the coming wrath of God that our sins deserve. How did Jesus accomplish our rescue? In Mark 10:45, Jesus told us, *"...the Son of Man came to give His life as a ransom for the place of many."* God loved us so much that He sent His own Son into the world to become one of us, fully human. And He came into the world for two reasons: to live the life we should have lived and to die the death we should have died. For everyone who commits himself to Christ, in the mind of God an amazing transaction took place 2000 years ago. On the cross, God treated Jesus as if He had lived your sinful life, so that forever He could treat you as if you had lived Jesus' perfect life. And then God raised Him from death.

How can you personally experience the rescue from God's wrath that Jesus died to accomplish? You must acknowledge like Paul did, and like Charlie did, not just that you do a few bad things, but that you are a sinner; in fact, the chief of sinners. And you must put your confidence in Christ and be willing to give up control of your life to Jesus. On Tuesday, Rocky Wyatt told me about his experience of flying with Charlie. Charlie showed him how to do a complete loop with the airplane, and then encouraged Rocky to try it. Charlie explained that to complete the loop without stalling, you first had to get enough downward air speed. The first attempt went great, so Charlie encouraged him to try again. But that time, they didn't get enough air speed. So as they approached the top of the loop, the plane lost its momentum, stopped, and then began to fall backward toward the earth. At this point, there were a few seconds of panicked silence. And then Charlie calmly and with that familiar smile in his voice said, "So, do you want me to take it?" Rocky said, "Yes! YES! I want YOU to take it!" It works the same way with the spiritual rescue that you need. Before Jesus can rescue you from your sin and its penalty, you must first recognize that you have violated not the laws of gravity but God's moral laws, and you can do absolutely nothing to save yourself. You must cry out to Him. You must let go of the controls of your life and commit yourself entirely to Jesus Christ. That is what Charlie would say to you because that is exactly the good news that Charlie embraced and that he spent his life sharing with others. Nothing would bring him more joy that to think that you came to embrace that truth at the celebration of his life. – *Tom Pennington*

The Words of a Fellow Soldier

(The Chaplain's address following the 21-gun salute at the Dallas-Ft. Worth National Cemetery)

What a great service of celebration and worship we had at the church. I was reminded of the words of 1 Thessalonians 4, encouraging us that though we grieve, we do not grieve as unbelievers who have no hope. Our grief, though real, is eclipsed by the brilliance of our hope in Jesus Christ. We have honored Charlie as husband, father, son, brother, brother-in-law, brother-in-Christ, friend, mentor, hero--and in countless other ways in our hearts and minds. What a great testimony to the power of the gospel that one day quickened Charlie's spirit, captivated his heart, and for the rest of his life constrained, controlled, compelled and consumed him. In these final moments together, we now honor him again as an airman, a wingman, and a patriot. It is a fitting tribute to his years of selfless dedication to the United States Air Force and to our nation. For that I am grateful. I will close our time together with the words of one of Charlie's favorite verses from Romans 1:16, *"For I am not ashamed of the gospel of Christ, for it is the power of God to salvation for everyone who believes, for the Jew first, and also for the Greek."*

Gracious God, Sovereign Lord. Your thoughts are not our thoughts, nor are Your ways our ways. For as high as the heavens are above the earth, so are Your ways higher than our ways and Your thoughts than our thoughts. Though we may not understand the timing or circumstances of Charlie's death, we rest in Your sovereign love and divine plan. Comfort us with the comfort You alone can give; grant us peace that surpasses understanding, and give us joy to be our strength in the midst of sorrow. For this, we give You all the praise and all the glory, in the name of Jesus Christ, our Lord. Amen. – *Chaplain Michael Coggins, USAF (brother-in-law)*

The Neighbors Remember

When all was said and done, our next door neighbors, Dave and Mary Ramsey, spearheaded the creation of a memorial that would remind the neighborhood of Charlie. Charlie spent many hours playing football and other games on our street with all ages of boys and girls. By now after twenty years, many were grown with families of their own, but there was also a younger generation of children, as some families had moved out and younger families had moved in. Over the years Charlie also taught many of the youngsters how to deliver a sales pitch. As the scouts, ball players, or band members would come to our house and try to sell us their fundraising "stuff," Charlie would spend time training each one on the "right way" to give a sales pitch. Then he would buy their "stuff." Most of the neighbors knew Charlie and often it was through his interactions with their children. Several months after the funeral, Dave and

Mary had a neighborhood party and unveiled the memorial, a park bench that was to sit at the entrance to the neighborhood at the spot where the kids wait for the school bus. The words engraved on the bench:

Charlie's Chair

C D Yates A Soldier for Christ

CHAPTER 14

The Baton is Passed

"...shepherd the flock of God among you, exercising oversight not under compulsion, but voluntarily, according to the will of God; and not for sordid gain, but with eagerness; nor yet as lording it over those allotted to your charge, but proving to be examples to the flock. And when the Chief Shepherd appears, you will receive the unfading crown of glory." (I Peter 5:2-4)

At the memorial service, Smedly, beloved son of Charlie, read the words that Paul wrote to his protégé, *"The things that you have heard pass these on."* Then Smedly challenged those who had come to remember and to be comforted. He said, "My Dad invested in so many people. There is a baton too big for any one of us to carry. There is an unfillable hole where my Dad stood, where my Dad served, where he spoke, where he loved. And it's going to take an army of people to carry the baton."

There is an army of people that picked up that baton. The testimonies that follow are representative of that those who were inspired to run the race well for the glory of God.

The Baton is Passed to His Students

Andrew

Charlie Yates taught me these things and so much more:

He taught me that renaissance men still roam the earth
He taught me to protect my glass with a skylight filter
He taught me production
He taught me videography
He taught me to slalom
He taught me how to back a trailer
He taught me how to drive his boat
He taught me how to treat the girl you love
How to treat people who love you
How to love God
Charlie Yates taught me these things and so much more,
with a textbook, lecture, lesson plan, microphone,
PowerPoint, podium, lectern, and whiteboard.

But I did not learn them because he used a textbook, lecture,
lesson plan, microphone, PowerPoint, podium, lectern, or
whiteboard.

I learned these things and so much more because:

Charlie was good at everything
He protected his glass with a skylight filter
He produced wonderful things
He shot beautiful pictures
He skied hard
He backed that trailer like he had been doing it for years
He babied his boat

He treated Diane like a queen
He was best friends with everyone
He loved God so hard – *Andrew Hale*

William

The pair of loafers was well-worn. They were not combat boots or highly shined dress-shoes or hiking boots or any other such kind of independently exciting footwear, just a thoroughly broken in pair of everyday shoes and they were sitting collecting a light layer of dust in a line of pairs of other shoes. I had seen these particular shoes before, tapping as the wearer kept time puffing on a harmonica in a little, but well organized, audio recording room in a suburban house in Grapevine, Texas five years before.

My words are not for people to learn about him. I am confident that those many other sides of Charlie "Rowdy" Yates will be covered in detail by people better qualified to commemorate all the dimensions of him. I am excited to read their portions and cry with them upon hearing their accounts and learning things I didn't know. My text is for people who already know him and knew him well, this is for them and for the person that is relationship, that third person between every two people who know each other, and this is dedicated to the person who *is* the relationship.

In Charles Dickens' classic novel, "A Christmas Carol," three ghosts visit a cruel miser named Ebenezer Scrooge in an act of divine intervention to save his soul from damnation and to teach him the importance of sacrificial love, giving, selflessness, and the virtues of contentment and gratitude. Scrooge's secretary, one Bob Cratchit, is a man of decidedly modest means, with a large family to take care of. His youngest son, Tiny Tim is a physically sick and feeble child, but Tiny Tim epitomizes a pure Christ-like spirit of generosity. Tiny Tim, for all his temporal disadvantages, has all the spiritual gifts that Ebenezer Scrooge lacks and what is more a desire to share the message of God's love with everyone with whom he comes in contact. The final ghost, the ghost of Christmas "Yet to Come," shows Scrooge a Christmas in the near future where Tiny Tim's illness has ultimately taken the life of the young evangelist child. The Cratchit home, usually a place of laughter and warmth, is quiet and somber. "Oh Spirit, not Tiny Tim, must there be a Christmas that brings this awful scene? How can the world endure it?" says Ebenezer Scrooge to the Ghost.

Scrooge and the Ghost look in through the window to see a grief-stricken Christmas dinner in the place of the once full of life family. Seeing his family around him Bob Cratchit speaks up, encouraging his family with the kind of Biblical wisdom that Tiny Tim was always so eager to share. Bob Cratchit: "It's alright children; life is made up of meetings and partings. That is the way of it. I'm sure we shall never forget Tiny Tim, or this first parting that there was among us."

God places people in our lives that comfort us when we are in pain like Tiny Tim or like Charlie, people who truly want to serve others when they don't know how to cope. When God takes people like these kind of servants home to be with Him it can be hard for all left behind to know what to do. Usually, when I was dealing with this kind of grief in times past, Charlie would come over and ask how I was and give me some serious, look me in the eyes, kind of Bible-grounded advice. Now that it is Charlie that I am missing it is hard to know whom to turn to. When Tiny Tim is gone, who is Bob Cratchit for me? Seriously though?

I looked around quite a bit to find out whose duty it was to give to me, to be there to help me through, to focus on my pain, the needs of "me." One time a few years ago my family was in need of comfort and my father called up Charlie, and Charlie and Diane rushed over to our house. They had received my father's call in the middle of their anniversary dinner. Charlie and Diane were not considering their "needs of me." First thing Charlie did when they arrived at our house was to find where I was, sitting on the stairs, and check to see if I was doing alright. "You doing alright son?" he asked. I mumbled "yeah." "No, you're not," he replied and patted my back. My mother was horrified to realize that we had ruined their anniversary dinner. Charlie said that there was no place that Diane and he would rather be. There is no "me."

I am wearing a pair of tan loafers tonight. After Charlie died, Miss Diane asked guys from the church to stop by her house and rummage through Charlie's clothes. One of Charlie's suits fit my dad. Chris took a couple of ties. Andrew took a couple shirts. Charlie's shoes fit me. Along the wall there were about eight or nine pairs of shoes, shoes for a variety of purposes. In 2008 Charlie recorded a song for a Vacation Bible School play that my mother and I wrote, "Sheep Story." In the video of the play there are a couple close-up shots of a tan-loafered foot tapping in time. This is that pair of shoes that I am wearing now, a pair of shoes broken in by someone else, filled with two new feet. Now that he is gone, it is time for the men, particularly the young men, in our church to fill some shoes. Ordinarily I would apologize for being a bit corny, but in writing about Charlie, it would be tragically ironic to apologize for being corny.

When I saw Andrew, Chris, and Kevin on that next Sunday, through the very long hugs and the storm of tears, it became apparent to me how I could honor Charlie and his life. I could love other people and give to them in the way that he gave to us, starting with those guys. Then we, as a generation of young men would extend to loving of Christ's church and giving of ourselves among God's people.

I would love to say something about high percentage kill shots, but I don't wear combat boots; I probably won't ever wear those kinds of shoes, but I can wear normal man shoes. I knew Charlie best as a highly giving and godly normal man, despite the many, many different specialized types of shoes that he wore during his life. Anyone who met Charlie would know that he was a man of SOP's, or Standard Operating Procedures. He believed in a life of procedural correctness. One action that Charlie believed must be done very properly was that of being a godly man. Be a man wherever God has placed you. Be a man by not worrying about being perceived as a man. Be a man by doing right by others regardless of how you think that you might look to the casual observer. Stay on target. Oh, and, "God Bless us, everyone." – *William Snider*

Chris

My relationship with Charlie Yates began in a way I never would have guessed. In fact, I didn't have much say in the matter. When I was seventeen years old Charlie came to me one day and told me that he had worked things out so I could be in his accountability group in the college ministry in which he served. I will never forget the day when he said to me, "I've taken a liking to you, son." The fact that this man had worked hard to start our friendship spoke volumes to me and touched me in a way that I'll never be able to explain. Over the next four years my relationship with Charlie deepened and he became a spiritual father and mentor to me. Charlie had always laid out tasks and challenges for me to meet, but in the wake of his departure from this life there are two specific batons that he handed down to me that stand out the most.

The first is to stand firm and take the lead as a man in whatever ministry I am in when biblical leadership is called for. Often times we would have dinner one-on-one, and there was not one meal that went by where he did not teach or instruct me on how to be a better decisive man of God in pursuit of the Kingdom. He told me many times that I was to have absolutely no tolerance for heresy or blasphemy. Charlie's deep love for the church and God's word was evident in how he charged me and many other young men with this task that cannot be taken lightly.

The second baton I was given is for the people of Kenya. Charlie had been to Kenya a few times on short-term mission trips and was burdened for the salvation of the people there. The Lord opened the door for me to go with him in the summer of 2012, and I was absolutely thrilled. About four months before we were to leave for Kenya I received a phone call from Charlie telling me that he was no longer able to accompany me due to work. I was crushed that my mentor wasn't going to be with me on this life-changing trip, but the next best thing happened over those few months leading up to my departure. I spent countless hours with Charlie in his home office studying lessons and preparing spiritually for the trip so I could be an effective instrument for the Lord. I now know that Charlie was not only preparing me for the trip but also for everything spiritual in life. He was the apostle Paul, and I was Timothy. So I went on that trip ready for what lay ahead because of Charlie's influence in my life. I returned from Kenya with amazing stories and encouraging reports for Charlie about the people there. We talked about one day returning to Kenya together as teacher and pupil, but that was not in the Lord's will. Charlie went home to be with the Lord only three months after my return. Shortly after, the Lord gave me my own deep longing and love for His people in Africa. No doubt because of the influence that Charlie had on me. I returned to Kenya the following summer to continue the work for which I had been trained and I look forward to going back again and again until the Lord completes my work there.

Charlie taught me that evangelism should be an ongoing pursuit, not just on mission trips. After Charlie's death it became customary for me to write the words "cinder block" on my hand on the twenty-second of each month in remembrance of the day that he passed away. "Cinder block" was a part of our personal handshake and yes; there is a story behind it. One day my co-worker saw the writing on my hand and asked me what it stood for. So I stopped and responded by telling her the same thing that Charlie told me a few years prior. "When you look out into outer space and you go a trillion, billion light-years past all the stars and all the galaxies and you come to the edge of the universe, what is there at the end?" Naturally my co-worker was baffled by this question and merely said, "I don't know. What is it?"

Feeling that smirk Charlie would so often give form upon my own face, I answered, "Well it's a cinderblock. I mean, what else could it be?" My coworker was less than amused but I went on before she had a chance to say anything. "Now you go in the other direction into the smallest nucleus of the smallest atom and at the very center what do we find holding it together?" "A cinder block?" she replied. I smiled and promptly said, "Nope. It's the Word of God. Because, Hebrews 1:3 tells us that all things are held together by the power of His Word." I was called away from my coworker but was able to talk to her later about the gospel of Jesus Christ. So those words serve as a reminder to me of the man that I greatly admired and greatly miss. They are also a reminder to preach God's gospel to all people even if the icebreaker I use is a little cheesy. – *Chris Ryan*

Bryan

I can't think of a more qualified runner in God's divine relay that has passed the baton to me than Charlie Yates. His legacy lives on in me and so many others it astounds me every time I think of him and his family. I would have never believed so many pivotal things could happen from one day. The journey has taken me from the mountains in Colorado to the streets in Atlanta reaching out to all those in need of the saving love of Jesus.

On September 22, 2012, my day started out early in the morning in Colorado Springs at Freedom Climb, an event that helps raise funds and awareness of the issues of human trafficking and slavery in the modern world. We split up into three teams to hike different areas in Colorado Springs. My mom and I chose to hike up Pancake Rocks which was a beautiful hike! We had wonderful times of prayer as we hiked. We remembered that each person trapped in slavery and forced prostitution has a name, real names like Tonya, Lydia, Jade, Anisha, or Hailey. The only number they should be considered is the number one instead of just a statistic. So we started counting our steps as one, one, one, one... as a reminder of how God sees them individually. It was lunch time when we reached the top. The beautiful scenery was all around us and we took in the splendor of God's wonderful creation. I climbed up to the top of this one rock to enjoy my lunch. It was a little after one o'clock when a bird flew up right next to me. I was surprised how close it was to me. I enjoyed its company and fed it a part of my sandwich. I like to name things so I named him Charlie. We both sat there for a while looking at the variety of trees and colors. We spent a good while together and then Charlie flew off. I didn't know it then, but I later learned this was around the same time Charlie's plane had gone down.

After lunch I joined the group to hike back down to our vans and drove back to the hotel. I had responsibility of picking up the other ladies at the different locations. So as I was driving back from Pikes Peak, I got a phone call from Christopher Ryan that I didn't answer because I felt I needed to pay attention to where I was going. It was a very full day, physically, emotionally, and especially spiritually. What I wasn't expecting is that night when it dawned on me to check my voicemail, I heard Christopher telling me what happened and I remember listening to it several times because I just didn't grasp what I was hearing. I remember lying there in bed, replaying what he had said and tears began to pour out of me that I didn't even know I had! The tears wouldn't stop. It felt as if a well that surrounded my heart was broken and the only thing that was flowing out of it was waves of tears.

That night I didn't sleep very well, however the next morning, friends at the conference (who didn't even know Charlie) heard what had happened the day before and prayed especially for the Yates family and for the pilot who was flying the plane. We started singing songs and one of the songs we sang was taken from Isaiah 40:31 which reminded me of Charlie's photography book about flying the F-15 Eagle. A few days after the celebration of Charlie going home, I was back in Atlanta and was invited to go to a conference called Catalyst, and it was there where I heard Christine Caine give a powerful talk about carrying the baton and making sure not to drop the baton in the exchange zone, which also means you have to be running while the baton is passed. During most of the talk I was thinking to myself how much Charlie lived with that urgency of carrying the baton. He knew the race that he was running; he knew who he was; he knew his calling; he knew the love he had experienced and the love he wanted others to experience.

A couple of weeks later another crazy thing happened. I attended a home group gathering for the first time in an area where I live. The meeting was an opportunity for people that serve in the church to get to know each other. I was telling the story of my friend and the accident, and the owner of the house asked me what his name was. I said "Charlie Yates." The man said to me "I flew F-15's with him in Alaska for three years and then worked at Delta with him as well." I thought, "Wow! I never realized how wide the lane was that God had given to Charlie." By God's grace I've been running full speed here in Atlanta, carrying what was passed to me by Charlie Yates, a lover of souls, a friend to many, a loving father and grandfather, a wonderful husband to Diane, and a fellow runner into the arms of Jesus.- *Bryan Cloin*

Drew

Out of all the memories - games of Crud, Ultimate Catch Phrase (hours and hours of Catch Phrase on the way to and from ski trips in Colorado), mornings out on the lake (it was a great day when I was officially an approved driver of the boat), and Sunday school lessons, I think my favorite memories are the ones on Wednesday nights in Charlie's small group. Once God's will was determined via the "dollar bill game," he would sit back and question or answer us as our discussions unfolded. Charlie's passion for the glory of God was always evident as he challenged us and encouraged us in our walks. He demanded that we "stop praying for discipline and start doing it." He never let up always pushing us to apply what we had been taught. It is this passion and love that I will always aim to imitate as I grow in my spiritual walk. - *Drew Irvin*

Matt

He was my Sunday school teacher, one of the people I met my first day at Countryside Bible Church. He taught me "the handshake," and the Five Lies of the culture: 1) Life is Random. (It's not; God is absolutely Sovereign.); 2) Truth is Relative. (It's not; God has revealed absolute Truth in His inerrant Word.); 3) Man is Basically Good, (We're not; just try to stop sinning if you believe that.);) You are the Only One Who Can Change Yourself. (You can't; only a supernatural heart transplant can do that.); 5) The Purpose in Life is to Seek Self-Satisfaction. (No, the purpose of our life and all of Creation is to glorify our Creator, and we do that by becoming a reflection of Jesus Christ.) He taught me the four possible ways to answer any question, and bragged on me for correctly answering "Has the sun ever risen in the west?" in the affirmative.

Charlie flew little turboprops in the weeds over Vietnam (just above the "speed of smell"), F-15s high in the Cold War skies (at the "speed of heat"), airliners for Delta, and many kinds of little airplanes all over everywhere. He was my Chief Instructor when I was a newly minted flight instructor. We flew around in an airplane together, he converting his extensive military and airline experience into a civilian instructor certificate and he passed on some of that knowledge to me, an aspiring commercial pilot. Among other important things, he taught me that even the lowly Cessna 172 has a "pipper." (It uses high-tech "imagi-vision" to project the pipper from the pilot's mind onto the windscreen, with remarkably accurate results.) He taught me the proper technique for rolling into a strafing run on a bulldozer in a field or a stock tank. He taught me to detest "buffoonery" and love clean mischief. He schooled me in the fine art of war stories.

Charlie was special to everyone. Yet everyone who knew him knew that they were special to him. He loved people, and he loved to teach. He didn't accept shortcuts or excuses: "It's a poor workman who blames his tools," or anything less than the exact runway centerline on approach: "If this plane crashes on final, I want the NTSB to come out here and find me on one side of the centerline, and you on the other." But he was amazingly patient with so many of us who, so many times, ought to have known better. He wrote job recommendations. He helped hire people. He expected that I, like he, try to avoid hitting reflectors in the road with my tires when changing lanes. He was the biggest personality in the room. He mercilessly picked on servers at any restaurant—and they loved him for it. He was irrepressible and, thankfully, incorrigible. He spread goofy jokes, bad puns, godly counsel, and—everywhere and to everyone—the gospel of Jesus Christ. He was a friend, a mentor and an example. He wasn't perfect, but always and everywhere you could not help but know Who it was that Charlie served, and Whose Word it was Charlie loved to study and expound.

As so many have noted if Charlie asked you how you were, he never let you get by with saying, "Good," because there is no one good, except God. However, as my friend Nat said, on Saturday afternoon, his Lord said to Charlie, "Well done, good and faithful servant." It wasn't Charlie's own goodness, but the goodness of God, lavished on Charlie, which had indeed made his life a testament to the glory of God, and a blessing and challenge to those of us left here. Indeed, the gaping size of the hole that he left reveals the thanks we owe to God for His goodness to us through the life of His servant. – *Matt Stutsman*

Dave

I am truly grateful and blessed to have been able to know Mr. Yates. I enjoyed interacting with him at church and hearing him talk about flying. The videos he put together for church functions were always something to look forward to and highly entertaining. His sense of humor and knowledge of the Bible made him a great teacher and mentor. Charlie had profound impact on my life. I had been interested in flying from a young age. More specifically, I wanted to fly fighters, and getting to meet and talk to a real Air Force fighter pilot was awesome. Mr. Yates was the first fighter pilot I knew personally and talking to him only cemented my desire to fly. I knew I wanted to be a fighter pilot, but wasn't exactly sure how to get there. During high school and college, Mr. Yates was instrumental in pointing me in the right direction. Charlie gave me great encouragement, even having his squadron commander from Vietnam send me a letter and control stick, which I still treasure. Mr. Yates always set a great example that being a Christian and a fighter pilot was possible. I understand now how difficult that can be at times, and he was a great role model to follow. Charlie will be greatly missed. I hope that someday I can have the same impact on a young aspiring pilot's life that he did on mine. - *Dave Snodgrass*

Nathan

Charlie Yates was a mentor, a teacher, and a friend of mine. Charlie invested in me. He led my accountability group when I was a college student, and then later guided me as I led the group. He and Diane took my girlfriend and me skiing and gave us advice on marriage. When she became my wife, we showed up randomly on the doorstep one evening and they took us in for dinner and gave us advice on parenting. I still remember sitting with friends when we found out Charlie had died. Those of us that knew him took turns describing him to the others there. Over the next week I was amazed at how many people were as impacted by the life of Charlie Yates as I had been. My experience with Charlie was repeated over and over again in the lives of those who had the privilege to know him. Charlie invested in people.

Charlie had finished the work God had for him and his departure left a huge hole for others to fill. I believe God used Charlie as an example and then took him so that others would have to step up to the standard we had witnessed. It was easy to sit back and watch as Charlie engaged visitors at church, boldly approached strangers in public to share the gospel, taught Sunday school, played music in worship service, and provided an example of a loving husband and father. Without Charlie to do all the heavy lifting, it is up to those he taught to carry on his legacy. We decided to start a Family Fellowship at our house every few months. It is a time for young families in the church to worship God and spend time together. At the first meeting I shared the vision I had for our group and the example of Charlie Yates. Our goal is to fill part of the hole of investing in the lives of fellow believers.

I look forward to being there when Charlie receives his crown - "*...shepherd the flock of God among you, exercising oversight not under compulsion, but voluntarily, according to the will of God; and not for sordid gain, but with eagerness; nor yet as lording it over those allotted to your charge, but proving to be examples to the flock. And when the Chief Shepherd appears, you will receive the unfading crown of glory.*" (I Peter 5:2-4) – Nathan Chandler

Alyssa

Mr. Charlie Yates was my buddy, my second dad, my mentor, and goofy friend. There are many great accomplishments he made in his life, but the most important ones are that he never ceased to love others or share his faith. The love that he showed, the love we have for him, and the love of Christ cannot fail. When I see him in glory, we will worship in joy forever.

I am not his only "little buddy." So let us be like Mr. Yates in the way he was like Christ and reach out to others in constant joy. Let us disciple others and find our own "little buddies' to shepherd so that many might be encouraged and might understand a little more about God's grace and God's heart of love. I will see Charlie again when my branches are pruned and my work is done. – *Alyssa Kern*

Hannah

"Brethren, join in following my example, and observe those who walk according to the pattern you have in us... for our citizenship is in heaven, from which also we eagerly wait for a Savior, the Lord Jesus Christ." (Philippians 3:17, 20) I can't believe that it has been a year since heaven gained a new citizen. Along with countless others, I still painfully miss Charlie, my "surrogate father." I pray that I would walk in the pattern he set forth of passionate, unashamed pursuit of Christ." I am blessed and thankful that God gave me the opportunity to know Charlie. –*Hannah Hale*

Jonathan

This letter from Jonathan was written on the one year anniversary of Charlie's death.

Dear Diane,

I just wanted to drop you a note this week and let you know that I was thinking about and thanking God for Charlie and for the ways God used Him in my life during the few years I got to know him this side of glory. Though I didn't think I could do it, Charlie taught me to waterski, just like he did many others. I am thankful for some encouraging lunches with Charlie and Nathan Simmons when I was just starting grad school and was still kind of new to the college group. I'm so thankful for the reminder, as we studied Genesis, that though the universe is rimmed with cinder blocks, Jesus is at the center holding it all together (Colossians 1:17, Hebrews 1:3). I loved being spurred on to greater "highs" as a tenor and being (I hope) a faithful "disciple" in the ways of the tenor rules. I also enjoyed exchanging puns with another punster like

Charlie, knowing I could share God-honoring laughter with him. To this day I am also conscious that I tie my tie without a "lazy" dimple near the knot. Once Charlie pointed something out to you, you didn't forget.

Above all these things I am thankful for the example he was to me of someone who was in the world but not of it, who loved to laugh, who loved people, who loved you and your family, and most importantly, who loved our Lord Jesus, His Word, and His people more than himself, and who had a passion that everyone would know Him, too. I pray that I will be just like Charlie in these areas.

I also thank God for you and your faithful ministry to our church and your testimony of day-by-day trust in the goodness and wisdom of our loving Abba Father. What a comfort that our God is acquainted with our grief. I am praying for you as you mark this first year without Charlie, that God would continue to be your comfort, hope, guide, and stay, and that He would overwhelmingly strengthen you with His daily sufficient grace to serve Him with your all until He calls you to Himself.

Remembering and rejoicing in the Lord with you at this time! With love, In Christ -*Jonathan Cooper*

The Baton is Passed to His Friends

Dusty

It was my privilege to serve alongside Charlie in the College ministry at Countryside Bible Church and to go on a mission trip to Kenya with Diane and him. My wife and I only knew Charlie for about five years but in that short amount of time the Lord used him profoundly in our lives. I have never met a man whose life was more driven by a love for Jesus Christ than Charlie. The Gospel permeated his every waking moment. He incorporated the truth of the Gospel into all of the things he loved in this life. When he taught our college students to waterski he used that as an illustration of the Gospel message. When we sat at a restaurant the conversation revolved around Christ, ministry, and the gospel. When we taught Pastors in Kenya Charlie magnified Christ and the gospel. Charlie went on many mission trips but he was no different on a mission trip than he was at any other time. Charlie's *life* was a mission trip. Even the things in this life that are seemingly the most temporal and trivial such as a hand shake or a greeting were quickly turned into eternal Gospel interactions.

I could list many examples of Charlie's faithfulness for Christ but one memory will never leave me. While we were in Kenya our group made a quick stop at one of the many "cure" shops to buy souvenirs. The group spent about 10 minutes there and then loaded up the van to head to our next church conference. But as we prepared to leave Charlie was nowhere to be found. The group waited impatiently for him to return but the minutes grew longer and longer. Didn't he know that we were on a "mission" trip? Didn't he know we needed to hurry and get to our next stop? Finally when Charlie returned the reason for his delay became known. Charlie had been sharing the gospel with the African man working the gift shop. One minute I was impatiently waiting for my friend Charlie to get in the van so that we could continue our "mission," the next minute I was convicted by the truth he had just taught me, not with his words, but through his life, "the mission never stops." I pray that this lesson is one that God will press upon my heart and mind for the rest of my life.

To say I will miss my friend and mentor Charlie Yates is a grand understatement. To me he will forever be "Dew Gew Yong Gew" which in Swahili means "my brother." I don't know if a day will go by for the rest of my life that I won't think about Charlie Yates, but that is just fine with me. I never want to forget that this life is short and that when it is finished all that will matter is the work I have done for Jesus Christ. Charlie was not a "good" man. He was a sinner saved by the grace of a good God. He would accept no glory for his actions in life or in death. I am confident that now more than ever he would confess, "Soli Deo Gloria." It is all to the Glory of God alone! - *Pastor Dusty Burris*

Charlie in Kenya (2010)

The Smith family

Diane, I share with you a testimony of Charlie's faithfulness to the gospel and a work that will follow him. In the very week that our Lord called Charlie home, Randy had the opportunity to share Christ and witness the miracle of salvation in the cockpit of a 737. Of course, as Randy shared what had happened, I immediately thought of Charlie and couldn't help but smile as God had brought "full circle" what had happened well over 18 years ago in the cockpit of a 727 where Charlie shared the gospel with Randy. When Byron called us Saturday night to break the news of earth's loss and heaven's gain, it truly was bittersweet. We know that a grand and glorious reunion is coming; it's just a matter of when. Until that time, we pray God's grace be multiplied during your time of sorrow. May you rejoice in knowing that Charlie fulfilled his calling and has his reward in full, "Well done, good and faithful servant." Diane, may you also know that your ministry alongside him has born much fruit for the kingdom of God and we are most grateful recipients. We trust that the Lord will continue to use you as His vessel to draw others to Himself. We thank God for the supreme honor of knowing both of you and bless Him for knitting our hearts and lives together. May God be glorified in Charlie's testimony and the words that follow him to this day. In His love, *Randy, Cindy, Hayden, Preston, Heather and Corie Smith*

The Kern Family

Charlie was my best friend. For the past 20+ years he was my best friend. I know that others also think of him as their best friend. That is okay with me. There was enough of Charlie to go around, enough to have several best friends, to be Big Buddy to many Little Buddies, to be a great husband, son and father, and still have time for others. How do we remember someone like Charlie? How do we not? There were many days on the boat with his family. He taught my children to ski. We had many other outings, serious talks, advice, and confidences. Some of his family traditions became my family's traditions. We heard all the stories and jokes so many times that we became complicit with him by offering leading questions or directing the subject so that he could tell one to some new, unsuspecting "victim." The jokes, the sayings, the one-liners, and the handshakes are all ways that we will remember him. But what was the purpose of these? What was the purpose of "Hey, let's keep this line moving?" It was to strike up a conversation with a total stranger and somehow bring the subject around to church or the gospel. This was Charlie's goal, engage people and tell them about the grace of God and Jesus Christ. We can remember Charlie by following his example. – *Randy*

His love and care for us was priceless, and his spiritual leadership became clear over the years. There were matchless gifts of time, prayer, and Bible lessons that I couldn't begin to count.

It is a debt that I can never repay. That example has many times kept me trusting in the Father when in my weakness I would have given up. That steady light will continue to shine in my heart and through his family. Yes, I did know Charlie. I am fairly well-schooled in his outlandish expressions and meticulous logistics. I received the steely glare many times if I played cards "like an old woman." I received the customized care and concern reserved only for his beloved brothers and sisters and everyone else. Many of us are aching for his greetings. He made the same magnetic impression on me that he made on us all, an exuberant life, sold out and utterly devoted to his Lord. Someone said "God gave Charlie 63 years, and he took 120." He was unstoppable, and we won't see another like him in this lifetime. No, there was only one Charlie. He lived life on purpose. It is not enough to say that I will miss him or that I loved him deeply. But maybe it is a start to say that his loss will change me. It is harder to waste the precious moments that I have. It is harder to see the world from anything but God's perspective. It is harder to overlook a stranger or a friend. – *Eileen*

The Turnbull Family

If only we had a poem or a story that would express our hearts about Charlie, but the truth is, it would never fit quite right because Charlie was one of a kind. He loved his country, his wife and his mama...fiercely. He never met a stranger and everyone who knew him became convinced that they were his "bestest buddy." He was always the first to stand up to do the right thing, and he encouraged everyone around him to do the same. He would circle the boat around to help you try again and again to get up on the wakeboard until you decided you were done, and then he always told you to try one more time. He told the same (great) stories again and again, and they got even better with the telling. He was Captain of the dinner cruises, working hard so all those aboard had a wonderful evening. Of all the great qualities about Charlie (and he was given more than his fair share), the one we loved and were encouraged by the most was his love for his Creator. He taught us with passion and intelligence, spurring us on to think deep thoughts about our great God. **That** is a good friend. Everywhere he went, every stop he made, every encounter with anyone meant another chance to share the Good News in the hopes of glorifying his Savior. God saw fit to use his obedience, over and over and over again. We are confident that Charlie's obedience will resonate for years to come and continue to encourage those who hear of it and will, in turn, continue to glorify God. Our lives were forever changed by knowing him and deeply affected by his going home. We will see him again, not in the funny papers, but in glory! Sola deo Gloria, Charlie! - *Ron and Beth Turnbull*

Gary

I met Charlie in 1969 when we were students at Texas Tech. He will always be my very best friend. He was there for me through good times and bad. His relationship with our Lord and Savior Jesus Christ was founded in the certainty that Christ died for him. It was a personal relationship that death could not quell, a relationship that is eternal. I remember years ago, we had been flying model airplanes, and Charlie looked at me and then up into a clear blue sky and said emphatically, "Man, today would be a great day for the Lord to come back!" At the time I knew I wasn't where I should be in my relationship with Christ, and on the way home, through tears, I begged the Lord for forgiveness and accepted Christ as my Lord and Savior. I am thankful that God gave Charlie to me as a friend to lead me to Christ. Charlie understood that God's grace through Jesus Christ was not something that was abstract, but instead was very personal. He came to live that personal relationship with Jesus Christ better than any man I have ever known and obviously his walk with Christ did not go unnoticed. He, with the tears of submission to Christ, understood the Lord's grace, and I can honestly tell you that his untimely passing has helped me and no telling how many others to understand that grace as well. We cannot know how many people saw the memorial service and now through the wonder of the Holy Spirit are coming to Christ. Charlie viewed his personal transformation with wonderment until God took him home on September 22, 2012. Now, thankfully, I get it! What a blessing! – *Gary Flynt*

Daniel

It was a sad moment for me, my family, and the entire On Board Ministry family in Kenya, upon learning of the death of our beloved brother, Charlie. A real hero has left the ministry to be with the Lord. I am a witness of him for the great things he has done in our ministry. Charlie has been a very devoted servant of the Lord in teaching sound doctrine. Many people have recommended his teaching style in that he revealed the real truth in the Bible. I personally thank him for shaping my spiritual life. He introduced a Bible program to me which has shown me how to maximize my study. I am now able to share this information with others. All to His Glory! – *Reverend Daniel Chizambo*

The Baton is Passed to Some He Did not Know

The Veterinarian

When Hobbes, our seventeen year old cat, died in April of 2006, we adopted a kitten. Charlie named the kitten after his brother Bill, who was nicknamed "Newton" by Charlie. Bill died in the fall of 2005. Charlie reasoned that he would remember his brother when he hollered at the cat. Newton disappeared a year before Charlie died, presumably the victim of coyotes that had been seen in the woods behind our house. There was great sorrow so we adopted Nelda and Buddy, named after Charlie's cousins. I took the kittens to a veterinary clinic near our home. Over the next several months Dr. Ford and I became acquainted and discussed such things as his wood carvings and heaven. Dr. Ford had been reading a book about heaven, and he asked if I had read it. I had not, but he told me about some of what he had been reading. Two days before Charlie's funeral I received an e-mail from Dr. Ford's office with the message, "Happy Birthday Nelda and Buddy!" I responded to the message and told Dr. Ford of Charlie's death, gave him the place and time of the funeral, and told him there would be a lot of talk about heaven. His Grapevine office was only two blocks from the church. Dr. Ford attended the funeral and then wrote the following letter.

Diane,

I have never been so touched by someone that I didn't even know. He seemed to live life with a mix of discipline, fun, and love. That must have been how Jesus lived: otherwise why would twelve men have followed him everywhere for three years. It sounds like Charlie mentored many people young and old, men and women. Your son said it best when he said, "I never knew until this week that I shared my dad with so many people because he never made me feel like I shared him with anyone else." If only I could treat my family like that. I, like Charlie, fill all of my spaces with activities, but it sounds like Charlie's passion and favorite activities were Bible and people. That makes him very special. It inspires me to want to fill my time with more Bible and people. My wife has told me several times that if I ever have to plan her funeral, to please sing "It is Well with My Soul." That song touched me deeply. I first recognized God through His Creation; luckily I had my dad (a biology teacher) to explain to me the God behind the Creation. The video that Charlie produced of Alaska reminded me of Romans 1:19-20. I felt his heart. I wish I had known him.

May God bless you and comfort you because I know Charlie is OK. Love in Christ, *Jed Ford*

The Venesky Family

I feel compelled to share with you how Charlie impacted my family and me. My reason for sharing with you was that I did not want even the little sliver of Charlie that the Venesky family enjoyed to get lost. It is important that people know how far and deep his reach was.

Chief among my instincts as a father and husband is family safety and security. When I realized that Francene forbade Beth to go on the African mission trip "unless Charlie Yates goes," I had a glimpse of the magnitude of impact this guy had already had; but it wasn't until his death that I realized how I underestimated that magnitude. As a 50 year-old-man, who lost a great father when I was 23 (he was 64), and 3 dear friends before the age of 40 (frankly a couple other fairly close acquaintances as well), I am familiar with somewhat untimely death. That said I surprised my own self at how much Charlie's death affected me. It was Ron Lenington who broke the news to me; I could sense the sadness in the church, which was overwhelming, as Ron tried to fight back tears. My last memory of Charlie was when he pulled me aside near the information desk in the church lobby to ask if Francene and I would be interested in serving as a "prayer couple" to assist folks following the service with prayer. I do believe this was the Sunday before he died. I'm embarrassed to admit that I did not act on that, however, I have expanded my church service activity elsewhere, thanks in part to this wake-up call. Following his funeral I performed somewhat of a pre-flight check (if you will permit me to use this phrase) on my life. Since Charlie's death, I have made a concerted effort to be more active in my faith (Men of the Word, music, evangelizing). I saw James 2:14-26 (especially verses 17, 20, 22, and 26) in how Charlie lived and I asked myself, "What am I waiting for?"

My daughter Beth loved Charlie. She considers it a rich blessing to have traveled with him to Africa. She often recounts events and memories of that experience. When Francene and I met with Charlie and Diane to review the slide show from the previous mission trip and have open discussion with them, Charlie told us that this trip to Kenya was a life-changing experience. There is no question that it had that powerful of an impact on Beth. I asked Beth to describe the impact of Charlie's death on her. She said, "It shook me to change, to change how I think about and live my life before death, and it made life after death become more real. Charlie's death was the jumpstart my heart and soul needed. His death and the death of two other friends gave me the push I needed to recognize my need and instigate my desire for the Holy Spirit to work actively in my heart."

My son Philip was being affected more invisibly, but quite radically just the same. Philip will tell you that he did not know Charlie during his life. But as he observed the impact Charlie's death had on our household and on each of us individually, Beth, Francene and me, it was then that the Holy Spirit began to transform Philip's life. I asked Philip to describe the impact of Charlie's death on him. He said, "I didn't even know him, but he is who God used to lead me to Christ. His death shook me out of my old life." His siblings will tell you that Philip's transformation has been tangible, the old Philip compared to Philip now. There's no other way to put it. You need to experience the faithfulness of this kid in conversation to understand how real his transformation has been. Only Philip, who knew the old self better than anyone, can tell you how extensive it was. Let me assure you that when I said previously that "Since Charlie's death, I have made a concerted effort to be more active in my faith," it is Philip who has not wasted a day over that same span in getting to work for His Kingdom on earth. And it all started with Charlie's death. Forgive the illustration if it elevates Charlie too much, but it is like a 15-year-old Philip received an evangelical-baton from a man he never met. He is truly missed by us. – *Paul Venesky*

Philip Venesky

Philip's Testimony at His Baptism Service - November 3, 2013

I live in a Christian home, and as a kid I was exposed to the gospel and forced to go to church on a regular basis. I always tried to outwardly fix what I heard about on Sunday, and I grew increasingly frustrated when I never could, because, as stated in Romans 6, I was completely enslaved to sin. As I grew into my teenage years, this enslavement grew stronger. I gave up on God and instead turned to myself; my philosophies, desires, and independence. Basically, I did things my way. I was consumed by my own arrogant, selfish, and lustful self. More than anything else, I was miserable. I knew I was headed for hell, and I hated God because He never answered my phony cries of rescuing me from it.

I went on a camping trip the weekend of September 21, 2012, still in complete rebellion against God. My dad picked me up on Sunday morning, the 23rd, and I learned of the death of Charlie Yates. I never knew Charlie, but I knew what he stood for. So his death shook me. I wondered how people like him could love a God who was, seemingly to me, so hateful. My question was answered when I came across the verse 1 John 4:10, *"In this is love, not that we loved God, but that He loved us and sent His Son to be the propitiation for our sins."* God changed how I saw Him by showing me His incomprehensible love; that He could send His Son, and that Jesus would come, to die for me even though I was so sinful and hated Him so much. For the first time, I submitted myself to God in repentance, understanding that only through Christ's sacrifice I could be forgiven. I was desperate to be rid of my sin, and comforted by the truth in 1 John 1:9, *"If we confess our sins, He is righteous and faithful to forgive us our sins and to cleanse us from all unrighteousness."* It all seemed too good to be true: freedom from, and forgiveness of, the sin that chained me to eternal punishment, and a relationship with the God of perfect love, all by a price I didn't pay.

My life since coming to know Christ is characterized by 2 Corinthians 5:17, *"Therefore, if anyone is in Christ, he is a new creature; the old things passed away; behold, new things have come."* God has made me completely new. I am able to grow closer to God my Father and move away from the sin that I could never separate myself from before. Joy, hope, and love have become a part of me, and unlike before, I have understanding through knowing the truth of God's Word. Instead of finding my satisfaction in the empty promises of the world that never fulfill, I find satisfaction in striving to be what God desires me to be. Spending time in God's Word, prayer, and joyfully attending church are a few of the things that opposed my nature before, but now I do regularly by God's grace. This is what God has done with a sinner like me, and why I am here to be baptized. – *Philip Venesky*

The Baton is Passed to His Family

His Wife

As Charlie's wife, I may have received several batons. From God's perspective Charlie's race on earth was finished; from my perspective there is some very important unfinished business. We have eight young grandchildren. Four of them will remember a little something about their Poppy who was so much fun. They will remember the games, songs, wrestling, tackling, and silliness. They will remember that they loved him. Four of the grandchildren are too young to have any memory of him. This book is for these precious eight children. I wanted them to know all about their grandfather and the God that he served. There is a lot to learn about God in the pages of his life.

It is hard to explain death to a young child. Grandson Reese was three years old when Charlie died. Reese's last memory of Poppy was of the two of them riding in the boat and swimming in the lake a few days before the accident. There were two benches reserved for family at the pavilion at the Dallas-Fort Worth National Cemetery where the official burial ceremony took place. I sat on the first bench and beside me was my son, Smedly, then daughter, Angela, and beside her was her son, Reese. Charlie's mother, his sister and her children sat on the adjacent bench. Other family and friends stood behind us. The honor guard solemnly and precisely folded the flag that had draped the fighter pilot's decorated casket. They placed the three-cornered, folded stars and stripes in my hands and expressed respectful condolences. The farewell volley of shots was fired. The chaplain, my brother Mike, choked back tears as he expressed the final words and ended with prayer. At the "amen" all was quiet, and then the small child voice of Reese could be heard, "Can Poppy come out of the box now?" I leaned over to him and said, "He's not in the box Reese; he's in heaven with Jesus." A few weeks later, Reese's Sunday school teacher talked about heaven. After class Reese said, "Poppy is there with Jesus. Mommy, they said Jesus. Poppy loves Jesus." A year later, Reese asked his mom, "Did you know that Jesus died on the cross and the rose from the dead? Angela replied, "Yes and He is in heaven with Poppy." Reese quickly responded, "No Mom, Jesus came back to earth and is alive!" Two-year-old Grace asked me if I had a daddy. I knew she was speaking of Charlie and that she knew something wasn't quite the same. Five-year-old Emet asked if Poppy would get to fly airplanes in heaven. Charlie had given Emet his first plane ride two months earlier. Seven-year-old Zoe asked with a big smile on her face, "Do you mean Poppy is with Jesus?" Nine-year-old Evi said, "But Poppy rode roller coasters with me. He played games with me. Poppy "wrastled" me, and Poppy taught me to waterski. Now who do I have?"

For now, they still have me. I will love them, and I will be a little more silly, and play more games, and ride roller coasters, and wrestle (as best a grandmother can), and throw the ball, and look at airplane pictures, and take them out in the boat and teach them to ski. But most importantly, I will teach them about God. Their parents will teach them, and I will be the "ditto" that rings in the ears of those children. One of my batons is like the one that Lois, the grandmother of Timothy, carried. The Apostle Paul wrote a letter to his beloved son in the faith and co-worker in the ministry of the Gospel. He reminded Timothy that he continued to pray for him; he encouraged him; and he penned these words, *"For I am mindful of the sincere faith within you, which first dwelt in your grandmother Lois and your mother Eunice, am I am sure that it is in you as well."* I must display my faith before my grandchildren. God's words must come from my mouth. I must earnestly and continually pray for Evi, Zoe, Emet, Grace, and Madeline Yates, and Reese, Ryder, and Piper Guthrie, that they would come to know and love God, so that forever **they will have God.**

His Children

Andrew Edward Yates, known as Smedly, loved to fly and he earned his pilot's license, but his calling was the ministry. He thought he would become a missionary pilot in some distant country, but God revealed that He had other plans. Smedly preaches and teaches the Word of God in the country of his birth, and he has opportunities to prepare others to go on the mission field abroad. He is running the same race that his father ran. He has a daily reminder as he goes about the business that God has given him to do, his dad's watch.

Doug Dunbar retrieved Charlie's watch from the site of the accident, cleaned it up, and had the damaged watchband repaired. He presented the watch that wouldn't quit to Smedly at the memorial service at the airport hangar. Smedly wears it every day. There are two peculiar things about that watch: the hands on the watch keep great time but the digital readout is permanently fixed at 1:00 p.m., about the time of the accident; and the digital alarm on the watch rings every day at 3:00 p.m., about the time of Charlie's death. Charlie must have had an appointment at three that day; he just didn't know it was with God. Smedly doesn't mind the reminder that he has the baton and is still running the race.

Angela Jean Yates Guthrie told her Pop that she was pregnant two weeks before he died. At the time, the other Guthrie children, Reese and Ryder were three years and one year old. The promise of the new life growing in Angela was a comfort. On Christmas day, Angela gave me a gift bag. As I pulled back the tissue, I saw that it was her Strawberry Shortcake doll #2. She received Strawberry Shortcake doll #1 from Santa Claus in 1983 when she was three years old. That doll went everywhere we did. She flew in our plane and went camping and fishing in Alaska. She went to the Grand Canyon in Arizona and Lake Powell in Utah. One of Angela's friends tried to clean Strawberry's face with nail polish remover. The dirt came off but so did the freckles and the eyes. I had to paint those back on. I had sewed her arms back on the soft body several times. I couldn't do anything about the once curly red hair that due to constant use and abuse stood straight up. The doll was quite a fright, but Angela loved her. When Angela was in high school, I went to a flea market and found Strawberry Shortcake #2. This Strawberry was the same make of doll, but she was like new in her clean pink dress with the red strawberries. Her hair was curly and framed her perfect face. She still smelled liked strawberries when you squeezed her. This doll was in a barrel of toys, and she had not been loved like Strawberry #1. I paid three dollars for her but I would have paid ten times that amount. Angela was thrilled. On Christmas Day, 2012, when I pulled Strawberry Shortcake #2 out of the gift bag, I knew that the baby Angela carried was a girl.

Over the next several months there was much discussion over the baby's name. Angela's husband, Ryan, wanted to continue his family's tradition of naming the children such that their initials were RAG (Ryan Andrew Guthrie, Reese Ambrose Guthrie, and Ryder Andrew Guthrie). They tried all kinds of combinations of girl names that would continue the tradition, but Angela didn't care for any of them. She knew what name she wanted, but she knew Ryan would have to decide. One day she came home from work and found Ryan and the boys sitting at the counter in the kitchen waiting for her. There was a vase of roses and a gift bag. The boys were really eager for her to open the bag. The gift was a Strawberry Shortcake doll, the 2013 version, which looks nothing like the other two dolls. Ryan said to Reese, "Tell Mommy the baby's name." Reese had been coached and he replied, "The baby's name is Piper Charlie."

Piper Charlie Guthrie was born May 10, 2013. Charlie's namesake will be a living reminder of the joy and inspiration he was to all of us.

The baton is passed. It is not the end.

Diane and the grandchildren,
(Clockwise from top right) Madeline, Piper, Zoe,
Reese, Emet, Evi, Ryder, and Grace (2013)

ABOUT THE AUTHOR

Charlie promised they would see the world. By way of his careers and their adventures, they saw a good part of it. Diane took notes, wrote letters, and saved stuff. These bits and pieces of their forty-two years together provided the framework for the rest of the story.

Made in United States
North Haven, CT
22 May 2023

36858963R00190